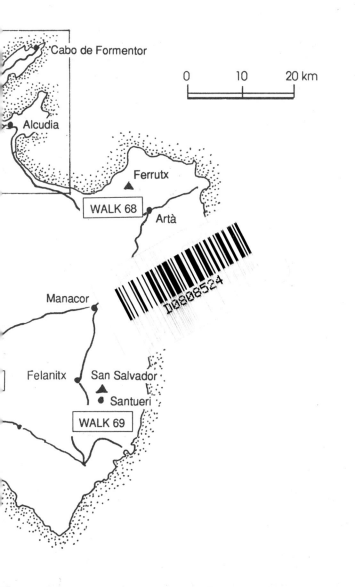

Cabo de Formentor

0   10   20 km

Alcudia

Ferrutx

WALK 68

Artà

Manacor

DB808524

Felanitx   San Salvador

Santueri

WALK 69

WALKING IN MALLORCA

WALKING IN MALLORCA

by

JUNE PARKER

CICERONE PRESS
MILNTHORPE, CUMBRIA

© June Parker
ISBN 1 85284 078 1
First published 1986
Reprinted 1988
2nd Edition 1991

Acknowledgements

June and Alan Parker would like to thank all the friends who have helped in trying out new walk descriptions or in making suggestions on itineraries. We would specially like to thank Mary Clarke and the late George Clarke, Stan and Jan Crawford, Jim and Ann Fielding, Brenda and Joe Lockey, Juan Noguerra, Charles Rhodes and group, David and Lily Rowe, Ernie Shepherd and friends, Stan and Margaret Thompson and Menna and George Vincent. Thanks too to all the walkers, too numerous to mention individually, who have written with comments on the book and the walks.

*All photographs by A & J. Parker
except where otherwise stated*

Front cover: In the Pareis Gorge (Walt Unsworth)
Back cover: Climbing the Puig de Maria (Walt Unsworth)
Frontispiece: Sa Calobra. Walk 28b

4

CONTENTS

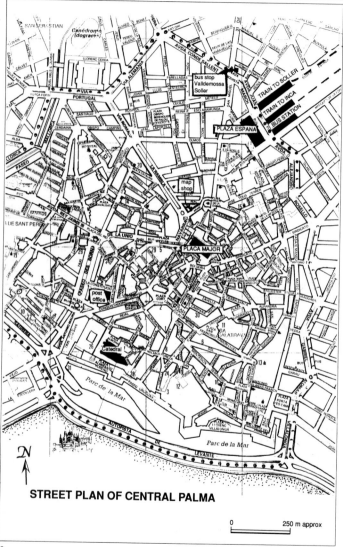

STREET PLAN OF CENTRAL PALMA

0   250 m approx

ROUTES

2·73 (handwritten annotation beside item 8)

7

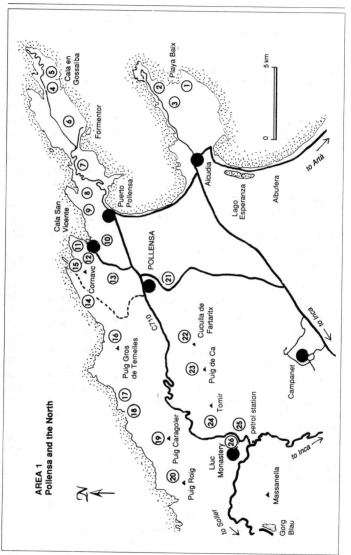

AREA 1
Pollensa and the North

26.2.93

.2.93

Got lost at 'T. Junction.'

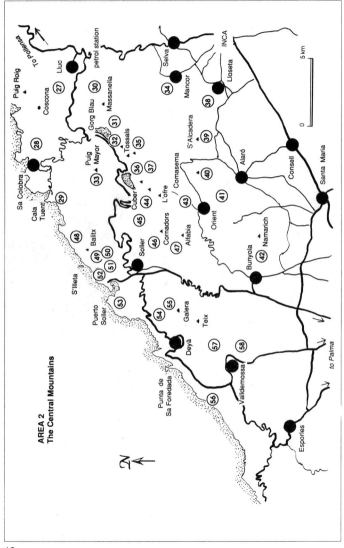

AREA 2
The Central Mountains

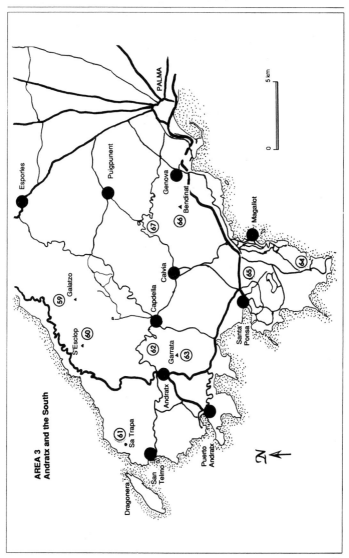

AREA 3
Andratx and the South

Dragonera
San Telmo
Sa Trapa ⑥⑴
Andratx
Puerto Andratx
Garrata ▲
Garrata ⑥⑶
⑥⑵
S'Esclop ▲ ⑥⓪
Galatzo ▲ ⑤⑨
Capdella
Calvia
Santa Ponsa
⑥⑸
⑥⑷
Magallot
⑥⑺
⑥⑹
Bendinat ▲
Genova
Puigpunent
Esporles
PALMA
0   5 km

N ←

11

QUERCUS ILEX (HOLM OAK)

*QUERCUS COCCITERA
(KERMES OAK)*

SKETCH MAPS

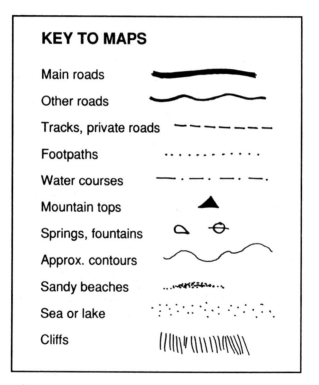

MOUNTAINS AND TOPS OVER 1000m

The heights are taken from the new IGN 1:25,000 maps where these are available. The criteria for separate mountain status are a separation of 1km or over and/or a re-ascent of 100m or more.

Mountains	Tops	Height m	Comments
1. Puig Mayor	Main top	1447	In military zone.
	Mitx Dia	1401	Outside military zone.
	West top	1358	
	Ses Vinyes	1105	
2. Massanella	Main top	1367	An enormous massif of
	Twin tops	1352	two long ridges sep.by
	Unnamed	1258,1239	two valleys leading to
	Unnamed	1169,1058	the high Coll des
	Ses Bassetes	1216	Prat.
	Galileu	1188	
	Sa Mola	1182	
	Es Fronto (w)	1009	
	Es Fronto (e)	1061	
3. Tossals group	Tossals Verds	1115	South of Gorg Blau
	S.top	1097	and east of Cuber.
	Sa Font	1069	
	Almallutx	1058	
	Es Tossals	1047	
4. Tomir	Main top	1103	At head of Pollensa
	South top	1086	valley.
5. L'Ofre	1091	1.8km	from Sa Rateta.
6. Sa Rateta	Main top	1084	
	Na Franquesa	1067	On ridge to L'Ofre.
7. Alfàbia	Main top	1067	Centre of long ridge.
	Palou	1049	1km NE of Alfàbia.
	'Antennae' top	1029	2.1km SW of Alfàbia.

Mountains	Tops	Height m	Comments
7 cont.	Sementer Gran Ses Hueres	1014 1051	At N end of ridge. Off-set from ridge.
8. Teix	Main top Teixoch Puig des Vent	1062 1062 1004	Between Deyà and Valldemossa. 0.75km N of Teix.
9. N'Alis		1035	Sep. from Massanella by Col de Sa Linoa
10. Galatzó		1027	Highest peak of SW of Mallorca
11. Cornadors		1009	1.6km NE of Alfàbia
12. Puig Roig		1002	Most northerly 1000m peak

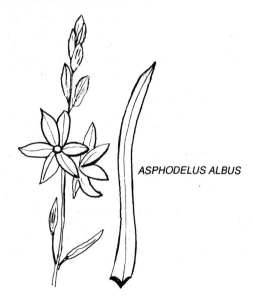

ASPHODELUS ALBUS

INTRODUCTION

General background

The Balearic islands lie in the Mediterranean between Barcelona on the coast of mainland Spain and Algiers on the North African coast. This favoured position is responsible for the sunny temperate climate attractive to both sun-lovers and walkers alike. Here it is worth pointing out that the temperatures in July and August which are ideal for sunbathing are far too hot for any serious walking by most people. These months are best avoided and the recommended 'season' for walkers is from the beginning of September to the end of May.

Mallorca is the largest of the islands and has long been well-known as a paradise for sun-worshippers. That it is also a paradise for walkers is slowly being discovered by those discerning walkers who enjoy the attractive and varied scenery, the equable climate and the opportunities for walking in quiet places where other people rarely go. Add to this the extensive Mediterranean flora, the spring migration of birds and the opportunities for photography and it is hard to understand why it has been neglected as a walking area for so long. One reason is the inadequacy of the maps, the almost total lack of signposts indicating the starts of footpaths and the absence of guidebooks in English written specifically for the experienced mountain walker. Since the 1st edition of this book a series of 1:25,000 maps has been published, but even these do not show all the paths and tracks. This new edition of the guide describes more than 70 walks, from very easy ones to some quite hard scrambles.

The main mountain chain in Mallorca is the Sierra de Tramuntana which lies along the north-west coast and reaches heights of over 1,000m in many places, culminating in the Puig Mayor at 1,447m. The Sierra de Levante in the east, although only topping the 500m contour also offers walks of surprising length and quality, having the same sort of high mountain characteristics as the Tramuntana. Many of the mountain tops of the island are almost bare of vegetation and the hard rough limestone gives excellent walking and scrambling with loose rock being extremely rare. There is a varied flora including dense evergreen forests, maquis and garigue in the arid zones, sub-alpine flora on the approach to the peaks, and an enormous number of beautiful flowering shrubs which give an extra dimension to many walks.

The small size of the island means almost every walk is enhanced by views of the coastline and the sea. The sea varies in colour from the palest greens and blues to incredible dark ultramarine and purple, often with small bays of white sand between steep cliffs which plunge dramatically into the water. In fact the coastal walks vie in attraction with the inland mountains and although they may not reach any great height often go through very wild and uninhabited country.

Many of the walks in this guidebook go through pathless and rough areas where some experience of route-finding is needed. Some make use of excellent tracks and paths which are very easy to follow. Most of these are a legacy of the past, being made by those who worked in the now defunct rural industries of snow-collecting and charcoal manufacture. Some of these paths are neglected, overgrown and difficult to find, but some have been repaired and waymarked. The maps are not entirely reliable in the matter of footpaths and these are rarely signposted, except those maintained by ICONA. If using the maps to plan your own walks, care is required. Steep cliffs or very complex ground can be encountered where the map gives no indication of this.

Scope of this guide

This book is written for the experienced mountain walker who is used to walking in mountains like the British ones in all seasons. It is not comprehensive but provides a selection of walks of all degrees of difficulty and should enable those limited to a short holiday to make the best use of their time. Circular walks have been described whenever possible, but often it is necessary to return the same way to the starting point. Most of the walks depend on the use of a hired car, by far the best means of getting about the island. Some walks can be done directly from Cala San Vicente, Pollensa, Puerto Pollensa, Soller and Puerto Soller. Occasionally public transport can be made use of, but in general the buses are more useful for getting to beaches than to the mountains.

Accommodation and travel (See also Appendix 1)

Although the development of the tourist industry in recent years has led to the spread of large concrete jungles, these are in the main confined to the coast around the bay of Palma, from Paguerra to El Arenal. However, there is no need to stay in this area, there being plenty of accommodation throughout the island in places that remain comparatively unspoilt. The resorts which are the best centres for walking will be described later.

Some people may like to stay in Palma, which has certain advantages. There is an excellent network of roads from the capital in every direction, and also a very good public transport system, provided you are fairly near the centre. Personally I do not like to be tied to catching a bus or train at the end of a walk, but if this doesn't bother you it can be a good system.

One advantage of the tourist development of the island is that a number of tour operators offer package holidays throughout the year, with the effect of keeping prices down to a reasonable level. By far the cheapest way to get there is to take advantage of any special offers that include the use of a car at a reduced rate. These offers only apply to the winter, but then that is also the best time to go for a walking holiday.

It is also possible of course to book a flight only and find your own accommodation independently. On the whole it works out more expensive to book in a hotel this way, but less expensive to take an apartment. There are an enormous number of apartment blocks, and some smaller ones often belonging to small bars and restaurants. It is easier to arrange this sort of holiday on a second visit when you know your way around and also if you are able to speak a little Spanish. English is always spoken in larger hotels, but by no means always in smaller places where cheaper accommodation is more likely to be found. Remember that some hotels close in winter, although those that do open are rarely full. The exception to this is Christmas and New Year and also Easter, when booking ahead is advisable.

Those who are able to take advantage of a long stay winter holiday can obtain extremely good rates for stays of up to four months. The best of these offers is usually from November to March, if you can get away for that length of time. There is a regular ferry service from Barcelona to Palma which may be worth considering for a long winter stay, but the costs of two ferries plus overnight stays on route make this quite an expensive option.

There is one official campsite on Mallorca, near Ca'n Picafort, at K8 on the Alcudia-Artà road. It is open all the year round and reservations can be made by telephone on 20-38-61. Those wishing to camp or bivvy in the mountains should ask permission at the nearest farm. Note that in many areas there is a prohibition against lighting fires because of the risk from dry vegetation. All walks can be done easily from a base in a small town or village, but longer two or three day backpacking walks can easily be devised. A popular annual event is organised jointly by walking clubs from Palma and Pollensa, in which a large number of walkers set out on a three day walk from south to north. The route is different each year, but always very tough and only a small number actually complete the whole course.

Choice of base

The best resorts for walkers are Cala San Vicente and Puerto Pollensa in the north, Soller and Puerto Soller on the west coast, and Puerto Andratx in the south-west.

Cala San Vicente is a small quiet resort with sandy beaches and a spectacular view of the steep cliffs of the Cavall Bernat ridge across the sparkling green-blue sea. It is surrounded by pinewoods, good for quiet walks, orchids and bird-watching. Several walks start from here and it is no great distance to drive to the starting points for other walks. There is a bus service, although very limited in winter. Walkers need to catch the 08.45 to Pollensa.

There are a number of apartments and several hotels, not all of them open in the winter. We can personally recommend the Don Pedro, which features in the brochures of several tour operators, and the Oriola, best booked independently. The Don Pedro is right by the sea, has self-service meals with an excellent buffet and friendly and helpful staff. The only disadvantage, as far as we are concerned, is the lack of a quiet area for reading and chatting, as there is music for dancing put on every evening. The Oriola is a very quiet family-run hotel by the pinewoods on the edge of the village. There is a home-cooked set meal in the evening and an attractive quiet lounge with a library of English books. Juan Noguera, the owner, is very knowledgable about walking and bird-watching and speaks excellent English. (Tel. 53-19-98)

Puerto Pollensa lies on the coast in a very sheltered position. There is a narrow strip of sand and quite a large marina. Much development has taken place here in recent years, so that those who remember it as a small fishing village will doubtless be horrified by all the changes. However, it has not been ruined as some of the resorts on the south and east coasts have been and it still remains an attractive place to stay. Nothing can spoil the splendid backdrop of the Cavall Bernat ridge and the quiet bay with its shallow water and sandy beaches. There are numerous hotels and apartments, a better bus service than Cala San Vicente, and plenty of shops and supermarkets. It is a good choice if there are children or non-walkers in your party. We have not tried any of the hotels here, but friends highly recommend the Flora Apartments.

Soller lies on the west side of the island between the mountains and the sea. It is an excellent centre for walks and has a good public transport system, with the train to Palma, a tram to the port, a bus service to Deyà and Valldemossa, and the bus over the mountains to Pollensa. There is a good old-established hotel near the station, the Guia, which can be personally recommended, but this sometimes closes in the winter.

Puerto Soller has many more hotels and apartments clustered round the attractive circular harbour. It is linked to Soller with a frequent tram service and is a good place for the independent walker. Unfortunately not many tour operators seem to offer holidays here, especially in the winter. A small one-star hotel which can be personally recommended is the Costa Brava, with excellent food and reasonable prices. Unfortunately this is only open from Easter to the end of October. We have also found the Hotel Monte Azul quite attractive, and this is open in the winter. Mixed reports have been received about the Hostal Es Port, which is highly praised by some although criticised by others on account of the food. It is in a very interesting old building set in an attractive garden. There are apartments to let, especially in the winter. See Appendix 1 under Accommodation for the name of an estate agent.

Banyalbufar is a small village about half-way between Soller and Andratx. It is set on a steeply terraced slope between mountains and sea and is a good centre for walking in the southern part of the Tramuntana range. The Hotel Mar i Vent is a family-run hotel with excellent cooking which can be personally recommended. It is open all year except for December and January. (Telephone 61-80-00) Two other hotels in the village are open in the summer months, the Baronia and the Sa Coma.

Puerto Andratx at the extreme south of the Tramuntana mountains is another picturesque harbour with a modern yacht marina. There are a number of modest hotels here and it is a good place for walking. The inland town of Andratx has been saved from development, like Pollensa in the north, by its distance from the sea. It is a charming old town, dating from the thirteenth century, with a weekly market on Wednesdays.

Climate and weather

The climate of Mallorca is a typical Mediterranean one: that is the winters are mild, the summers are hot and dry and there is plenty of sunshine all the year round. The relative humidity is said to be constant throughout the year at about 70%. This together with the sea breezes, makes even the hottest summer days pleasant and enjoyable, provided you are not trying to walk uphill. There are almost 300 sunny days during the year and even in the winter months there is an average of five hours of sunshine each day. When rain falls it often does so in sharp heavy showers that soon clear up, except for occasional whole days of torrential rain which can occur in the late autumn and early spring. There can, of course, be different weather conditions in different parts of the island. Naturally the rainfall is greatest over the highest mountains, varying from 1,000mm per year near the Puig Mayor to less than 400mm on the south coast. It is thus often possible to find a sunny or sheltered place to walk by avoiding the higher tops on bad days.

Snow is quite common on the mountain tops, or used to be. So common that it was formerly collected during the winter months to make ice for use in the summer (see p.42). At sea level it is very rare and there was great excitement when several inches fell in January 1985. Local people said it was the first time this had happened for 29 years. That year the snow-fall in the mountains was tremendous and much damage to trees was done, many roads also being blocked for days both by the snow and fallen trees. When the roads were cleared, people from Palma were driving up to the mountains to make snowballs and loading snow on to the tops of their cars. (See photograph taken on the Puig de Maria at 333m.)

The central plain, protected by the high Sierras to the north-west enjoys an almost sub-tropical climate. In winter the average mid-day temperature here is 10°C, whereas it is 6°C on the north-west coast.

The following table gives a rough indication of what to expect, but remember that these are averages and apply to Palma. In February 1990 there were 25 days of perfect 'summer' weather and most days the lunch-time temperature was 18-21°C. Then it shot up to 28°C, and plummeted to 5°C two days later.

Temperatures in °C and number of rainy and sunny days each month

	Jan	Feb	Mar	Apr	May	Jun	July	Aug	Sept	Oct	Nov	Dec
Max. temp.*	14	15	17	19	22	26	29	29	27	23	18	15
Min. temp.*	6	6	8	10	13	17	19	20	18	14	10	8
Average	9	8	11	13	17	21	26	24	22	18	12	14
Sea temp.	13	13	15	16	18	21	24	26	22	19	17	15
Rainy days	8	6	6	7	4	2	2	1	5	8	8	9
Sunny days	23	22	25	23	27	28	29	30	25	23	22	22

* Min. temp. at dawn, *Max temp. at midday

GEOLOGY AND SCENERY

These notes are necessarily very brief and the emphasis is on the scenery. Those interested in the geology are strongly recommended to obtain the field guide by A.E.Adams listed in the bibliography. This gives details of ten itineraries which are easy to follow and which cover most of the events in the geological history of the island.

Brief geological history

The Balearic islands lie on a submarine sill extending north-eastwards from Cap Nao on mainland Spain and are an extension of a chain of mountains in that area known as the Baetic Cordillera. These mountains are part of the Western Mediterranean block, pushed up in a major mountain-building episode at the end of the Carboniferous period, the Hercynian orogeny. It is thought that a ripple fold in a north-east/south-west direction was then thrown up by pressure from the northern land mass and that this fold underlies the main mountain chain of Mallorca, the Sierra de Tramuntana.

Subsequent earth movements raised and lowered this block a number of times, with various land bridges uniting it temporarily with Europe and Africa. It is these land bridges that partly account for the variety of flora and fauna on the islands.

Major events in the Mesozoic period were the laying down of thick deposits of Triassic clays and marls, followed by Jurassic and Cretaceous limestones, when all southern Europe, the Mediterranean and North Africa was a synclinal basin under the sea known to geologists as the 'Tethys'. Even during these times there were periods of uplift when the high land in the north was above water. During the Cretaceous there was probably a land bridge with Catalonia.

In the Eocene period massive earth movements caused folding of vast areas of southern Europe and North Africa. It was at this time that both Alpine and Himalayan folding and uplift occured. In Mallorca the pressure against the Hercynian block was responsible for further folding on the same axis as the original ripple fold. This and later folding and faulting along the same axis gave rise to steep scarp slopes facing north-west with gentler slopes on the south-east side. A series of lakes was formed at the foot of these slopes when surface water was trapped above impermeable Jurassic rocks. Alluvial deposits dated at 50 million years, or late Eocene, are evidence of this.

A mainland bridge is believed to have existed in the lower Oligocene, then in the Miocene there was a further submergence with deep sea deposits being laid down over a wide area. At the end of the Miocene further elevation brought the mountain chain again up to its present height. The story after this is uncertain, except that the the islands did not achieve their present form until the Quaternary.

Surface features today

Although large areas of the exposed rocks on Mallorca are limestones of various ages and Triassic clays and marls, mention must be made of other rocks that will be observed from time to time when walking in the mountains. There are a number of minor igneous intrusions of a dark doleritic rock, probably of Triassic age, seen for example in the Ternelles valley. In the north-east of the island there are extensive areas of a very coarse conglomerate in which rounded pebbles and boulders with all sorts of angular fragments are well-cemented together, giving a 'pudding-stone' appearance. This will be seen on the walk to the Puig de S'Aguila, Walk 11. Here too there is an outcrop of an attractive pink, white and black rock, not a true marble, but the result of pressure and percolating solutions acting on the limestone. Occasional outcrops of cross-bedded sandstones are also seen, for example in the picnic area of the pinewoods at Cala San Vicente.

There are three distinct areas of Mallorca which can be considered as structural-morphological units; these are the main mountain chain known as the Sierra de Tramuntana, the central plains and the mountains of the south-east, the Sierra de Levante.

1. The Sierra de Tramuntana

The Tramuntana is a chain of mountains some 80km long which lies in a north-east/south-west direction along the line of the original ripple fold. There are 12 peaks and 37 tops more than 1,000m in height. There are many ridges showing the same directional trend as the whole chain. The Cavall Bernat ridge (Walk 9) is one of these. The steep north-west scarp slopes are a striking feature, particularly the coastal scarp which makes much of the shoreline inaccessible. This feature is well seen on the circuit of the Puig Roig, (Walk 20), and on the approach to the Puig Gros de Ternelles, (Walk 16). As pointed out elsewhere, these scarps are not always marked on the maps and this should be borne in mind when planning independent walks.

Many of the rocks at the surface high up in the mountains are deep sea calcareous rocks dating from the Miocene. They are hard medium-grey rocks often sculpted into fantastic pinnacles and with conspicuous 'flutings' due to rainwater erosion. This phenomenon can easily be seen when driving along the C710 from Pollensa to Lluc, here developed on massive conglomerates. There are many areas of typical karst or limestone pavement, where percolating water has enlarged the joints of the rock into deep fissures called grikes. The ridges between, known as clints, can be knife sharp, and negotiating this sort of terrain calls for great care from walkers. By far the most badly dissected limestone we have ever seen is up on the Puig Gros de Ternelles (Walk 16) between the summit and the Coll de Tirapau. It is so bad that this descent is no longer recommended. Walks 17 and 18 both traverse areas of impressive rock scenery and are highly recommended.

There is only one major watercourse on the island. This is the Torrente de Pareis (Walk 28), and it has worn through great thicknesses of rock to expose earlier Jurassic strata of a very dense, hard limestone, sometimes dolomitic.

2. The central plains

The central plain or *es pla* consists of Miocene and late Plio-Pleistocene deposits which are poorly exposed. Large areas are completely flat and covered with a layer of terra rossa, a red and very fertile soil consisting of the insoluble residue left behind after the solution of limestone by ground water. The red colour is due to the accumulation of iron oxides. When recently ploughed this earth is bright red and makes a striking contrast to the pale blossom of the almond trees or the dark green of the carobs.

Elsewhere there is an undulating relief, and at the south-eastern border of the Tramuntana is a belt of low hills derived by erosion from the Sierras themselves. Occasional inliers of folded Triassic and Jurassic rocks rise up prominently from the central plain, such as Randa (Walk 70).

3. The eastern hills

The Sierras de Levante are a lower range of hills running from the Artà peninsula towards Manacor and Felanitx. They only just exceed 500m in height. The folding here is considered to be more recent than that of the Tramuntana. Triassic and Jurassic strata are overlain by Cretaceous limestones and by the mid-grey Miocene limestone. There are extensive areas of karst and some large Jurassic cave systems near the coast. These are the caves of Drach, Hams and Artà: all open as showcaves.

25

Mallorca: simplified geolgical history

PERIOD	EPOCH	EVENTS	MYA
Quaternary	Recent Pleistocene	Mallorca sep.from Menorca Ibiza sep.from Formentera.	2
	Pliocene	Bridge betw.Ibiza and Mallorca broken.	7
	Miocene	Elevation & uplift to present height. More deep sea deposits.	19
Tertiary	Oligocene	Partial re-submergence, but with land bridges.	38
	Eocene Paleocene	Major folding & earth movements.	63
Cretaceous	Upper Lower	Land bridge to Catalonia. Deep sea limestones dep.	136
Jurassic		Deep sea limestones dep.	190
Triassic		Thick deposits of clays and marls laid down.	225
Permian		Ripple fold in NE/SW direction.	280
Carbonif.		Hercynian mountains formed.	345
Devonian		Fossil plants show earliest evidence of life.	410

MYA = Million years ago

NATURAL HISTORY

The pleasure of walking on Mallorca is greatly enhanced by the rich variety of plant and animal life. Wherever you go you cannot fail to notice the immense variety of flowers and shrubs and how different the vegetation is from that seen in Britain. Ornithologists have been visiting the island for many years, mainly in the spring and the autumn to catch the migrants, but there is plenty to interest the walker with a casual interest in bird-watching all the year round. The notes which follow are necessarily very brief and the reader is referred to the bibliography in the appendices for further reading.

Flora

Only five varieties of native trees are found in the woodlands of Mallorca; pine, oak, olive, carob and dwarf fan palm. Others, such as black poplar, London plane, ash, elm, hawthorn and blackthorn will be observed on the banks of streams. A striking feature of the forests is how green they are in winter, not only because of the preponderance of evergreens but because the autumn rains wash off all the summer dust which gives a drab grey appearance to the trees. Both the pines and the oaks are perfectly adapted to the long hot and dry summers: the pines having leaves reduced to narrow grooved cylinders and the oaks having thick leathery leaves with a waxy coating, so that both types of tree cut down on loss of moisture by transpiration.

The Aleppo pine, *Pinus halepensis,* grows from sea level up to 1,000m and is abundant everywhere. It can be 20m high with a straight trunk but is frequently bent and twisted in windy situations. It often grows in fairly open stands but is sometimes in mixed woodlands with evergreen oaks. Two other pines are seen but are not common; the Stone Pine or Umbrella Pine, *Pinus pinea,* recognisable by its umbrella shape, and *Pinus halepensis var.ceciliae* recognised by its upwardly growing branches.

Of the five different evergreen oaks the most common is the Holm Oak, *Quercus ilex.* It has been much used in the past for the making of charcoal (see p. xx) but is still abundant. Other varieties are the Kermes Oak, Cork Oak, Lusitanian Oak and *Quercus rotundifolia.* Bonner gives full details of how to recognise them and where to see them all.

It is not known whether the olive, *Olea europea,* existed wild on the island before it was domesticated. The sub-species *Oleaster* does exist and it is believed that the cultivated olive was developed from this in Syria. Another sub-species, *var.sylvestris,* also grows on the island.

The cultivated olive grows up to 10m in height and has a distinctive silver-grey foliage. Olive trees are seen everywhere, on the central plain and on terraces levelled out of the mountain slopes, where they will be noticed on many of the walks. Some of the trees are very old, 1,000 years or possibly older and their gnarled and twisted trunks are very striking.

The carob tree is also very common. It is a beautiful tree with thick shiny leaves. The new growth is a lighter green than the old, so that the tree often has a two-toned appearance. The fruits are conspicuous, being large pods which are green at first but become brown on ripening and eventually almost black. They have a high sugar content and are used to feed cattle.

The dwarf fan palm, *Chamaerops humilis,* is most distinctive with its sharp lance-like leaves arranged in fans. It occurs only in three localities in Mallorca, but is abundant in these areas which are the north-east around Pollensa and Alcudia, Artà, and the south-west near Andratx.

Although trees are few in variety, there is such a wealth of flowering shrubs that it is impossible to list them all here. Of the more outstanding ones which are to be seen on the walks in this book, the most common is the Lentisk or Mastic Tree, *Pistacia lentiscus,* a dark spreading evergreen shrub which grows from 1-3m high and has a resinous smell. This grows in all situations from sea level to high in the mountains. It is said that keeping a sprig between the lips wards off thirst on hot days. The leaves have 3-6 pairs of dark green leaflets with blunt tips. The flowers occur in the leaf axils and are either reddish or brown, followed by fruits which are first red and then black.

Very noticeable too are the beautiful deep blue flowers of the common rosemary, *Rosmarinus officinalis,* a dense aromatic shrub which seems to bloom somewhere all the year round. The deepest blue flowers have been noticed on Formentor and on the Serra de San Vicens, with swarms of bees humming around each plant.

In March and April the yellow brooms burst into flower, making golden splashes of colour across the hillsides. First seen is *Genista lucida* in March, localized in the Artà area and the south-west, then the thorny broom, *Calicotome spinosa,* in April, easily recognised by its trifoliate leaves and by its long sharp spines.

Hypericum balearicum, an endemic St.John's wort is another common shrub found on mountain slopes, in woodlands and by the roadside. The yellow flowers may be seen sporadically all the year round but it is at its best in spring. The leaves are deep green, narrow and crinkled. There is another endemic St. John's wort, *Hypericum cambessedessii,* which grows in the beds of mountain streams. It has the same flowers as *Balearicum* but the leaves are long and flat and of a beautiful pale almost luminescent green.

Asphodels are everywhere, growing along roadsides and on barren wasteland from the seaside to the mountain tops. The tall spikes of white flowers with a reddish-brown vein on each petal are very conspicuous. In spite of its name, *Asphodelus microcarpus,* it may grow as much as 2m high. The plant is not eaten by animals and its presence is a sign of neglected and overgrazed ground. There is a smaller variety, *Asphodelus fistulosis,* which is less common. The flowers may be pink, but it is most easily identified by the leaves which are round in cross-section, those of microcarpus being V-shaped.

One of the most attractive groups of shrubs are the rockroses which are commonly found in the oak woods as well as in more open spaces. Most common is *Cistus albidus,* or grey-leaved cistus which has velvety leaves and large pink flowers with a crumpled appearance. It flowers in April-June and is very aromatic. *Cistus monspeliensis* or narrow-leaved cistus with smaller white flowers is also common and starts to flower in March. Slightly less common is the sage-leaved cistus, *Cistus salvifolius,* with large white flowers.

The strawberry tree, *Arbutus unedo,* is not a tree but a striking tree-like shrub with big shiny leaves and fruits which turn first orange and then deep red in October and November. The fruits, which are edible but tasteless, ripen at the same time as the white flowers of the following year's crop are in bloom.

Tree heather, *Erica arborea,* grows up to 3m high and is dense but feathery looking with hundreds of tiny white or pale pink flowers in terminal heads. Some of the euphorbias are very striking, especially the tree spurge, *Euphorbia dendroides,* which forms hemispherical bushes with bright yellow glands surrounding the flowers. *Euphorbia characias* is smaller, but very attractive with reddish-brown glands. Bonner says there about twenty different species in the Baleares but only these two are easy to identify.

Two 'hedgehog' or 'pincushion' plants will be noticed by all walkers. Their sharp spines are an adaptation to wind as well as a protection against being eaten by grazing animals. These are *Teucrium subspinosum* and *Astralagus balearicus* and they are very difficult to tell apart when not in flower. In fact in Mallorquin they are both called *coixinets de monja* or nuns' sewing cushions.

Smilax aspera or European sarsaparilla is a climbing plant with hooked spines on the stems, growing up through shrubs and hedges to 1-2m high. The leaves vary enormously in size according to the conditions, being very large in cool shady places and small and narrow in sunny ones. *Smilax balearica* is an endemic variety growing in the mountains. It has minimal leaves and is extremely prickly, becoming a great nuisance to walkers as it often fills the crevices in otherwise bare limestone. The backward curving thorns are notorious for lacerations to flesh and clothes and are one good reason for not wearing shorts on some of the rougher walks. The Mallorquin name is *Aritge*, and there are thousands of them on the aptly named 'Pla des Aritges' crossed on the walk along the archduke's path, Walk 57.

One of the commonest mountain plants is *Ampelodesmus mauritanica,* a pampas-like grass. It's easier to use the short Mallorquin name, *carritx,* for these grasses which form enormous clumps covering large areas. From a distance a green hillside sometimes gives the illusion of being close-cropped turf, but it never is. The tall narrow leaves curve over to reach the ground and it is very easy to step on them with one foot and trip over them with the other. You soon learn to lift your feet high when walking on a narrow path between clumps of *carritx*. So far we have concentrated on the trees and shrubs and some other plants which make their presence obvious to the walker, but there are a number of smaller, less conspicuous plants which are well worth seeking out. A tiny plant, *Crocus minimus,* shows its lilac-pink flowers before the leaves as early as December, for example on the approach to the west top of the Cavall Bernat ridge. The very common but delightful and delicate little *Cyclamen balearicum* can be found in flower in March, if you look under the sheltering leaves of other shrubs, on the mountains and in the woods. The leaves, not unlike house plant cyclamens, are a mottled greyish green and will be seen everywhere. They are a little like the leaves of another common plant, *Arisarum vulgare,* or Friar's Cowl, which flowers in winter and is very common. Similar in leaf shape are *Arum italicum*, *Arum pictum* and *Dranunculus muscivorum.* The latter is particularly striking with a spotted reddish-purple 'spadix' and 'spathe' and strangely incised leaves. (A spadix is a fleshy spike bearing flowers and a spathe is a large bract enclosing the flower head.)

There is no space here to describe plants of other habitats such as the sea-coasts, the sand dunes, the cliff faces and the marshlands. For these the reader is referred to the books listed in the bibliography in Appendix 4. Before beginning the next section though there are two striking plants which deserve a mention although they are not native. One is the prickly pear, which is sometimes used as a dense protective hedge and whose fruits are edible, and the other is *Agave americana*. This plant has huge leathery leaves which may be as long as 2m. After about ten years it send up an enormous tree-like flower spike up to 10m high, after which it dies. Finally, Mallorca is a wonderful place for orchids, flourishing in the pinewoods near the sea, inland in the mountains and even thrusting up through tarmac at the side of the road.

Birds

These notes are written for walkers and not for experts, who are referred to the books listed in the bibliography. Even those with a minimal interest in birds are likely to find this interest stimulated by the number and variety of birds to be seen on nearly every walk. Binoculars and an identification book are a must. Some of the walks described coincide with good birding areas e.g. Na Blanca (No.6), Atalaya de Albercuitx (No.7), Boquer valley (No.8), and Castell del Rei (No.14). There is a good chance of spotting birds on many of the other walks too. In fact the only birds missed would be ducks and waders etc, some of which can be seen at the S'Albufera in north-east Mallorca. A visit to this area is highly recommended; see Note 1. at the end of this chapter.

The best time for birdwatchers to visit the island is the peak migration season in April and May with the last half of September and the first two weeks in October as a second choice. Bird meetings are held at the Hotel Pollentia on the sea-front at Puerto Pollensa, every Monday and Friday during these periods, starting at 9.0 pm., when others birdwatchers can be met and information exchanged. Graham Hearle, who runs these meetings, is also the GOB/RSPB representative and can be contacted at APTDO 83, Sa Pobla. Telephone 86-24-18. Graham also leads small groups on birdwatching excursions.

There is a local birdwatching organisation on the island, the Grupo Ornithologia Balear, or GOB, based in Palma, which is very active. Amongst other things they are responsible for the management of the Albufera, have acquired land at Sa Trapa for conservation, cooperated on the Black Vulture re-establishment programme, (see Note 2.), and produce an annual review and other publications. Incidentally the filming of nesting birds is subject to Spanish law. Anyone planning to do this should ask advice from GOB or SECONA.

Although GOB is well supported locally, many other local people are more interested in shooting birds for the pot, both in and out of the official season which is from the end of August to the end of January. Thrushes are regarded as a serious pest in the olive groves and the traditional practice of *caza a coll* or thrush-netting is still allowed. Thrushes may be seen hanging up in bunches on market stalls. A plateful of robins has been sighted in a domestic refrigerator. However, many birds are protected by law and if any illegal shooting is observed it should be reported to GOB with evidence such as photographs or car-numbers. All eagles, vultures, harriers, owls and flamingoes are protected. Eddie Watkinson described how, with the help of GOB, two men were heavily fined for shooting a flamingo.

Of all the birds of Mallorca, the Hoopoe always arouses great interest even after many sightings. It is extremely striking with its barred black and white wings and tail and erectile crest. It is quite common in many localities, and is often flushed out of hedges as you drive along. Most exciting of all the birds on the island though are the large birds of prey, especially the Black Vultures which may be seen soaring over the Tramuntana, for example on Tomir. (See Note 2.)

Besides the resident Black Vultures, other raptors to be seen in winter are Red Kites, Peregrines, Kestrels and Booted Eagles; more rarely the Golden Eagle and Short-toed Eagle. Marsh Harriers are resident and breed on the larger marshes. Hen harriers and Montagu's harriers are occasional visitors. Ospreys are frequently seen on the marshes and sometimes inland at the Gorg Blau and Cuber reservoirs. One of the most interesting birds is the Eleanora's Falcon which breeds in large colonies on the coastal cliffs all the way from Formentor in the north-east to Dragonera in the south-west. These birds arrive in late April but do not breed until later in the summer. The young birds then feed on tired migrants, an activity which may be observed during September and October in the nesting areas.

Other birds of the mountains include the fairly common Crag Martin which might be seen on Walks 28 and 38 and many other places including the marshes, where flocks of about 1,000 may be seen catching insects on mild winter days.

Alpine Accentors may be seen in small flocks in the northern mountains, but personally we have only seen them singly. One accepted

In the Boquer Valley (Walk 8) (W.Unsworth)

Cala San Vicente and the Cavall Bernat Ridge (W.Unsworth)
On the ridge of La Coma (Walk 10a) (W.Unsworth)

some of our lunch high up on Massanella on a cold New Year's Day. The Blue Rock Thrush is resident in fair numbers, but not easily seen. In spite of its bright metallic blue plumage it tends to disappear behind rocks or bushes as soon as sighted. Pallid Swifts breed on the cliffs and small colonies of Alpine Swifts may be seen in a few places, such as the Artà peninsula, near the Puig Mayor and on the Castell del Rei walk.

In the woodlands the most common winter residents are Blackcaps, Black Redstarts, Crossbills and Goldfinches. Also White Wagtail, Meadow Pipit, Hoopoes, Serins and Greenfinches, Linnets and Great Tits are common, and robins and chaffinches are abundant. Firecrests and Blackcaps are found as high as 800m. Rock Doves are fairly common and nest on cliff faces e.g. at Formentor, as well as in the woods.

The many areas of maquis and scrubland are the preferred habitat of a large number of birds including many warblers. The Sardinian Warbler is a very common resident, as is the Fantailed Warbler. The Marmora's Warbler is resident but somewhat elusive. It may be seen in the Boquer valley and Walk 6 to Na Blanca passes the nesting sites near the Cases Veyas valley.

During the winter there is a big influx of birds from further north in Europe, including starlings, thrushes, finches, waders and wildfowl. Goldcrests are numerous and may even outnumber the resident firecrests.

Other wildlife

July and August are the poorest months for wildlife, apart from grasshoppers and cicadas, but walkers will want to avoid these two months anyway. Even in midwinter there are numerous butterflies and moths and they are abundant the rest of the year. Parrack (1973) mentions that 32 species of butterflies and 250 of the larger moths have been observed. Red Admirals may be seen in the winter, Clouded Yellow and Painted Ladies more commonly in the spring. Some exotic species such as the Two-tailed Pasha arrives in May from North Africa, and the Mediterranean Skipper is found from May onwards. (See Note 3 on the processionary caterpillar.)

Other invertebrates include the shell-bearing molluscs, with the gastropods or snails being of particular interest. In the mountains snails form the basic diet of the Blue Rock Thrush and it has been noticed that the colours of the shells vary in different areas and from season to season. This colour variation is probably of survival value, depending on the colour of the background vegetation.

A large number of frogs live in the marshes and up to a height of 800m in the mountains. Many breed by the outlet from the Cuber reservoir. Most of the frogs are an endemic form of the marsh frog, *Rana ridibunda*, but there is also a green tree frog and three species of toad; the Green Toad, the Natterjack and the Midwife Toad. They mostly hibernate in winter, but can be heard croaking on mild days at the Gorg Blau or below the dam at Cuber.

There are four species of snake: Grass Snake, Viperine Snake, Ladder Snake and Cowl Snake, non of them capable of causing fatalities. The only snake I've ever seen was high up on the south ridge of the Puig Roig. It was no more than two feet long and slithered away into a rock crevice so fast I could not recall its appearance afterwards. It should have been hibernating, but must have come out to enjoy the hot sun.

Two species of broad-toed lizards or geckos are found. The Wall Gecko lives mainly in lowland areas but it is the Disc-Fingered Gecko which is more common in the mountains. The latter is the more bold of the two, but they both disappear quickly when approached. Both are eaten by Hoopoes. Both hibernate, but also come out of hibernation on sunny winter days.

There are few large mammals on Mallorca due to two natural calamities since the severance of the island from the mainland some 800,000 years ago. The first of these was a rising of the water level with widespread flooding and the second was climatic changes associated with the mainland glaciations during the Quaternary. After this the final doom to a number of species was brought by man, not only as a hunter but as a destroyer of the forests through charcoal burning and cultivation. The wild boar and the red fox probably survived until this century. The pine Marten and the genet survive along with true wild cats, feral cats and weasels. Pine martens are still being trapped or shot. (Once we saw one hanging by its neck from the branch of a tree.) Of the smaller mammals shrews, hedgehogs, bats, rabbits, the brown hare and various rodents are quite common. Rabbits provide food for man as well as the birds of prey who also do well off the smaller rodents. (Although extra food is being provided to aid the survival of the black vultures.)

The feral goats are the animals most frequently met with on mountain walks, and the tracks they make through the prickly scrub and the *carritx* are often a help to the walker. They are frequently hunted.

From some of the cliff walks it is worth looking out to sea for whales and dolphins. There are occasional sightings of Sperm Whales and Killer Whales but mostly it is the common dolphin and sometimes the Bottle-nosed and Risso's Dolphin that are seen. Pilot Whales are rare and

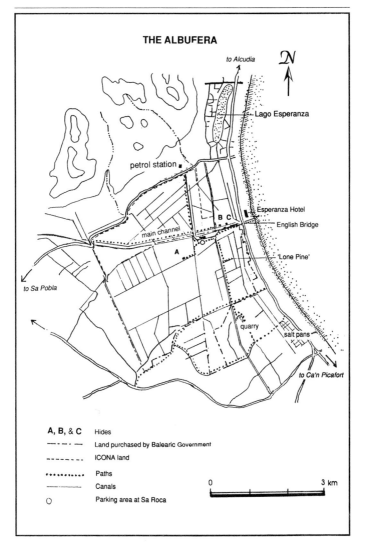

THE ALBUFERA

to Alcudia

Lago Esperanza

petrol station

Esperanza Hotel

B C

English Bridge

main channel

'Lone Pine'

A

to Sa Pobla

quarry

salt pans

to Ca'n Picafort

A, B, & C	Hides
— · — · —	Land purchased by Balearic Government
— — — — —	ICONA land
• • • • • • •	Paths
————	Canals
○	Parking area at Sa Roca

0   3 km

Rorquals more likely. On rare occasions they have been beached after heavy storms.

Note 1. The Albufera

The Albufera is the largest wetland area in the Baleares and one of the most important in Spain. It is on the north-east coast of Mallorca between Alcudia and Ca'n Picafort and covers an area of about 4,000 acres. In the 1960's the northern part came into the hands of property developers and at one time it was thought this might be the fate of the whole area. However, in 1985 the autonomous Balearic Goverment purchased a large area (almost 2,000 acres) and it is now a well-managed nature reserve with an information centre, three hides and an observation tower. More than 200 species of birds have been observed. Most of them marsh birds, but also woodland species and others among the dunes and the trees bordering the canals.

It is well worth spending some time here and there are many paths and tracks providing quite long walks. A circular walk can be made by returning along the coast which is bordered by pinewoods. The reserve can be reached by bus from Puerto Pollensa. Ask for 'El puente Inglesos' (The English Bridge), or look out for the Hotel Esperanza on the left just before the bridge. If driving, start signalling a right turn before the bridge, as it is a very sudden and narrow turn. There is a car park (with toilets) near the information office. (See map.p.35)

Note 2. The Black Vulture recuperation programme

Since the beginning of the century the resident population of Black Vultures on Mallorca has seriously declined. In recent years attempts have been made to reverse this tendency and already some success has been achieved. The first and simplest method has been to put out food for them high up in the mountains. Since tractors have replaced horses and mules there is less carrion which would have been a natural source of food in the past.

The second method has been the introduction of immature and injured birds recovered on the mainland. Twelve of these were introduced between 1984 and 1987.

The third method has been to release chicks hatched in captivity into the wild through the technique known as 'hacking'. Fledgling chicks are put into an artificial nest with a tame vulture who cannot fly. They are fed under cover of darkness so that they do not become accustomed to human beings. The chicks teach themselves to fly and already a number of them have successfully integrated with the local population.

These birds live, breed and feed in the high mountains. They are wonderful and exciting to watch but it is essential that they are not disturbed. For this reason, walkers in the area between the Puig Roig and Ternelles should take special care to keep to footpaths, to avoid undue noise, and preferably to limit numbers in walking parties to less than six. The area of Mortitx is particularly sensitive and permission to walk in this area should be sought from the information office at the Albufera. Hopefully some time in the future observation hides may be provided so that the vultures can be seen without disturbance.

Note 3. Processionary caterpillars

A number of curious features will be noted when walking through pinewoods. These include strange grey nest-like objects hanging from branches, wooden boxes also suspended from branches, and in some areas large numbers of dead pine trees lying on the ground and riddled with holes.

The fact is that the pinewoods of Mallorca are under serious threat by attacks from 'processionary' caterpillars. The caterpillars get their name from their habit of walking in single file when searching for food, and can form chains many metres long. They have voracious appetites and devour the leaves of pine trees (and other trees) and eventually the trees die. They secrete fine silk threads which are used for returning to the nests, which are the grey bags seen in the trees.

Various attempts have been made to eradicate the caterpillars at enormous cost. At one time cartridges were issued free by the Ministry of Ag. and Fish to encourage people to shoot the nests out of the trees. This was stopped when it was found the free cartridges were being used in normal hunting pursuits. Cutting off and burning branches with nests on has been tried but is only effective if the burning is done on concrete, as the caterpillars can burrow into the ground and chrysalids can survive there for a year, to emerge as moths. Large areas have been treated with insecticides, but the best results are being obtained with biological control, using traps containing pheromenes. These are the boxes seen on the trees in many woodlands. The pheromenes attract the female moths, who can lay up to 200 eggs. They get trapped in the lure and die. No damage is done to other flora and fauna.

MAN AND HIS IMPACT ON THE LANDSCAPE

There is evidence that Mallorca was inhabited more than 6,000 years ago, making use of natural caves. In the 1960's bones of extinct antelopes mingled with human remains were found in the Cueva de Muleta near Soller. The human remains were dated at 3985 B.C.+ 109 years. This cave is in a Jurassic limestone outcrop and consists of two levels connected by a vertical chimney, forming a natural animal trap. Another major site, even older, is that of Son Matge, near Valldemossa. This is dated at about 4730 B.C. and has been used as a corral for animals, then as a habitation, a burial site and a workshop.

These caves are not easily accessible, but in the village of Cala San Vicente there are some caves partly natural and partly man-made, the former probably dwelling caves and the latter long rectangular rooms, probably burial chambers. These caves are to be found in a small park full of flowering shrubs, at the western edge of the village. The date of these is probably about 2,000 years later than the Muleta cave.

In 1979 a very important find was made on the ridge of La Punta which separates the San Vicente valley from the road between Pollensa and the Port. Local climbers found the entrance to a large cave which had been used as a burial chamber. It was very carefully excavated and the objects found sent to various museums on the mainland for evaluation. Some have now found their way back to the museum in Pollensa. The most interesting finds at La Punta were the remains of two wooden bull-like creatures with hollow bodies. These have been carbon-dated at 320 B.C. and are assumed to have contained human ashes. Reconstructions of these can be seen at the museum.

Some time during the 2,000 years before the Romans arrived, the Balearic people progressed from living in caves to building stone dwellings, megalithic structures containing towers or *talayots*. Not a great deal seems to be known about these times, but there are a number of sites where they can be seen. Near Artà there is the Talayot de Ses Paisses, but the largest and best documented is that of Capacorp Vey or Vell, near Lluchmayor. This is maintained as a national monument by the Institute of Catalan Studies and is well worth a visit. It contains 28 dwellings and five *talayots*, two square and three circular. One of the square *talayots* has an opening at ground level from which a low tunnel descends in a spiral to a small room partly roofed by olive wood branches. (To go in here means hands and knees and a torch held between the teeth.) The function of this room was probably religious. This village has been dated at about 1000 B.C. and was thought to be occupied well into Roman times.

Mallorca has no mineral resources, so the finding of ingots and bronze implements, such as the bronze button at La Punta shows that trading must have occurred with merchants from the civilisations of the eastern Mediterranean. There would have been settlements on or near the sites of most of the present ports. The Carthaginians provided garrisons to protect their trading posts, recruiting from among the local warriors armed with slings. The name of the islands, the Balearics, comes from the Greek verb, ballein, meaning 'to throw'. The leather slings fired stones the size of tennis balls, carried in a leather pouch. Legend has it that boys were trained in this art by having to shoot down their daily food from where it had been placed high up in the trees.

The Romans invaded the island in 123 B.C. They built the cities of Palma and Alcudia (then known as Pollentia). The remains of the Roman town of Alcudia include the theatre on the road to Puerto Alcudia and other buildings near the Tucan crossroads. In the Pollensa area there is a Roman bridge on the north side of the town, near the starting point of several walks in the area. The remains of a Roman aqueduct, which was thought to take water all the way to Alcudia, are seen in the Ternelles valley.

The fact that there are so few Roman remains is partly due to the depredations of the Vandals after the island was abandoned by the Romans. During this time too the main setlements began to develop a few kilometers inland from the ports, which is why today there are still the towns of Pollensa, Alcudia, Soller and Andratx each with its own port. Watch towers too were built on headlands and hills so that warning of approaching invaders and pirates could be given These watchtowers or *atalayas* are seen on many walks. They are usually circular and can often be climbed by iron ladders to a viewing platform at the top. One of the best preserved, and recently restored, is that of Albercutx, Walk 7.

After the rout of the Vandals in North Africa by the Byzantine general Belisarius the Balearics were incorporated into what is now Tunisia. Mallorca again became a trading post protected by military stongholds, this time of the Byzantine Empire. This period was followed by very unsettled times and constant strife between the Moors and the Christians, beginning with Arabic raids in 707 A.D. This is still re-enacted today in various folk festivals, such as is held in Pollensa every 2nd August.

Arabic influence on the development of agriculture during times of peace is still to be seen in the countryside They introduced the *norias* or water-wheels used to pump water from underground reservoirs and wells, and the *seguias* or open water channels used to irrigate the fields. They also began the terracing of the steep hillsides with massive dry stone walls that enable cultivation of otherwise impossible places.

Placenames on the map are another legacy of the Arabs. *Bini* in a name means 'the house of', as in Binisalem and Biniaraitx. In Palma the arches of the Almudaina palace and the Arab baths are still to be seen and there is a Moorish influence on many country houses.

The modern history of Mallorca dates from 1229 when Jaime I of Aragon (known as 'the conqueror') led an expedition of 150 ships and 16,000 men to re-claim the island. The landing was made at Santa Ponsa, after storms diverted them from the original plan of landing at Puerto Pollensa. After several months the reconquest was complete and a new state proclaimed in March 1230. Although a modern style government was introduced this was not the end of Mallorca's troubles but the beginning of new ones. When Jaime I died in 1276 he left his estates of Aragon, Catalonia and Valencia to his eldest son Pedro III and the Balearics, Rousillon and Montpellier to his younger son Jaime II. Pedro III's son and successor, Alfonso III, then invaded Mallorca and proclaimed himself king. The castle of Alarò (Walk 40) was one of the last strongholds to hold out against him. Alfonso committed such terrible atrocities in this siege that he was excommunicated and eventually Jaime II returned to the throne and proved an excellent ruler.

During his reign Palma cathedral was built and so was Bellver Castle. He patronised the great scholar Ramon Llull who founded the hermitage on Randa and wrote his major works there. He encouraged the development of trade and agriculture by granting charters to 11 market towns. His son Sancho continued his father's enlightened policies, but owing to bad health had to spend much time away from state affairs. The Aragonese under Pedro IV again invaded the island in 1343 at Paguerra. Sancho's nephew and heir Jaime III tried to regain possession but was killed in battle in 1349. That brought to an end the reign of the independent kings of Mallorca, which became part of Aragon. (In 1716 Mallorca lost the title of kingdom and became a province of Spain.)

From 1349 until the present Mallorca had a chequered history, with invasions, rebellions, and natural disasters such as earthquakes, floods, and outbreaks of cholera and bubonic plague. This chapter is not a history of Mallorca, but aims to point out the significance of some of the features seen on the island, so for further details of the history, see some of the books listed in the bibliography. The castles and the watchtowers are some of the most striking features, but other buildings also found on mountain tops are the *ermitas* or sanctuaries. One such is on the Puig de Maria, near Pollensa (see Walk 21). Many others are in use and some of them offer refreshments and accommodation. (See San Salvador, Walk 69.)

Cultivation

One of the most impressive sights in Mallorca is the blossoming of the almond trees in early spring when large areas of the island become pink and white. If you arrive by plane during daylight in February you may even observe this from the air. There are said to be over six million trees and most of the crop is exported. Planting of the almonds began in 1765, but the olive tree has been cultivated for much longer. Some of the trees are believed to be 1,000 years old or more, and their gnarled and twisted trunks will be seen on many of the walks. Sometimes you may see almonds or olives being harvested, the almonds being shaken from the trees onto sheets spread on the ground and the olives being knocked down by long poles.

Orange trees and other citrus fruits too are another sight to delight and interest the walker. The main crop is in January but fruit seems to be on some trees all the year round. The scent of the blossom is wonderful. Sometimes in the winter you can see blossom, green unripe fruit and bright orange (or yellow) ripe fruit all at the same time. Soller is famous for its orange groves, but they can be seen in many other parts of the island too, for example in the *huertas* or market gardens near Pollensa on the way to the Ternelles valley in Walks 14 and 15.

Potatoes are another crop grown for export, many of them on the central plain near Inca and Sa Pobla, including earlies for export to England. Strawberries are already ripening here under cloches in February and March. Other fruits grown are mandarins, peaches, apricots, melons and figs. Vines grow at Binisalem and near Felanitx where some very good wine is made. Fresh vegetables grow all the year round, thanks to the sunshine and the irrigation system. Often vegetables such as broad beans and peas are grown on terraces between the fruit trees. Several crops can be grown in succession and the first peas and beans will be harvested in February. The village markets all have a fine display of fruit and vegetables, most of them grown locally. It is a splendid treat to buy delicious fresh oranges, still with leaves attached, two or three kilos at a time.

The methods of cultivation too are a pleasure to watch. Horses and mules can still be seen pulling a primitive plough along narrow terraces where it would be impossible to use a tractor. Seed too is often hand sown from a sack hanging round the neck in a manner which may be archaic but is obviously still efficient. Corn and cereal crops are grown too, and grass for grazing is often sown on the olive terraces

There are few cattle on Mallorca and much milk and dairy products are imported from Menorca. However there are large flocks of sheep and many goats in the mountains. These are usually belled and sometimes hobbled. Pigs are sometimes seen foraging about in oakwoods in a semi-wild state. Besides acorns they dig up roots and can make a real mess of some of the woodland paths in their search for food. One of the main animal markets is at Sineu, near the centre of the island and is held on Wednesdays. Here can be seen magnificent rams, tiny lambs and goats, cages of birds and all manner of livestock.

Rural Industries

There were two major 'rural industries', the remains of which will be seen time and again on many walks in this book. In fact they are intimately connected with these walks because many of the footpaths were made by workers in these occupations. These two activities were snow-collecting and charcoal-burning and knowing something about these adds greatly to the interest of the walks.

(a) Snow collecting

The highest man-made paths on Mallorca were all built by the *nevaters* or snow-collectors. Snow was collected on all the highest mountains to make ice for use in the summer, and conserved in pits or buildings known as *casas de nieve*. There were 7 on the Puig Mayor, 7 on Massanella, 2 on Tomir and on Teix and several on the Alfabia ridge. Most of them were at a height of over 900m. These structures are sometimes circular and sometimes rectangular, usually partly or wholly below ground level. The most unusual is the one on Tomir, below the Coll dels Puig des Ca, which is roofed over.

In winter when the mountains were covered with snow, groups of men from the nearest villages went up to gather the snow in carriers and baskets made from cane or grass. To make collecting easier flat platforms were often made and cleared of vegetation. These can still be seen. Here the snow was arranged in layers and trampled down hard to pack it into ice, in time to the following rhyme:

pitgen sa neu, pitgen sa neu
i tots estan dins ses cases
peguen potades, peguen potades
en Toni, en Xisco, en Juan i N'Andreu

tramp the snow, tramp the snow
and throw it in the pit
Beat it down, beat it down,
on Tony, Harry, John and Andrew.

The packed snow was put in the pit and each layer covered with thin layers of grass (probably *carritx*), to make it easier to extract the blocks when required. When the pit was full, it was protected with a layer of ashes and finally a thick covering of branches. One man remained on duty all the year to maintain the covering in perfect condition. In the summer nights, huge blocks of the snow-ice were taken down on muleback to the villages and towns. It was not only used for ice-creams and cooling drinks, but also medicinally. An emulsion with olive-oil was used for dressing wounds and was believed to stop bleeding.

The local authority controlled the price and limited the production of ice, supposedly to prevent speculation. There was a specific tax on it. Sometimes ice had to be imported from Cataluña by boat, but other years there was overproduction and ice was exported to Menorca. It appears that the last occasion in which a snow-pit was used was in 1925 on the Puig de Massanella. The *casa de nieve* on the Son Moragues estate was built in the seventeenth century, but abandoned in the eighteenth century as it was not really at a high enough altitude. This one is seen on Walks 55 and 57. Nearby, the hut where the *nevaters* lived has been made into a shelter for walkers.

(b) Charcoal production
Many other paths used by walkers today were made by the charcoal workers. Almost every wood of evergreen oaks was formerly used in the production of charcoal and there are still plentiful signs of this activity. The former charcoal hearths or pitsteads appear as flat circular areas often ringed by stones and covered with bright green moss. Many have been pointed out as landmarks in route descriptions. They are known as *sitjes*, (singular *sitja*). The production of charcoal in Mallorca continued until butane gas became popular, roughly in the 1920's, although in some

areas it continued for longer and there are still people alive today who worked in this industry in their youth. Occasionally pieces of charcoal can still be found on the sites. Its only use in Mallorca was for cooking, preferred rather than wood because it gives a cleaner and steadier heat.

The charcoal burners began work in April and lived and worked all summer in the woods with their families. They could not leave the site because charcoal burning is a delicate operation and everything could be ruined in a moment of neglect. For this reason they built huts to live in, the remains of which are often seen in the woods, together with a stone oven used to bake bread. These ovens are a beehive shape, instantly recognisable. They can be seen on Walks 31, 32, 57, 58 and others.

The process of making charcoal began with the felling of large oaks, of a diameter stipulated by the landowner. Each *carbonero* had his own area known as a *ranxo*. Axes and enormous two-handed saws were used to fell the trees. Meanwhile a perfectly flat and circular site had to be prepared. Stones were carefully arranged so that sufficient circulation of air would carbonise the wood without igniting it. On this platform the cut logs and branches were arranged in a 'cupola', leaving a narrow central chimney. Over all this was arranged a covering of gravel and clay. A ladder was needed to reach the top of the chimney through which the *carbonero* dropped live coals to start the process, and to feed the fire from time to time with small pieces of dry wood. Constant vigilance and expertise were needed on the part of the worker.

During the process the weight of the wood was reduced by 75-80%. Each firing lasted for 10-12 days, and would produce around 2,800 kilograms. When the operation was complete the covering was removed and very hot pieces extracted with a shovel and rake. Sieved earth was used for quenching as using water caused a loss of quality. Finally the charcoal was sorted into a number of different grades and taken by muleteers for sale at special shops in the villages. As a by-product, bark from the oak trees was collected and used for tanning.

A fine reconstruction of a charcoal-burning structure can be seen on the Son Moragues estate in Walk 57.

(c). Lime-burning

Brief mention must be made of the lime kilns which will be seen from time to time. There are three of them in the Cairats valley, Walk 57, but they will be seen in almost every woodland. They are rather different from those seen in the British Isles in that they are normally cylindrical. Lime is used for whitening houses, something which used to be done every year, and also for making mortar in the construction industry. Great heat is needed to initiate the reaction $CaCO_3 \rightarrow CaO + CO_2$, so these *hornos de calc* were always built near a plentiful supply of wood. Great destruction of woodland was often the result. Although there is a vast amount of limestone on Mallorca, stones used to produce lime were always chosen very carefully and were known as *piedra viva* or living stones.

From the base of the circular pit used as a kiln, a cupola was built up of large stones with spaces left between them so that the flames could pass through. Above the cupola the rest of the oven was built up of stones and the space between the cupola and the outer walls of the kiln filled with pieces of limestone for calcining. The whole structure was then covered with slaked lime and soil. The interior was filled with wood and the fire lit. It was kept burning for a period of time varying from nine to 15 days, wood being thrown in continually. The quantity required is impressive: up to ten tons of branches during one firing. A firing would produce around 100-150 tons of lime. It was very hard work, the fire needing to be fed day and night. Nor was it financially rewarding, according to the old proverb *'Qui fa calc, va descalc'* (he who makes lime goes barefoot).

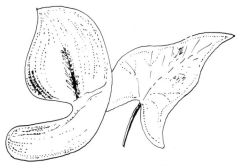

ARUM PICTUM

WALKING IN MALLORCA

Equipment and clothing

Although the winters in Mallorca are mild and the weather is normally ideal for walking, bad weather is not unknown as in any area of high mountains. There are days when a warm sweater, anorak, hat, gloves and waterproofs will be appreciated especially on the higher tops. There will always be days when these extra clothes will stay in the rucksack even in January, the coldest month, but it's as well to be prepared. Boots are advised for most walks, although for those graded 'C' some may prefer trainers or strong shoes. Shorts are not advised because of the extremely prickly vegetation unless long trousers are taken along too. Sunglasses and a sunhat might be needed even in winter for those sensitive to hot sun. It is advisable to carry water or other drinks as dehydration can be very unpleasant and debilitating. The local oranges are both thirst-quenching and cheap.

Snow falls on the high tops most years, but it is very rare for it to fall at sea level as it did in December and January 1984-5. When this happens, the roads to the mountains are cut off for days on end, not only by snow but by fallen trees. The snow is usually wet and soft, so ice axes and crampons can be left at home. Of standard walking equipment take a whistle, compass and torch. Darkness falls early in midwinter, 17.30 on the shortest days and some of the walks are long.

This book deals only with walks and occasional scrambles, none of which require a rope, although some parties prefer to take a short length for the Torrente de Pareis, Walk 28. The whole island abounds in steep rock and there is much good rock climbing, with many crags hardly developed. (See *Costa Blanca Rock* by Chris Craggs, Cicerone Press.)

Maps

One of the best maps for getting about the island is the Firestone map, *Baleares: Map Turistico*, scale 1:125,000. This is available at petrol stations, newsagents and some general stores throughout the island. Another good general map is *Majorca Leisure Map: What to see - where to go,* scale 1:120,000. This has the bonus of 66 coloured photographs on the back of places of interest, with brief descriptions. This is also commonly available.

There are no ordnance survey maps of the high standard of the

46

British O.S. maps or the French IGN maps. However, since the first edition of this guidebook, new Spanish IGN maps have been published on the 1:25,000 scale. These are based on an aerial survey of 1979, and the contouring seems more accurate than on the military maps which were the only ones available previously. However, it is disconcerting that many roads and paths are missed out, especially where they are hidden by trees. Not only when they are in woodlands either, as even the well-known path up the barranc from Biniaraix to the Cases de L'Ofre is missing. This means that the really serious walker will want to have both sets of maps. The military maps are available on the scale of 1:50,000 as well as 1:25,000. To avoid confusion when ordering it is best to quote the quadrant by compass point rather than number. A list of the relevant military maps with the IGN equivalents is given at the end of this chapter.

The most important maps for walkers are Pollensa, Soller and Inca on the 1:50,000 scale. Of the 1:25,000 maps Son Marc, Pollenca, Soller, Esporles, Alarò and Selva are the most relevant. All maps, folded and in a plastic wallet, can be ordered from The Map Shop, 15 High Street, Upton-upon-Severn, Worcs, WR8 0HJ. When in stock they will be supplied by return of post. (£1.95 each, plus postage, at time of going to press). Stanfords' International Map Centre at 14 Long Acre, London also stock them, or they can be bought in Palma at the Libreria Fondevila at 14 Calle Arabi. A climbing shop in Pollensa, attached to a hardware shop, the Ca'n Morou in the Calle Costa i Llobera also stocks them.

When using any of the maps for exploration, remember that the terrain is frequently more complex than is indicated by the map. Steep cliffs and crags are not always shown, new roads appear and old ones fall into disuse. Always leave time to get back to your starting point in case of unforeseen difficulties.

Grading definitions

All the walks in this book have been done by the writer. An attempt has been made to assess the difficulties in such a way that anyone using the book can form a reasonable idea of what to expect. Such assessment is obviously very subjective and can be influenced by weather conditions at the time and many other factors. When heavy rain occurs dry stream-beds can become raging torrents, landslips may occur, rocks can fall and the ground can become very slippery. At such times it is better to wait for things to improve, and once the sun is out again all the surface water quickly disappears.

Assuming normal conditions, the walks have been graded into three categories which can be called difficult, average and easy or A, B and C. These categories refer to the terrain and the route-finding difficulties. The approximate times, distances, and heights involved are given separately in addition to the grading. Under the heading 'type of walk' a description gives details of what is involved. It cannot be over emphasised that much of the walking in Mallorca is over very rough ground and this often takes much longer to negotiate than expected. Even the paths are usually rough and stony and require care. The walking times allow photography, some birdwatching and flower identification but do not include long stops for refreshments. On the whole they are for slower than average walkers, more interested in enjoying the scenery than setting up speed records.

The grades

   A   A strenuous walk, often pathless in places and on rough ground with considerable route-finding and/or some scrambling. Normally only for experienced walkers.

   B   An average mountain walk which may call for some skill in route-finding, but mainly on paths.

   C   Easy walking along well-defined paths or tracks and with no route-finding difficulties.

Access

Many of the walks in this book go across private land. The maps do not show rights of way. However, by Spanish law, there is a right of way on any track leading to the sea, to a mountain top, or to monasteries, hermitages, towers, castles, or other famous landmarks, which just about covers every walk. That is the theory, but in practice it seems to be slightly different. For example access restrictions have been imposed on the Ternelles valley and visitors are only allowed through the entrance gate on Saturday. In certain areas walkers have even been threatened in a very unpleasant manner. However, we personally have met with nothing but friendliness from the landowners we have encountered. On occasion they have gone out of their way to point out routes, and obviously appreciated our attempts to speak a few words of their language.

   One fact worth knowing is that the ubiquitous sign *coto privado de caza* only means 'private hunting' and can be ignored by walkers. However, if there appears to be a lot of shooting going on, it might be more prudent to choose another walk. The black and white rectangular sign divided diagonally often seen on fence posts and gates also means private hunting.

Many tracks have a standard 'no entry' sign which means that cars are prohibited and this must be respected, but should not stop walkers. Often access gates or stiles are provided when the gate is a locked one, but more of these are needed. On the other hand there are some private estates where walkers are distinctly unwelcome. Exploration stops short when faced with three metre high fences and heavily padlocked gates topped with barbed wire and iron spikes.

There is no access to the summit of the highest mountain of Mallorca, the Puig Mayor, because it is occupied by a military radar station. The western spur, the Penyal de Mitx Dia, is outside the boundary and the ascent has been described in Walk 43. At one time there was a popular annual excursion to the top of the Puig Mayor itself to see the sunrise at the time of the summer solstice. A long walk was made of it, starting at Biniaraix and following the old road up to Monnaber, going up at night to avoid the scorching heat of the sun.

Walkers' 'country code'

It should go without saying that all walkers should have the utmost respect for the countryside through which they walk and for the people who live and work there. Although the vast majority of walkers have this ingrained in them, the fact remains that there are always a few people about who are careless or antisocial and by irresponsible actions can do serious damage to natural resources and private property. For this reason I am spelling out this code here, in the hope that the responsible readers of this book will not only continue to abide by the code themselves but take an active part in seeing that others do so. Even if this is only in minor ways, such as taking back an extra bit of litter, or closing a gate left open by others it can all help. Watching out for carelessness in use of matches in dry areas could even prevent the devastation of a fire.

The Country Code

1. Guard against all risk of fire.
   Forests, woodlands and scrub are all highly inflammable. Take every care with matches and cigarette ends and do not light fires except in recognised fireplaces.

2. Fasten all gates.
   Even if the gate is found open, unless obviously fastened open by the farmer.

3. Keep dogs under control.

Keep dogs on leads whenever there is livestock about. Some farms have clear pictorial signs not allowing dogs at all.

4. Keep to the paths across farm land.

Crops can be ruined by people's feet.

5. Avoid damaging fences, hedges and walls.

Repairs are costly. Keep to recognised routes, using gates and stiles.

6. Leave no litter.

All litter is unsightly and some is dangerous to livestock, such as glass, tins and plastic. Take all litter back to the town.

7. Safeguard water supplies.

Avoid polluting water supplies in any way. Never interfere with wells, springs or cattle troughs.

8. Protect wildlife, wild plants and trees.

Wildlife is best observed, not collected. To pick or uproot flowers, carve trees and rocks, or disturb wild animals and birds not only destroys other people's pleasure but can irrevocably damage the ecology.

9. Go carefully on country roads.

Country roads have special dangers: blind corners, high walls, deep drops at the edge, slow-moving tractors, sheep and goats. Drivers should reduce their speed and take extra care; walkers should keep to the left, facing oncoming traffic.

10. Respect the life of the countryside.

Set a good example and try to fit in with the life and work of the countryside. This way good relations between walkers and landowners are preserved and those who follow are not regarded as enemies.

The importance of the Country Code cannot be too strongly emphasised. There is already some evidence that increasing numbers of walkers have resulted in landowners being antagonised and discouraging access across their land. Large parties should take special care over closing of gates, as it is only too easy to assume that the next one through will see to it. Leaders should try to ensure there is a responsible person at the rear. Large parties in

themselves, with their tendency to chatter and spread out over a long line can be resented as an intrusion into the landscape. Every effort should be made to keep numbers in guided parties to a minimum.

ICONA

This is the national institute for nature conservation. (El Instituto Nacional para la Conservacion de la Natureleza.) They are doing a lot of good work on the island and have acquired several tracts of land which are being conserved for public use, constructed some excellent paths and provided well-equipped picnic sites with shelters, cooking facilities and toilets. One of their largest undertakings is the purchase of the Son Moragues estate near Valldemossa which has become an openair museum with reconstructions of charcoal-burning sites etc (See Walk 57).

SECONA

This is the nature conservation office of the Balearic government.

Mountain Rescue

There is no mountain rescue organisation on the island. In the event of an accident the Guardia Civil should be contacted. (Telephone number 46-51-12). Walking alone in the mountains is not recommended. There are many places where you could break a leg or worse and not be found for days or even weeks.

Guides

1. Pere Llobera, Calle Costa i Llobera, 40, Pollensa. Tel.53-03-65. Walking, rock-climbing and caving. Also sells guidebooks and maps.

2. Biel Ordinas, Calle Jaime I, 24, Santa Maria. Tel. 62-01-62. Walking and rock-climbing.

Relevant military maps and their IGN equivalents

Military maps	IGN maps	
1:50,000 645 645 IV (NW) CABO FORMENTOR	1:25,000 645 I (NW) Cabo Formentor 645 III (SW) Aucanada	1:25,000 Cap de Formentor 645 III (SW) Alcanada (n.y.p.)
644 POLLENSA	644 I (NE) Cala de San Vicens 644 III/IV (SW) Son March 644 II (SE) Pollensa	644 II (NE) Cala de Sant Vicenc 644 III (SW) Son Marc 644 IV (SE) Pollenca
670 SOLLER	670 I (NE) Soller 670 III (SW) Esporlas 670 II (SE) Alarò	670 II (NE) Soller 670 III (SW) Esporles 670 IV (SE) Alarò
671 INCA	671 IV (NW) Selva 671 III (SW) Inca	671 I (NW) Selva 671 III (SW) Inca
698 PALMA	698 IV (NW) 698 III (SW) Calvia	698 I (NW) Sa Vileta 698 III (SW) Calvia
697 ANDRAITX	697 I & IV (NW & NE) Dragonera 697 II (SE)	697 II (NE) n.y.p 697 IV (SE) n.y.p.

1. PLAYA BAIX, ALCUDIA

The Playa Baix is a small, sheltered and unspoilt beach on the Alcudia peninsula where the sea is an incredible turquoise colour. It is not safe for bathing as there is a very strong undertow, but it is an excellent place for a picnic on a sunny day in winter or early spring. The approach through a sheltered valley with both woodland and open scrub is good for birdwatching.

To reach the starting point, take the Mal Pas road from the second traffic lights in Alcudia. If approaching from the direction of Puerto Pollensa, this means going straight on at the first lights, then at the second lights turn right and immediately left as the junction is slightly offset. Drive along this road for almost 2km then turn sharp right at a minor crossroads where there are two bars, the Bodega del Sol and Ca'n Tomeu. Keep straight on along this narrow country road to the Parque de Victoria, going through the double iron gates (usually open) and parking just inside.

Type of walk: A short easy walk along a level forest track with a gentle rise to the Coll Baix. The narrow path down to the sea is a good one, but there is some rough bouldery ground where it reaches the beach. (This path passes below steep cliffs with some loose rock; beware falling stones.)

Starting point:	Parque de Victoria entrance
Time:	3hr
Distance:	9km
Highest point reached:	148m
Total height climbed:	211m
Grade:	C
Map:	Aucanada 1:25,000

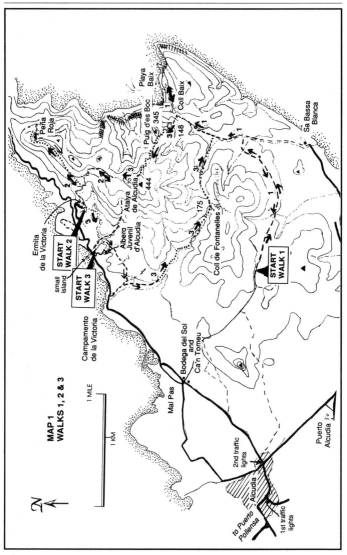

MAP 1
WALKS 1, 2 & 3

1 MILE

1 KM

N

Ermita
de la Victoria

START
WALK 2

small
island

START
WALK 3

Campamento
de la Victoria

Peña
Roja

Atalya
de Alcudia

Albera
Juvenil
d'Alcudia

444

Puig d'es Boc

Playa
Baix

Coll Baix

345

148

175

Coll de Fontanelles

START
WALK 1

Sa Bassa
Blanca

Mal Pas

Bodega del Sol
and
Ca'n Tomeu

2nd traffic
lights

Alcudia

Puerto
Alcudia

1st traffic
lights

to Puerto
Pollensa

Follow the main forest road into the park ignoring all side turnings. At first there are pinewoods on the left, then open scrub, and fields with almond trees and carobs on the right, sheltered by a low ridge. Further on the track runs through more pinewoods which are fairly open and have an undergrowth mainly of lentiscs and narrow-leaved cistus. There are dwarf fan palms, carritx, euphorbias and asphodels and a few giant orchids too.

About 30 minutes after the start there is a private road on the right signposted to Sa Bassa Blanca. Ignore this and keep on the main track which soon rises up to the Coll Baix, where there is a shelter provided by ICONA. Follow the path down to the beach. This goes quite a long way to the right before descending in zigzags, to avoid the steep and loose cliffs which are in the way of a straight descent from the col to the beach.

Park entrance - Coll Baix	1hr 5min
Coll Baix - Playa Baix	20min
Playa Baix - Coll Baix	30min
Coll Baix - park entrance	1hr 5min

(The Atalaya de Alcudia can easily be ascended from the Coll Baix by a good path if a longer walk is wanted. See Walk 3.)

2. PEÑA ROJA AND ATALAYA DE ALCUDIA

The Alcudia peninsula lies between the bays of Pollensa and Artà. It is hilly and wooded and although the Cap del Pinar at the end is a military area and out-of-bounds, part of it forms a national park and provides some easy and very attractive walks. Although only a low stump some 2m high is all that remains of the original watch-tower, it is still a wonderful viewpoint. There is a shelter below the top with a well on the flat terrace outside. The first part of the walk to the Peña Roja makes a worthwhile short excursion on its own, along an attractive path undulating below red cliffs and overlooking the sea. The barrel of an old cannon still lies on the flat circular top. At one time this had a low stone parapet and a cobbled floor.

Leave Alcudia by the Mal Pas road by going straight on at the second traffic lights if coming from the Puerto Pollensa direction. The junction is slightly off-set so that it is necessary to turn right then immediately left. Follow the coast road, turning right after approximately 4km to the *Ermita* where there is a large parking area, picnic places and a restaurant with a terrace overlooking the sea.

Type of walk: Easy, along wide tracks and well-made footpaths kept in good repair by ICONA. There are even handrails along the exposed places. The last ten minutes to the top of the Peña Roja is by a rocky path which is a little steep and a bit of a scramble.

Starting point:	Ermita de la Victoria
Time:	3hr 10min
Distance:	6km
Highest point reached:	444m
Total height climbed:	409m
Grade:	C+
Map:	Aucana 1:25,000 or
	Cabo Formentor 1:50,000

Go up past the *Ermita* buildings by a wide track from the corner of the car park. After 20 minutes this makes a sharp bend to the right. Almost immediately turn left along the Peña Roja path which is signposted. This path contours along the base of the reddish cliffs and eventually rounds the end of the ridge by going through a short tunnel. Round the corner the path leads to an old stone shelter with an empty water storage tank behind it. Near this is found the start of the rough steep path which leads up in about ten minutes to the top of the Peña Roja.

Return by the same way to the wide track, turn left along it and continue up to a broad col at 315m. From here a stony ascent leads to a well-built path with protective handrail. This winds up to easy ground below the summit. Near the top, by the *Ermita* signpost, will be seen a very good path coming up from the Coll Baix, used in Walk 3. From the top, drop down a short way on the south side to reach the shelter.

Ermita - Peña Roja	1hr 5min
Peña Roja - Atalaya de Alcudia	1hr 15min
Atalaya de Alcudia - Ermita	50min

3. ATALAYA DE ALCUDIA BY FONTANELLES

This is a circular walk making use of a disused footpath in the Fontanelles valley which goes over the Coll de Fontanelles to join a forest road on the south side of the Atalaya. The road formerly a forest track but surfaced in 1991, leads through the forest and up to the Coll Baix where there is an ICONA shelter. A footpath goes down to a small beach from here, described in Walk 1, and this could be followed if a longer walk is wanted.

From the Coll Baix there is a good path built by ICONA up to the Atalaya. This is an excellent viewpoint, described in Walk 2.

Leave Alcudia by the road to Malpas, by doing a right and immediate left at the second traffic lights if arriving from the direction of Puerto Pollensa. The starting point is 4km further on from here. It is found 700m after crossing a stream-bed next to a disused bridge and almost immediately opposite a small island close to the shore. Turn right into the track leading to the hostel and then immediately left into a rough car park in the pinewoods. If doing this walk when the sea is warm, there is a small shingly beach here with picnic tables and barbecues.

Type of walk: Fairly easy on tracks and paths, but route-finding quite difficult in places, especially if trying to do the walk in reverse.

Starting point:	Alberg Juvenil d'Alcudia
Time:	4hr
Distance:	9km
Highest point reached:	444m
Total height climbed:	559m
Grade:	B
Map:	Aucana 1:25,000 or
	Cabo Formentor 1:50,000

Start the walk from the rough car-park in the pinewoods, about 35m from the road leading to the hostel. Go up the low pine-covered ridge between this road and the track in the valley floor. The path is not obvious at first being obscured by pine-needles but soon becomes evident at the point where it levels out. Follow it through open ground with newly-planted trees and ignore a cross-track. About five minutes after this cross-track turn right at a T-junction and roughly one minute later turn left along a track coming from the Campamento de la Victoria. The tennis courts at this children's holiday place are seen from here.

Follow the track across fairly level ground towards some new houses on the far side of the Fontanelles valley where the old and little-used track is picked up. Although slightly overgrown it is easy to follow and continues right up to the col.

At the col two paths will be seen. Take the left-hand one, which leads down through a narrow wooded valley to meet a forest road at a T-junction. Turn left and in about 15 minutes the Coll Baix will be reached. The path to the beach begins on the far side of the shelter, although it is probably best left for a separate excursion. The path to the Atalaya rises up through the trees on the north-west side of the col. This well-made path passes close to the top of the Puig des Boc which is an excellent viewpoint, before going on to the top of the Atalaya with its shelter and well.

From the summit return to the signpost and go straight down the steep path to a wide col, from where a forest road leads down to the *ermita*, below which is a large parking area. The last part of the descent begins at the corner of this car park at the exact point where the forest track joins it. No path is seen at first, but after a very short but quite steep descent a good path will be found. This leads down steadily to a stream-bed which is crossed and re-crossed and eventually joined and followed to reach a wide cross-track. Turn right along this to return to the starting point in a further five minutes.

Youth hostel - Coll des Fontanelles	1hr 10min
Coll des Fontanelles - Coll Baix	40min
Coll Baix - Atalaya de Alcudia	1hr 10min
Atalaya de Alcudia - Youth hostel	1hr

4. EL FUMAT AND ROCA BLANCA

The Fumat is a spectacular peak which overhangs the Formentor road near the tunnel. This short excursion is mainly pathless but not very difficult and on a good day the views are outstanding. It can easily be combined with Walk 5 to the Cala en Gossalba and this is strongly recommended. Alternatively there are easy walks down to the sea at Cala Murta and Cala Figuera which are quite short. The route makes use of an old track which was used to reach the lighthouse before the new road and tunnel were constructed in 1968. To reach the starting point drive through the tunnel towards the lighthouse and park at the viewpoint on the cliff-edge at K14.9.

Type of walk: Although only short the pathless nature of this route gives it a 'B' grade.

Starting point:	Viewpoint, Formentor road
Time:	2hr 35min
Distance:	4km
Highest point reached:	334m
Total height climbed:	300m
Grade:	B
Map:	Cap de Formentor 1:25,000

The Fumat on the Formentor peninsula

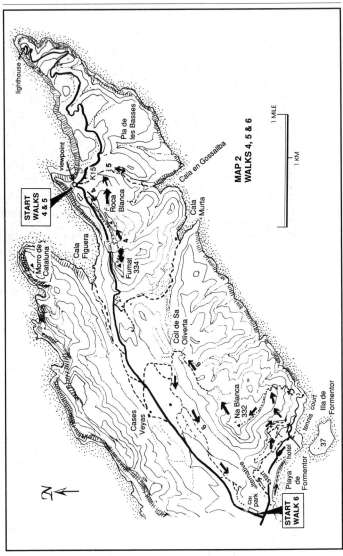

MAP 2
WALKS 4, 5 & 6

lighthouse

viewpoint

START
WALKS
4 & 5

K15

5

Roca
Blanca

4

Fumat
334

Cala
Figuera

Morro de
Cataluna

Pla de
les Basses

Cala en Gossalba

Cala
Murta

Coll de Sa
Oliverta

6

Na Blanca
332

6

Cases
Veyas

Illa de
Formentor

tennis court

37

Playa
de Formentor

hotel

car
park

START
WALK 6

1 MILE

1 KM

N

Cases Veyas valley from the Fumat

Walk back along the road from the viewpoint towards the tunnel and at a point marked by a cairn scramble up the hillside to reach the old lighthouse track which is just above the road. Follow this narrow track which leads up to the col between El Fumat and Roca Blanca at a gentle gradient. The top of the Fumat is reached quite easily from this col, up rock slabs and stony ground at an easy angle. After enjoying the view descend to the col and go straight up the ridge ahead to the Roca Blanca. There is no path but there are no particular difficulties. From the last top on the ridge continue downwards in the same direction, avoiding steep rocks when necessary on the south side. The ridge ends in a short cliff, but an easy way down can be found leading back to the right.

Once on easy ground walk along to the foot of the cliff, then make for a large pine tree in the valley below. Follow the red earth path back left to the viewpoint, or turn right to reach the Cala en Gossalba as in Walk 5.

Viewpoint - El Fumat	45min
El Fumat - col	15min
Col- first top Roca Blanca	25min
First top - last top	25min
Last top - viewpoint	45min

61

5. CALA EN GOSSALBA

This tiny bay of bright water on the south side of the Formentor peninsular is an unspoilt gem. Fortunately it is inaccessible by car, unlike the adjacent Cala Murta which has been spoilt by an access road and a large private house. The excellent path down to Cala en Gossalba was used to supply the lighthouse in the days before the new road was built, and also for the extraction of wood from the forest of pine trees. Some of these pines still stand to provide welcome shade in hot weather. This walk is ideal for a lazy day, or it can be done after the walk over the Fumat and Roca Blanca to give a longer excursion.

Type of walk: Easy, on a well-made path.

Starting point:	Viewpoint at K14.9, Formentor road
Time:	1hr 15min
Distance:	3km
Total height climbed:	Descent and re-ascent of 176m
Grade:	C
Map:	Cap de Formentor 1:25,000

Go down the path from the viewpoint: it is slightly indistinct at first, but soon develops into an excellent and well-made mule track. It follows the river bed, which it occasionally crosses. There are no turnings and no cross tracks, and the path ends on some rocks on the right-hand side of the little bay. To reach the shore, which is of boulders large and small, go down the last part of the stream-bed.

6. NA BLANCA

This pleasant hill on the Formentor peninsula provides a delightful and varied walk. The broad and rocky top overlooks the colourful waters of the Formentor beach and on clear days there are views across to the Alcudia hills and beyond them to Artà. The return route passes the nesting-sites of the Marmora's Warblers and goes through the sheltered wooded valley near the Cases Veyas where migrants rest during the spring and autumn migrations. During the winter this is a good place for residents such as Hoopoes, Black Redstarts, Firecrests, Crossbills, Linnets and Great Tits.

The Atalaya de Albercuitx from Na Blanca

Type of walk: Mainly easy walking on paths and tracks, but there is a pathless section on the ascent and it is rough and rocky for a short distance on the top.

Starting point:	Formentor car park
Time:	3hr 30min
Distance:	8km
Highest point reached:	332m
Total height climbed	342m
Grade:	B
Map:	Cala de Sant Vicenc 1:25,000 and Cap de Formentor 1:25,000

Walk along the sea-front or the beach in front of the Formentor hotel. Although the grounds are private it is permissible to walk past them along the coast. At the end of the grounds go round the end of the fence and follow the road inland. Take the second turn to the right, after passing the hotel tennis courts. The road goes through a gateway with a chain for cars and ends by the gates of a house on the Punta Caseta. Immediately before the gate and on the right of a stream-bed, go through the bushes and up some rough ground. An old path is very soon found, leading back right to the wooded ridge near an old gate. Follow the path up the ridge. It is well-marked with cairns. Higher up avoid following a branch path off to the right and keep going up the ridge, where a stony path leads along the edge of steep rocks to the top.

Alternative start:

Walk towards the Formentor hotel along the road and take the first turn left about 100m past the landing stage. About 20 minutes after the start join another track coming from the left. About one minute later turn left where the main track descends to the right, just after passing a house called Quinta Bareta. The track now keeps at a fairly constant height and makes a sharp bend left at a point where a private chained road goes straight on. The track then rises before crossing a torrent bed, branches right and re-crosses the torrent bed to contour again A workman's hut is passed and in five minutes the track rounds a corner and comes to an end. Exactly at this point look out for red paint marks on rocks and pine trees. There is no path but it is easy to pick out a route using the paint marks to give the general direction. Make for a metal pylon supporting electric cables, the first metal one above some wooden ones. From the pylon look uphill and further red marks will be seen ahead. When a group of cairns on a large rock slab are reached it is best to traverse right to join the ridge which rises from the Punta Caseta.

From the top, follow the ridge down in a north-easterly direction to join a path at an unnamed col at 188m. A few cairns mark the way, which in any case is well-defined by the proximity of steep crags on the left. Follow the track along from this col to the Coll de Sa Oliverta and continue down into the wooded valley below. Ignore a right and then a left turn, but take the left fork at a junction reached about ten minutes after leaving this col and at the corner of the cultivated fields. Take another left fork after a further ten minutes. Ignore a right turn which leads to the road and continue to a flat sports field, the 'Campo de Desportes, Formentor.' Cross the field at its left-hand edge to find a track leading to the right. After 100m fork left at a minor cross-track and follow this down to the car park.

Car park - Na Blanca	1hr 50min
Na Blanca - Coll de Sa Oliverta	50min
Coll de Sa Oliverta - Car park	50min

Rafal de Ariant (Walk 17) (Author)
On Puig de Maria (Walk 21) (W.Unsworth)

In the Pareis Gorge (Walk 28b) W.Unsworth)
On the approach to Massanella by the Coll des Prat
(Walk 30) (Author)

7. ATALAYA DE ALBERCUITX

This old watch-tower on the Formentor peninsula is a splendid viewpoint, easily reached. In 1984 it was presented to the town of Pollensa by the Capllunch family and it was repaired and restored in 1990. It is now quite safe to climb the iron rungs on the outside wall, go through an entrance into a circular room, then up a ladder on the inside wall to emerge on the top platform around which is a parapet.

Since the first edition of this book the track up from the Mirador d'es Colomer has been upgraded to a surfaced road and many people drive up, hence it is best to avoid weekends. The walk has been described from Puerto Pollensa for the benefit of those who do not use a car. Some road walking is involved so again it is advisable to choose a quiet day in midweek. An alternative if a car is available is to park at the Mirador, from where it is about 1hr 30min to the Atalaya and back, then go on to do one of the other walks on Formentor.

Near the watch-tower there are the ruins of a former barracks. Before reaching them an old tunnel leading to an ammunition store is passed on the left. This is about 200m long and quite safe to investigate with a torch, as there are no drops and ventilation shafts to let in a little light.

Type of walk: Very easy, along surfaced roads and a newly made stepped path near the top. (A variation is to walk up the southwest ridge which runs parallel to the road, from the low Coll d'en Vela at K3.6, joining the Atalaya road at a sharp bend. There is no path but the gradient is reasonable and the terrain not difficult.)

Starting point:	Puerto Pollensa
Time:	4hr 15min
Distance:	14km
Highest point reached:	375m
Total height climbed:	373m
Grade:	C (Variation, B)
Map:	Pollensa 1:25,000 and
	Cala de Sant Vicenc 1:25,000

Walk along the sea front as far as possible: then turn left to reach the Formentor road. Follow this up to the Mirador d'es Colomer. It is worth making a diversion here for the view down to the detached rock 'El Colomer' and across the bay to the Cala Vall de Boquer, where the steep rocks at the end of the Cavall Bernat ridge dip into the sea. Go up the road opposite the Mirador car park. It soon swings round to the other side of

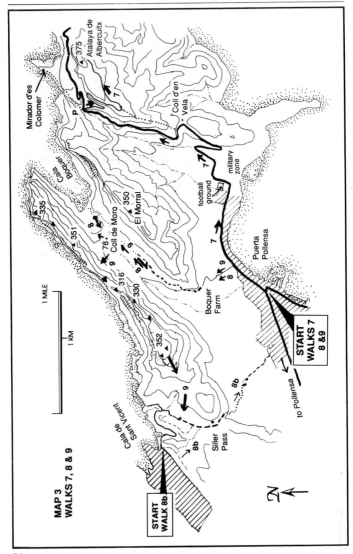

MAP 3
WALKS 7, 8 & 9

1 MILE

1 KM

START
WALK 8b

START
WALKS 7
8 & 9

to Pollensa

N

Siller Pass

8b

8b

9

352

330

316

9

9

78.

8

Coll de Moro

351

335

Boquer Farm

8

9

7

7

8

9

Puerta Pollensa

football ground

military zone

Coll d'en Vela

7

375

Atalaya de Albercuitx

Mirador d'es Colomer

P

El Morral

350

Cala de Boquer

Cala de Sant Vicent

the hill with views of Formentor. After passing the barracks it makes a sharp left turn to reach the highest of the old buildings. From here the new stepped path leads up to the tower.

Puerto - Mirador d'es Colomer	1hr 30min
Mirador - Atalaya de Albercutx	1hr (inc. tunnel)
Atalaya - Mirador	30min
Mirador - Puerto	1hr 15min

8(a). BOQUER VALLEY FROM PUERTO POLLENSA

This attractive and sheltered valley is much favoured by migrant birds, and in winter is always a good place for seeing some of the residents such as the beautiful Blue Rock Thrush. It is also interesting botanically and the flowers of *Cyclamen balearicum* can be found within a few feet of the valley wall under the shelter of other shrubs. The valley is bounded on the north-west by the splendid Cavall Bernat ridge in which there are several spectacular holes or windows. One of these is easily seen from the path. There is a good path right down to the small shingly beach of Cala Boquer. The end of the Cavall Bernat ridge dips steeply into the sea and there are views across the bay to the detached rock of Es Colomer. (The beach itself is disappointing, with debris washed in by the sea.)

Type of walk: Very easy, along good paths.

Starting point:	Puerto Pollensa
Time:	2hr
Distance:	6km
Highest point reached:	84m
Total height climbed:	168m
Grade:	C
Map:	Cala de Sant Vicenc 1:25,000 and Pollensa 1:25,000

If arriving by car, turn left where the Pollensa road meets the sea front and park here. Walk along the sea front to the left and go straight on along a footpath in front of a terrace of small hotels. Turn left along the Avenida Bocharis at the end of this terrace and cross the main road opposite the stone gateposts at the entrance to the Boquer farm track. The avenue of old trees that once led through the fields is now surrounded by building sites, but the trees have been preserved. Follow the track to the farm and pass in front of the farmhouse to go through the iron gate at the end of the courtyard.

Turn right immediately, go through another gate and follow the track between some immense boulders into the Boquer valley. The track then continues through gaps in the stone walls and over the low Coll de Moro, from where it continues as a narrow and less defined path down a wide shallow gully to the sea. It is possible to walk on past a fisherman's shelter to a small platform overlooking the bay.

8(b). BOQUER VALLEY FROM CALA SAN VICENTE

Walkers staying at Cala San Vicente can get to Puerto Pollensa by public buses, or sometimes by a courtesy bus provided by the Hotel Don Pedro, or else over the Coll de Siller, an easy walk taking one hour.

From the Molins beach go up the steps behind the telephone booth* to reach an unsurfaced track. Turn right at the top, then left past the small hotel Los Pinos and turn right again. Go through an old gate at the beginning of a level section, then turn left by an electricity sub-station, then first right by a red arrow. This leads to a cairned footpath across level ground. After going down into and up out of a little stream-bed this re-joins the main track. (This track is a continuation of the road running south along the coast from the Molins beach, which can be followed for easier walking or for variety.) This wide track continues past the white Water Board building on the Siller pass for about 200m then ends abruptly.

From the end of the track there are several alternative ways all marked by a superfluity of cairns. Go roughly straight on, all paths leading to the left of a large private house. Go through the iron gates at the side of the house and follow the lane to a T-junction at the Siller gateway. Turn left and keep following the road, unpaved at first, until the main road is met. Turn left towards the sea front.

In returning to Cala from the port, the easiest way to find the Siller track is to walk along the Pollensa road to a small bar almost opposite the petrol station and turn right there.

* The telephones were washed out to sea by floods in 1990, but the steps are still there.

On the Cavall Bernat ridge, looking towards Formentor

9. SERRA DEL CAVALL BERNAT

The Cavall Bernat ridge lies between the bay of Cala San Vicente and the Boquer valley. Although its maximum height is a modest 350m it has very steep cliffs and those on the Cala side plunge the full height vertically into the sea over a length of two kilometers. In the evening light the slanting rays illuminate their intricate structural detail and they glow with changing shades of amber, orange and pink. A most spectacular and beautiful sight. From the other side it is also a splendid back-drop to Puerto Pollensa, seen to particular advantage when driving along the coast road from Alcudia. The double tower about half-way along the ridge looks quite astonishing from many viewpoints. The traverse of the full ridge from end to end is a major undertaking, requiring rock climbing experience.

Type of walk: The route described here is not long, but includes exceedingly rough walking and some quite difficult scrambling. The ascent of the tower is not technically difficult, but it is sensationally exposed and requires a good head for heights. It could be classed as an easy rock climb rather than a walk. Nevertheless it is highly recommended to experienced scramblers who will find it interesting, strenuous and enjoyable.

Starting point:	Puerto de Pollensa
Time:	4hr 20min
Distance:	8.5km
Highest point reached:	352m
Total height climbed:	466m.
Grade:	A+
Map:	Cala de Sant Vicenc 1:25,000 and Pollensa 1:25,000

Leave Puerto Pollensa by walking along the sea front and into the Boquer valley as in Walk 8. Continue along the Boquer valley track as far as the second wall crossing the valley; this is opposite the obvious col on the ridge to the right of the impressive double tower in which lies one of the 'windows'. A narrow path on the inland side of the wall leads to some ruined buildings. From the corner of the fields here find a way up a shallow gully towards the col using goat tracks and scree between the vegetation.

From the col turn left and climb up the steep rock tower near the edge overlooking the sea. This is a very spectacular and exposed situation, but easier than it looks. The topmost section of the tower is avoided by taking to a sloping ramp leading up to the left. This arrives at a cairn quite near the top. From this point onwards the exhilarating route continues westwards along the ridge. To reach the 'window ledge' it is best to go over the top of the window first, then carefully descend the steep ground at the western side, regaining the ridge the same way to continue the route.

An alternative way to reach the window without climbing the tower is by the 'Ledge Route'. From just below the col turn left and follow an obvious rocky ledge at the foot of the tower. This becomes narrow in places, but is not difficult and leads across a subsidiary ridge to a broad sloping shelf below the window. Walk along this, passing below the window until it is possible to scramble up to the top of the ridge. Walk back along the ridge to find the way down to it at the western side.

Continuing westwards along the ridge, the most difficult part is an awkward move on the descent of the double tower. Perhaps this is technically the most difficult part of the route. It has to be said that even after making several traverses of the ridge that finding the best way is not easy. In places there are cairns and flattened vegetation to indicate the way, but trial and error as well as route-finding skills will be called upon.

A second window, is found just before reaching the last col. On the rise up to the final top, either continue along the edge of the cliffs, or choose easier walking in the shallow valley lying between the main ridge and another on the left. A short way up this valley and on the right a large hole in gently sloping ground penetrates the sea-cliff to form another impressive window. The final top is double and a line of cairns can be followed down from the dip between the two peaks, crossing a wall. Turn right along the second wall to pick up another descending line of cairns at the end of it. These eventually drop over into the shallow depression on the right. When the cairns end, make a slightly rising traverse towards a white building on the Siller pass road and turn left here to return to Puerto Pollensa, or right to Cala San Vicente.

Puerto Pollensa - col on ridge	1hr 30min
Col - 375m top	1hr 30min
375m top - Coll de Siller	50min
Coll de Siller - Puerto Pollensa	30min

10(a). LA SERRA DE LA PUNTA: RIDGE ROUTE

This low ridge with several tops (named La Coma on the military maps) lies between the Cala San Vicente valley and the main road between Pollensa and its port. Some years ago local cavers found a hitherto unknown cave in this area which proved to be a most important archeological find. Reconstructions of the wooden burial urns in the form of bulls found in the cave can be seen in the museum in Pollensa.

As a walk, people seem either to love it or to hate it. Those who like wandering along easy paths should give this one a miss, but it appeals to others who like the challenge of making their way over rough country. The terrain is almost wilderness, yet it is within sight and sound of the road and village of Cala San Vicente.

Type of walk: Easy walking along tracks and road to the beginning of the ridge, then pathless on difficult ground, but no route-finding problems. Sometimes easy walking on bare rock, but some boulder hopping and negotiation of scrub cannot be avoided. (Wrongly graded C+ in the 1st edition of this guide.)

Starting point:	Cala San Vicente
Time:	4hr 30min
Distance:	8.5km
Highest point reached:	315m
Total height climbed:	393m

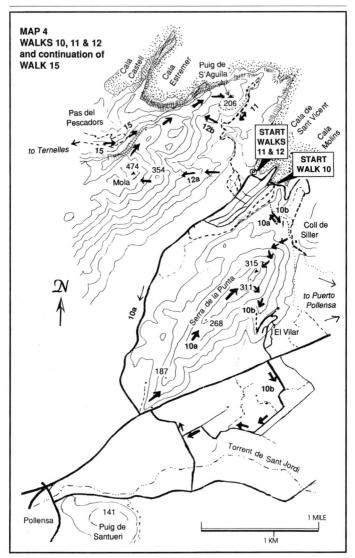

MAP 4
WALKS 10, 11 & 12
and continuation of
WALK 15

Cala Castell

Cala Estremer

Puig de S'Aguila

Pas del Pescadors

206

11

to Ternelles

15

15

15

12b

Cala de Sant Vicent

Cala Molins

START WALKS 11 & 12

START WALK 10

474

354

Mola

12a

12a

10b

10a

Coll de Siller

N

315

311

to Puerto Pollensa

10a

Serra de la Punta

268

10b

El Vilar

10a

187

10b

Torrent de Sant Jordi

Pollensa

141

Puig de Santueri

1 MILE

1 KM

Grade:	B+
Map:	Pollensa 1:25,000

From the Molins beach go up the steps behind the telephones (missing after floods in 1990) and turn right along the track through the woods. Follow this track through a gate and cross the stream to join the main road just outside the village. Turn left and follow the road to the junction with the road to the port. Go up behind the notice boards and follow the well-defined ridge over several tops. Most people are surprised by how long and rough this ridge is.

The last top has a distinctive cairn standing on a circular wall. Follow the ridge down towards the Coll de Siller. The easiest way is to keep to the ridge at first, then look out for a way off to the left, following the white cairns which avoid the steep lower end of the ridge. The well-marked path leading down to Cala San Vicente is then followed.

Cala San Vicente - road junction	50min
Road junction - main top	2hr 25min
Main top - Cala San Vicente	1hr 15min

10(b). LA SERRA DE LA PUNTA: FROM SILLER PASS

This alternative route is much shorter and less strenuous than the ridge route. It follows the ridge leading up to the highest top from the pass, but avoids the lower part of it which is very steep and rocky. All the same it is still no hands in the pocket stroll and provides a good introduction to the type of terrain often encountered in Mallorca. If the suggested return route is followed then typical market garden countryside is also seen.

Starting point:	Cala San Vicente
Time:	3hr 40min
Distance:	8km
Highest point reached:	315m
Total height climbed:	315m
Grade:	B
Map:	Pollensa 1:25,000

Start either from Cala San Vicente or Puerto Pollensa and go up the Siller pass by the ordinary way. Some 200m on the Cala side of the pass a white arrow points to the start of the route, and some conspicuous white cairns can be seen higher up. There is no path, but it is easy to choose a way using the cairns as a general directional guide. A large white mark indicates the place where the ridge is most easily gained and followed to the top.

From the top walk along the ridge for about five minutes to the second little top. Make a sharp left turn here and the houses of El Vilar soon come into view. Go down the broad ridge, heading between a prominent house on the left and what appears to be a narrow path on the right. Easy walking is found near the remains of an old electric fence with its ceramic insulators still attached. After reaching some cairns on a rocky outcrop bear right to pick up the path, which is in fact the edge of a wide but overgrown track. Follow it down to the road, through the houses of El Vilar.

To return to Cala San Vicente without walking on the busy main road, turn right then immediately left towards the Club Tropicana. At the end of the straight road by a black gate, turn right, then left, then right again. After 500m turn right where another road comes in from the left. There are good views of the ridge route on this stretch. The road now makes several bends before swinging right at a fork and then turning left. Turn right at a T-junction by a square-arched gateway and follow the road along until it re-joins the main road about 100m from the Cala road junction. Either walk back into Cala San Vicente or wait for a bus.

Cala San Vicente - summit	1hr 30min
Summit - road at El Vilar	1hr 10min
El Vilar - road junction	1hr

11. PUIG DE S'AGUILA

This small hill overlooking the sea makes a worthwhile short excursion from Cala San Vicente. There are excellent views, especially in the afternoon when the sun is shining on the magnificent rocks of the Cavall Bernat ridge across the bay. This view is irresistible to painters and photographers. Take a torch if you are interested in exploring the rock tunnels leading to some old ammunition stores.

Type of walk: Easy, along a good but stony track as far as the tunnels; then a narrow path to the top, only a short distance but steep and loose.

Starting point:	Cala San Vicente
Time:	1hr 45min
Distance:	4km

Highest point reached:	206m
Total height climbed:	200m
Grade:	C
Map:	Cala de Sant Vicenc 1:25,000

From the Hotel Don Pedro go north along the sea front and follow the road where it turns left to go inland. In about 100m turn right up a flight of steps between two houses. At the top of the steps fork right to reach the locked gate at the entrance to the quarry road. Access is through a gap in the wall and the track is a good one all the way to an old quarry where a beautiful white, pink and black rock has been extracted. Further on the track makes a sharp turn left and leads past three tunnels excavated into the rock. The first of these runs straight in for some 40m, then makes a right turn and divides, one part going straight on and the other turning left, then right and right again to meet up with the first part. Daylight can be seen above where the shafts open up on the hill. The second tunnel is usually knee deep in water, but from its position appears to lead to the shaft sunk down from the top of the Aguila. The third tunnel is very short and has no vertical shaft.

A narrow path continues past the third tunnel and leads up to a col on the west of the Puig de S'Aguila, from where it is only a short distance to the top. The position of the shaft is quite obvious, as are those of the next two shafts reached in a further few minutes. From these shafts a vague path continues down towards the sea, curving right to meet the quarry road at a sharp bend. Return by the same way, or explore the area between this road and the coast, which although pathless is quite easy walking.

12. MOLA

The area between Ternelles and Cala San Vicente is mountainous and uninhabited except for wild goats. The mountains are not high, but give some very rough walking. They are in the form of parallel ridges with very steep cliffs on the north-western side. Mola, at the eastern end of the Serra de Sant Vicenc ridge is the most accessible of the tops and this circular route is a good introduction to the sort of terrain often encountered in Mallorca.

Type of walk: Rough and rocky ground with occasional traces of paths. Easy return along the quarry road from the Puig de S'Aguila.

(a) Normal way by the east ridge

Starting point:	Cala San Vicente
Time:	4hr 15min
Distance:	6.0km
Highest point reached:	474m
Total height climbed:	493m
Grade:	B+
Map:	Cala de Sant Vicenc 1:25,000

Begin the walk as for Walk 11. From the Don Pedro Hotel take the road along the sea front and follow it round to the left. Immediately after going through the wall by the locked gate, turn left on a rough path going inland. After about 100m leave it and make for the ridge to the left of the end tower. Walk up the first section of the ridge on easy bare rock to reach a cairn, then cross a stretch of level ground to the right to reach the offset continuation of the ridge. At the top of this section there is another cairn. Continue up in the same direction, passing the top of a gully which goes down steeply on the right. Go up the broken ground ahead towards a shoulder slightly to the right of the little peak ahead. Occasional goat tracks and some outcrops of solid rock are a help. From this shoulder it is worth making the short diversion to the little top on the left from where there is a clear view back down the ridge to Cala San Vicente and the Cavall Bernat ridge.

Ahead is a rock tower, steep at the bottom. Cross the little col and go up to the left of the tower on easy rock and scree below the steepest rocks. A path is beginning to develop and there are some cairns. Higher up look for a break in the steep rocks which allows a rising traverse right to be made to the top of Mola. This top is the highest of the three, all marked as 457m on the old maps, now promoted to 474m on the new IGN map.

Leave the summit by descending to the north and cross the hollow straight ahead to a small rocky top on the far ridge. Turn right (NE) along this ridge and descend on good rock, keeping to the edge of the steep ground on the left. After about 500m make for a low rocky outcrop in the middle of a slight hollow, following bare rock ribs when possible for easier walking. Continue in the same general direction, getting closer to the edge of the cliffs again. A short rise is followed by a descent towards a wall. Ignore the red arrow pointing towards the right. A cairn marks the beginning of quite a good but narrow path going up along the edge of continuous and impressive cliffs overlooking the sea. This leads towards

76

Cala San Vicente from Mola

an indefinite top from which can be seen two further tops. Make for the left of these and continue on to the Puig de S'Aguila. On this top is a hollow and a deep shaft and further on a group of three shafts with an easy path on either side.

Reach the quarry track either by keeping straight on towards the sea and bearing slightly right, or go down the path on the west side of the top used in the ascent of Aguila. At the end of the quarry track, go through the gap in the wall by the locked gate and turn left to reach the steps back down to the road.

Cala San Vicente - Mola	2hr
Mola - Puig de S'Aguila	1hr 30min
Puig de S'Aguila - Cala San Vicente	45min

(b) Mola by a rock scramble
This route gains the Serra de San Vicenc ridge by a pleasant scramble up an unnamed rock tower, reaches the top of Mola from the north-east, then descends the east ridge of Mola back to Cala.

Starting point:	Cala San Vicente
Time:	4hr
Distance:	5.5km

Highest point reached:	474m
Total height climbed:	480m
Grade:	A+
Map:	Cala de Sant Vicenc 1:25,000

Leave Cala San Vicente by the quarry road as for Walk 11. In about 20 minutes two bridges are reached, close together. Follow the dry stream-bed from the first bridge and make for the foot of the right-hand rocky peak at the valley head.

The route goes up by the ridge which forms the right-hand skyline and this can easily be gained if the rock is dry by climbing the head of the gully direct. If wet, go up diagonally left, then back right to the notch above the steep section. The ridge is mainly good clean rock with ample holds, although there are one or two patches of dense and trying vegetation.

The scramble ends at a pleasant little rock tower. From the top cross two small rocky knolls and keep going in the same direction to a wall. After crossing the wall continue up the vague ridge ahead, choosing bare rock for the easiest walking and making for the cliff edge on the right as soon as desired. From this cliff there are spectacular views down to the sea and up the Ternelles valley to the Castell del Rei, with the steep face of Cornavaces forming the continuation of the cliffs.

Follow the ridge up until the ground levels out a little with a rocky top on the left. Go up this by a small but obvious groove to reach one of the three tops of Mola, which have between them a grassy depression. Cross over to the east and highest top which has a prominent cairn. To descend, go down at first towards the south-east to avoid some steep ground and find the obvious break in a little escarpment, then down to the right to reach some bare rock ledges. From here go back left and continue in this direction at the foot of some steep rocks to arrive at a small col. Cross this col to the left of a small top ahead and continue down by easy rocks and boulders to another small col. Continue over the next little top and on down towards the end of the ridge. Descend to easy ground on the right before reaching the final tower and make for the gate to the quarry road.

Cala San Vicente - Unnamed top	1hr 10min
Unnamed top - Mola	1hr 20min
Mola - Cala San Vicente	1hr 30min

13. CUIXAT GORGE (a) RETURNING BY TERNELLES

This intriguing gorge lies between the flat Cala San Vicente valley and Ternelles, connecting the two over the Coll de Cuixat at 367m. Tantalising glimpses of a detached pinnacle low down on the left of the gorge are often had from the main road between Cala and Pollensa when the lighting is right. The hidden valley leading up to the Coll is wild and rough, typical of the terrain in this area. (Note that the way into the gorge described in the first edition of this guide cannot now be used.)

Type of walk: Some scrambling up rocks and boulders, but the one difficult place can be avoided. Easy return along the Ternelles valley. (Only permitted on Saturdays, but see alternative walk described later.)

Starting point:	Pollensa
Time:	4hr 45min
Distance:	11km
Highest point reached:	367m
Total height climbed:	307m
Grade:	A
Map:	Pollensa 1:25,000

Leave Pollensa by the road near the Roman bridge and turn right towards the east. Take the first turn off to the left and follow this until after about 600m another road is met at an angle. Turn left and follow this road round several bends until it winds up through an area of newish houses known as Sa Font. This road ends at a turning circle. Before reaching there, leave it at the last bend and traverse across carritx covered ground for about 200m. Then slant downhill in an approximately north-easterly direction, passing a large cave. There is no path but some cairns mark a feasible route. Make for some large rocks quite low down, which appear to be the remains of some talaiotic buildings on a small spur.

From the talaiots, continue downhill but bear left, finding the easiest walking at the edge of the low and rather dense shrubs that grow in the valley bottom outside the cultivated area. With luck, or possibly imagination, it is possible to discern a faint path which leads to the foot of the gorge. Clamber over a low wall and go through the trees to find the good path in the narrow Cuixat valley. Follow this up to a small hanging valley. A scramble up some steep rocks on the left at the head of this leads to a small ledge from where it is easy to drop down into a hidden valley. Turn left and follow the stream-bed up to a junction, where the right branch should be taken and followed until a rather steep little chimney is

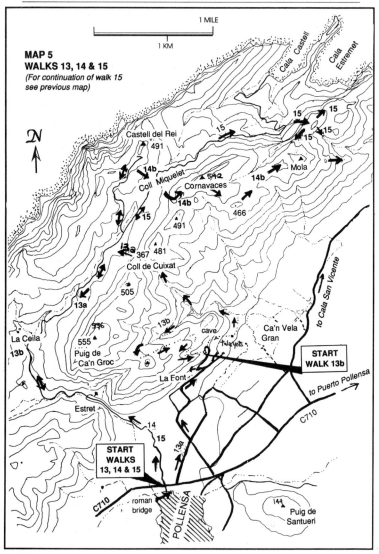

MAP 5
WALKS 13, 14 & 15
*(For continuation of walk 15
see previous map)*

1 MILE

1 KM

N

Cala Castell

Cala Estremet

Castell del Rei
491

14b

Coll Miquelet

542
Cornavaces

15

14b

14b

466

15

15

15

15

15

Mola

491

13a

367
481

Coll de Cuixat

505

13a

736

555

Puig de
Ca'n Groc

13b

cave

talayots

Ca'n Vela
Gran

START
WALK 13b

to Cala San Vicente

La Font

La Ceila

13b

Estret

14

15

13a

to Puerto Pollensa

C710

START
WALKS
13, 14 & 15

C710

roman
bridge

POLLENSA

14

Puig de
Santueri

encountered. This is the only difficult bit and it can be avoided by going out to the left and then back right into the bed of the stream. At the next junction, again take the right-hand branch and continue up until a little head wall is reached. Easy climbing up this wall leads to a valley sloping gently upwards. The Coll de Cuixat is reached in a further ten minutes. From this col there are excellent views of the Castell del Rei and the Puig Gros de Ternelles (Walks 14 and 16).

Go down from the col, steeply at first and then across the valley on a forest track to reach the Ternelles valley road. Turn left here and follow the road back to Pollensa. (Drinking water is available from a tapped spring on the left of the track, after about one hour of walking down the valley and just before reaching the large house.)

Pollensa - foot of gorge	45min
Foot of gorge - Coll de Cuixat	2hr 25min
Coll de Cuixat - Pollensa	1hr 35min

13(b). CUIXAT GORGE: A SHORT ROUND FROM LA FONT

This walk avoids the walk down the Ternelles valley which is limited to Saturdays. Those who dislike road-walking and have the use of a car may drive to the road end above La Font and park there. (B+, a good 2 hours.)

Follow the above route into the Cuixat gorge, but half-way up take the left-hand instead of the right-hand branch of the stream and continue up to the 309m col overlooking the Ternelles valley. From this point descend in an approximately east-northeast direction down a narrow valley parallel to the one just ascended. There are cairns marking this route which leads to a col at 242m. There are traces of an old path here and again more cairns point out the way, which doubles back right into another stream-bed, at one point following a natural rock ledge. Follow the route down the valley floor and back to the turning circle at the road end.

A way of extending this walk would be to include the ascent of the Puig de Ca'n Groc (555m) from the 309m col. There is no path but the terrain appears reasonable.

14(a). CASTELL DEL REI

The situation of the ruined Castell del Rei, overlooking the sea from the edge of very steep cliffs is extremely impressive. It was an important stronghold of the Arabs, but was taken by Jaime I in about 1230 by offering good terms to the defenders. Later it was besieged by Aragonese invaders in 1285 and again in 1343, but eventually had to surrender. The ruins cover an extensive area and it is well worth spending some time here. Black Vultures are sometimes seen on this walk, especially up near the castle.

The walk goes through the wooded and beautiful Ternelles valley which is privately owned. Although according to Spanish law there is a right of way to visit historic monuments such as this, access has recently been restricted to one day per week, at first Mondays and then Saturdays. Sometimes conditions have been imposed, such as showing of passports at the gate or obtaining a permit in advance. At the time of writing the practice is for the guard to make a note of the name of your hotel and the number of people in the party. It is recommended that before setting out on this walk enquiries are made locally as to the current position. These restrictions only apply to visitors. Residents are allowed access at any time but may have to show identity card or passport.

Type of walk: Although quite long, the walk is easy along country roads and a forest track. The uphill gradients are mainly gentle and nowhere very steep. Only the last five minutes require a little effort up a stony path.

Starting point:	Crossroads on C710 near Roman bridge, Pollensa
Time:	4hr 15min
Distance:	13km
Highest point reached:	491m
Total height climbed:	430m
Grade:	C
Map:	Pollensa 1:50,000

The narrow road to Ternelles begins just outside Pollensa at a signposted crossroads on the Lluc road C710, near the Roman bridge. It is possible to park in the town near here, by going into Pollensa from the crossroads and turning first left. (N.B. To walk here from the bus station, turn left and go up through the main square, the Plaza Mayor, up to the right of the church, then right into a small square with a distinctive cockerel fountain, left here, then right into the Calle de la Huerta. Follow this long street to the edge of town where it crosses a bridge to reach the crossroads.)

On the way to Ternelles the road goes through a very attractive area of market gardens with almond orchards and orange trees. As it enters the 'Narrows', the remains of a Roman aqueduct may be seen. At the entrance gates to the Ternelles property, there is a guard on duty who may ask to see your permit or your passport or want to write down the name of your hotel.

After going through this gate, the road becomes unsurfaced. About 100m after passing the large house drinking water may be obtained from a brass tap on the right. This is spring water which local people collect in large plastic containers.

Another access gate is provided at the second locked gates, after which the track begins to rise. Shortly after crossing a cattle grid the track divides into two; take the right fork which is signposted 'Castell del Rei' and continue uphill until the trees thin out and the castle can be seen in the distance. The left turn that leads to the castle will be found 100m beyond the start of a fenced area on the right. (The main track continues over the Coll de Miquelet and down to the sea at Cala Castell.) The track to the castle ends at a flat area from where a narrow path leads to the gateway arch which is the entrance to the ruins.

Return by the same way. It is possible to vary it slightly by walking along the ridge running south-west to the Coll d'es Colom and descending to the Ternelles valley from there. However, this is rough going and not recommended.

Pollensa - Castell del Rei	2hr 15min
Castell del Rei - Pollensa	2hr

14(b). CASTELL DEL REI AND CORNAVACES

The steep northern face of Cornavaces is part of an almost continuous line of cliffs extending eastwards right to the Puig d'Aguila. It is a fine viewpoint, guarding the Ternelles valley on the east as the castle does on the west. This walk starts in Pollensa and ends in Cala San Vicente. There is a morning bus from Cala to Pollensa at 08.45 and an evening bus at 18.45.

Starting point:	Pollensa crossroads near Roman bridge
Time:	6hr 30min
Highest point reached:	542m
Total height climbed:	727m
Grade:	A
Map:	Pollensa 1:25,000 and Cala de Sant Vicenc 1:25,000

Go to the castle as in Route 14(a).From the broad track just below the castle go down the hillside to the Coll Miquelet. There is no path but it is not difficult ground. Go up the hillside opposite on the outside of the wall bounding the cultivated area. Turn right along the wall from the corner and then strike up to the col between Cornavaces and Barrancada. Turn left at the col and follow the edge of the cliffs up to the top. Keep near the edge for striking views of the north-east face of Cornavaces.

From the top it is an easy walk across a dip and up to the 478m top of the Serra de San Vicens ridge. Follow this ridge along to Mola, a triple top with a high point of 474m being the most easterly. Go down the east ridge to Cala San Vicente as in Walk 12(b).

Pollensa - Castell del Rei	2hr 15min
Castell del Rei - Cornavaces	1hr 45min
Cornavaces - Mola	1hr
Mola - Cala San Vicente	1hr 30min

15. PAS DELS PESCADORS

(This walk is subject to Ternelles valley access restrictions. See Walk 14.) The Pas dels Pescadors is a moderately difficult scramble and requires a head for heights. It is only recommended to experienced walkers for whom it provides an interesting variation to the normal Castell del Rei walk. By using the bus service betwen Cala San Vicente and Pollensa a circular route can be made.

Type of walk: Easy walking to the Castell del Rei and down a good track towards Cala Castell, then the scramble up to the cliff top, followed by rough walking to the Puig de S'Aguila.

Starting point:	Ternelles crossroads, near Roman Bridge, Pollensa.
Time:	5hr 40min
Distance:	15km
Highest point reached:	491m
Total height climbed:	641m
Grade:	A+
Map:	Pollensa 1:50,000 or Pollensa 1:25,000 and Cala de Sant Vicenc1:25,000

Follow Route 14 to the Castell del Rei. From here go down the hillside to the Coll Miquelet. There is no path but it is not very steep and not difficult to pick a way between the clumps of *carritx*. From this col, walk down the good track towards Cala Castell as far as a sharp hairpin bend. There are some red circles painted on the rocks to mark the start of this route.

A rising traverse is made across rough but quite easy ground towards an obvious grassy ridge forming the skyline on the far side of the intervening valley. The route goes up the cliffs roughly at the top of this grassy ridge. There is hardly a path, but if a good line is picked out then the painted marks will be noticed from time to time. Near the cliff the ground becomes steeper, and at the beginning of the rock scramble there is a very large red circle and an arrow pointing to the way up.

Be very careful to follow the marks, which go up right at first, then back left. About half-way up a ledge goes horizontally from left to right for about 25 yards. From the end of the ledge a deep groove or chimney slopes up obliquely to the left. The easiest way to surmount this is by the left or outer edge, where there are good holds. This is the part where a sense of exposure may alarm the inexperienced.

A cairn on the cliff top marks the place to begin the descent if this route is being reversed. (This is a good deal more difficult and not recommended unless an ascent has been made previously.) From the cairn on the cliff top there are three different ways of reaching Cala San Vicente.

The first, the real fishermen's route, crosses over the ridge in a south-easterly direction to a flattish col on which is a shallow pool of water. Some cairns mark the way down but there are only traces of paths and it is rough going.

The second way, which is further but easier walking and recommended, is to turn left and follow the edge of the cliffs along to the Puig de S'Aguila and return by the quarry track as in Walk 11. A third alternative, slightly more strenuous, is to turn right along the cliff top to Mola, then descend by the east ridge as in Walk 12(b).

Pollensa - Castell del Rei	2hr 15min
Castell del Rei - Bend in road	40min
Bend in road - cliff top	1hr
Cliff top - Puig de S'Aguila	1hr
Puig de S'Aguila - Cala San Vicente	45min

16. PUIG GROS DE TERNELLES

Although the Puig Gros does not have the status of 1,000m it is a very impressive mountain with steep northern cliffs and no easy way up. There are extensive views from the rocky summit, especially to the north-east. On the way up there are some fine situations overlooking the sea and because of the difficulties involved it is rare to meet other walkers. In fact Black Vultures are more likely to be seen than people. (N.B. There are access restrictions in the Ternelles valley See Walk 14 and enquire locally before attempting this walk.)

Type of walk: Some very rough and trackless ground with difficult route-finding. The route as described is only recommended to very experienced walkers. In fact, the terrain from the top of the Puig to the Coll de Tirapau is so difficult to negotiate that a return by the route of ascent is to be preferred. In this case the Grade becomes 'A' and the time reduced by one hour.

Starting point:	Roman bridge, Pollensa
Time:	8hr 40min
Distance:	15km
Highest point reached:	839m
Total height climbed:	810m
Grade:	A+
Map:	Pollensa 1:25,000 and Son Marc 1:25,000

Leave Pollensa by the Roman bridge. By car, take the Lluc road and turn into Pollensa at the crossroads, then turn first left where it is usually possible to park.

Follow the Ternelles road as for the Castell del Rei, Walk 14. After the first cattle grid, take the left fork. (The right fork is signposted Castell del Rei.) About five minutes after crossing a bridge turn right up a path at the side of a stream-bed. This soon goes left then right to cross an old aqueduct leading to a spring. A track leading to the right will be found near here. After a sudden increase in gradient this track narrows and levels out before rising again towards the Coll d'es Colom. Watch out for a right turn where a painted sign on a rock is almost obscured by vegetation. The path, now very narrow, becomes confused with animal tracks, but it is easy enough to make for the col which is an obvious cleft on the left of a rocky outcrop. Here there is a sudden and dramatic view of the coast and the next part of the route, with a look back to the cultivated area of

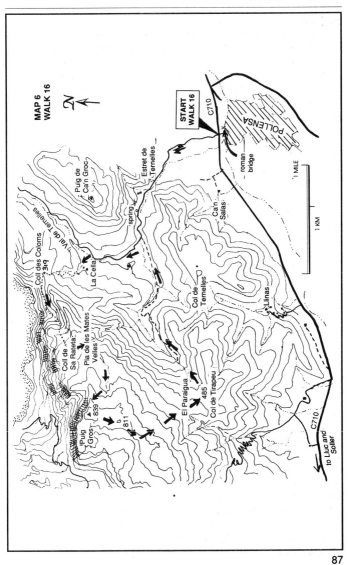

MAP 6
WALK 16

2N

START
WALK 16

C710

POLLENSA

roman
bridge

1 MILE

1 KM

Ca'n
Salas

spring

Estret de
Ternelles

Puig de
Ca'n Groc

Col de
Ternelles

Llinas

Coll des Coloms
319

Vall de Ternelles

La Cella

Col de
Sa Rateta

Pla de les Mates
Velles

Puig
Gros
839

D
811

El Paraigua

485

Col de Tirapeu

C710

to Lluc and
Soller

87

the Ternelles valley and the surrounding woods.

The way ahead at first sight seems difficult, but looking down towards the sea a narrow path will be observed contouring the foot of the crags and disappearing round the corner. Follow this path which leads along the sloping shelf between the crags above and the steep ground falling towards the sea below. After about 15 to 20 minutes this path turns left and goes up a wide gully through prickly scrub to a flat rocky outcrop. (This makes a good place to aim for if a shorter and less strenuous walk is wanted.) From here the route becomes harder going, up an unstable scree slope. The easiest walking is found close to the vegetation on the left. High up, cross over to a vegetated area on the right and continue upwards on traces of an old path. Eventually some level ground is reached at a cairn. This is the so-called Coll de la Rateta and a careful note should be taken of this point if a return is to be made this way.

The top of the Puig Gros can now be seen above some impressive cliffs, but in order to reach it a circuitous route must be followed. Turn left and cross the small plain, the 'Pla de les Mates Velles', heading in the general direction of a prominent rock at the foot of a steep ridge. Go past a narrow defile on the right and continue towards a second defile leading into a narrow valley on the right. There is quite good going here with some built-up sections of path. Some vegetation is encountered, but the path continues into a large amphitheatre where it peters out. Keep roughly to the right of centre of this area, trying to locate a cairn near a stone wall. With luck, a rough path up a sort of gully may be found leading to the ridge on the east of the summit. Turn left and scramble up the rocky ridge to reach the top. Besides the summit cairn there is a metal plaque inscribed 'Grup Excursionista d'Inca'.

Although a return by the same way is recommended, the alternative route is now described. Be warned that this is extremely demanding! The way lies almost south, (170°). The ground is very rough indeed and it is nowhere easy to pick the best way. In places there are razor-sharp rocks with deep clefts between them which make progress very slow. At first, the easiest ground is found near to the watershed with the Ariant valley. Approaching the Coll de Tirapau (485m) make for the right-hand side of the 'Umbrella' rock which is marked on the map (El Paraiagua) and visible for some distance. Once on the col, turn left (north-east) down the valley, still rough going until the forest track is reached. In 1990 a big fire had burnt off the vegetation in this area making walking a little easier. Follow the forest road down to reach the main track in the Ternelles valley by some stepping-stones over the stream.

Pollensa - Coll d'es Colom	1hr 30min
Coll d'es Colom - Puig Gros	2hr 40min
Puig Gros - Coll de Tirapau	2hr 30min
Coll de Tirapau - Pollensa	2hr

17. MORTITX GORGE AND RAFAL DE ARIANT

The area of the Mortitx gorge is one of the roughest and wildest places in the Sierra de Tramuntana. The area is important ecologically and is now under the protection of ICONA. The property occupies some dozens of square kilometers, sloping down from the foot of Tomir towards the sea. There are incredible rock formations in the karst landscape, and old olive trees with gnarled and twisted trunks. The sea cliffs are pocked with caves and holes. The gorge itself is interesting botanically with plants that prefer moister conditions than those that prevail elsewhere.

The abandoned house Rafal de Ariant is situated on a flat shelf overlooking the sea, where sheep graze on the once cultivated fields among a few almond and fig trees. Remote, quiet and utterly peaceful, this place is about as far removed from the crowded and noisy resorts of the south of Mallorca as it is possiible to be. As such it has an irresistible appeal to all lovers of wild country and solitude.

Type of walk: Very rough and rocky, with difficult route-finding.

Starting point:	Mortitx gates, K10.9 on C710
Time:	4hr
Distance:	8km
Total height climbed:	275m descent and re-ascent
Grade:	B+ (A to return by the gorge)
Map:	Son Marc 1:25,000

There is room for several small cars by the Mortitx gates at K10.9. Go through two gates, pass the tennis court, then turn right through another gate on the left of a stone building and continue between orchards to another gate with an access stile over the fence. After passing a fig tree the path rises slightly to yet another gate. After this take the first fork to the left. (The prominent and colourful marker stone which previously marked this point has disappeared.) About 50m further on a cairn marks a branch path on the right. Follow the path down through olive trees, thorny broom and other shrubs. There are a few red paint marks and cairns, but they are not very easy to see.

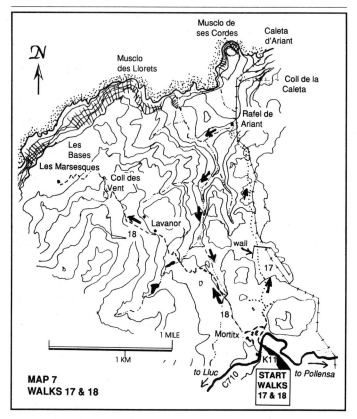

MAP 7
WALKS 17 & 18

Go through a gate at a junction of two stone walls and continue to follow the path through this wild and rocky area. Cairns and red paint marks will be found in places, but it is still difficult to find the way. The path twists and turns in a tortuous way through the incredible landscape, but makes steady progress downhill towards the coast. Look out for two places where the path makes a sharp right turn.

Eventually the path goes through a gap in a stone wall and makes a big sweep right, then left. Take a short cut straight down a steep bit from the gap if preferred. (If going the longer way round, don't miss the left turn

90

to reach the same point. If you come to some stones across the track which goes straight ahead you have missed this turn.)

The path now turns left and descends a cliff in tight zigzags to the plain behind Rafal de Ariant. From the house it is a further ten minutes or so to the edge of the cliffs with a view of an impressive cave high up on the right. Another narrow path leads from the house over the low Coll de la Caleta and then descends towards the coast. This becomes steep and loose, but is worth the effort for the view of the coast at the Caleta de Ariant. (Caleta = small bay.) The Cova de Ses Bruixes, or witches' cave, is high up in the cliff on the left and cannot be seen except by crossing very rough ground on the right of the path, leaving this at a very large boulder encountered some 20 minutes after leaving the house. Allow an extra hour if you want to do this.

Most walkers will be content to return to Mortitx by the same path used on the descent. Finding the way back is not all that easy owing to the confusing nature of the ground; it is as well to pay attention to the twists and turns on the way down. However, a return by the Mortitx gorge makes a rewarding and slightly more adventurous alternative. This involves some easy scrambling, and it is not recommended after recent rain which makes the rocks slippery.

From the ruined house follow a path leading west through an area of old fruit trees near the stream and finally turn into the stream-bed itself. Turn left after about 400m to enter the main torrent. (If you pass this you soon come to a deep and beautiful but impassable pool, worth a diversion to look at.)

The only difficult part of this route occurs quite near the beginning. A pool of water forces one to get across a steep slab on the left (looking up). This can be done close down near the water using a crab like technique, or higher up where it is easier but more exposed. After this there are no further difficulties, but some bouldery scrambling is involved. Cairns often show the easiest way. At the first fork take the right-hand branch and at the second fork take the left-hand one. Higher up the path flattens out before going over a stile and turning right to join the wide track which leads from Mortitx to Lavanor. Blue arrows point to this path for anyone deciding to descend the gorge. Turn left and follow the main track back to the entrance gate. Going back this way takes about the same length of time as returning by the ordinary route.

18. LAVANOR AND THE COLL DES VENT

The area of Mortitx is of outstanding natural beauty and of great scientific interest for its flora and for its geology. Although this walk goes through wild and spectacular scenery it is entirely on a narrow road and is highly recommended. This road was being improved in 1990 and although there are three sets of gates to prevent vehicular use, each had a pedestrian access stile. This route is in the centre of the area where black vultures live and it is essential that these rare and magnificent birds are not disturbed. Visitors are requested to keep to the road and only to go in small groups.

Type of walk: Very easy on a narrow road, but rough ground at the end for 20 minutes.

Starting point:	Mortitx gates, K10.9, C710
Time:	4hr 30min
Distance:	11km
Highest point reached:	502m
Total height climbed:	400m
Grade:	C
Map:	Son Marc 1:25,000

There is room at the entrance gate for several small cars to park but this can be difficult at weekends. From the entrance gate, or the access on the right if it is locked, follow the main track round past the tennis courts. After passing some buildings the track swings right and heads towards the coast. Ignore a branch left and keep on the main track all the way. Orchards of peach trees and other fruit will be noticed on the left, and a blue painted sign which shows the way to the top of the Mortitx gorge on the right.

The track has been level up to now but soon begins to rise and then passes by a small reservoir fringed with reeds. It continues to rise to reach Lavanor, where there is a small house and a flat cultivated area, conspicuous in the wilderness. After more uphill work the road dips down before rising to the Coll d'es Vent. From here there is a steep descent towards another flat field, and the road swings left alongside this to end by a ruined shelter. There were originally two gateways here, now fenced, with piled stones making a rough stile.

To reach the cliff edge and find a lunch spot involves some 15-20 minutes of rough walking, but is worth the effort.

19. A CIRCUIT OF THE PUIG CARAGOLER DE FEMENIA

This rocky massif lies between the well-known Puig Roig and the Puig Gros de Ternelles, in a wild and virtually uninhabited area north of the Pollensa-Lluc road. The route described is not as popular as the circuit of the Puig Roig but is extremely attractive and deserves to be better known. The views are extensive and varied. At first, the outlook is across the plain to the bay of Pollensa, then the eye is drawn to the steep and craggy Puig Gros de Ternelles. From the Coll Ciuro to the Coll des Pinetons there is a rocky wilderness sloping down to the sea. At the coll des Pinetons the whole of the north-eastern slopes of the Puig Roig come into view across a trackless valley. Finally, from the Coll d'els Ases, there is a view of Tomir bathed in the late afternoon light.

Type of walk: No steep gradients, but partly pathless and route-finding experience is essential. Not recommended in mist.

Starting point:	K14.2, Pollensa-Lluc road
Time:	4hr
Distance:	10km
Highest point reached:	676m
Total height climbed:	310m
Grade:	B+
Map:	Pollensa 1:25,000

The route begins at the entrance to Femenia Nou on the Pollensa-Lluc road. Although parking for one car may be found about 100m further on towards Lluc there is not much space anywhere else nearby. It.is better if possible to arrange to be dropped off here and picked up at the end of the day. The main gate is usually locked, but there is an access stile on the left. In a short distance take a left fork and go through the gate behind Femenia Nou, continuing to Femenia Vell where the track appears to end. It does not end, but doubles back near the house to enter the pinewoods on the east side of Puig Caragoler.

This wide track ends at a spring, the Font d'en Quelota, where water gushes out of a rock into a stone trough which is roofed over and gated. A glass tumbler is provided inside! From the spring a rather narrow and overgrown path leads on to the Coll Ciuro, at first descending slightly and then contouring before rising towards the cliffs of Caragoler.

From the Coll Ciuro an old path goes left to circumnavigate the grassy hollow ahead. Go straight across here and pick up the path by a cairn on a large boulder. Although little used the path is marked by cairns and red

93

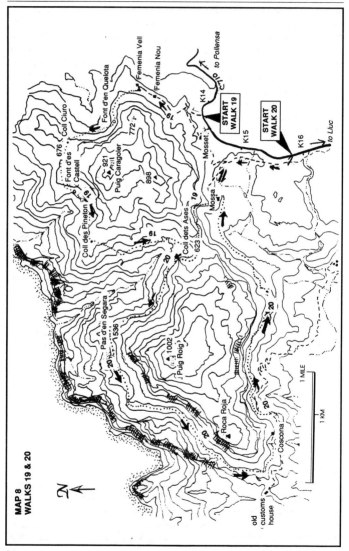

**MAP 8
WALKS 19 & 20**

N

to Pollensa

START WALK 19

START WALK 20

to Lluc

K14

K15

K16

C710

Mosset

Mossa

Femenia Vell

Femenia Nou

Font d'en Quelota

Coll Ciuro

676

Font d'es Castell

Coll des Pineton

921

Puig Catagoier

898

772

61

19

623

Coll dets Ases

19

20

Pas d'en Segara

1536

1002

Puig Roig

20

20

20

Roca Roja

Coscona

20

20

old
customs
house

1 MILE

1 KM

paint. It contours at about the same height as the col, going through a gap in a wall and passing a ruined building. A few minutes after this building there is a choice of ways. The old way goes down to some old terraces near a spring, the Font d'en Castell, which is roofed. From above this can be recognised by the green damp area below it surrounded by a wall. To continue from the spring, descend slightly to cross the stream-bed and then up pathless ground towards the Coll des Pinetons.

The alternative way misses out the spring but avoids losing height. There are some cairns showing the best route, which crosses the same stream-bed at a higher level, and the two ways re-join before reaching the Coll des Pinetons. As this col is approached avoid the right branch to another small notch in the ridge.

At the Coll des Pinetons turn left and make a slightly rising traverse following a line of cairns. Then bear right, descending into a shallow carritx-filled valley. Follow the cairns for the easiest walking. The route divides to go either above or below a rocky outcrop, then re-joins, traversing again before descending in the same direction. Further on a narrow rocky gully is descended, where traces of a carefully-built mule track will be found. This leads into a hollow where there is a *sitja*. Leave the hollow by the stream-bed on the right. When a flat area is reached, turn left and then go up towards the Col d'els Ases. The route is a bit vague here, although there are some cairns and traces of a very overgrown path.

Once on the col, the excellent path descending to Mossa is followed. From Mossa, follow the track towards the C710, in a few minutes turning left at an acute angle to go behind Mosset and join the Femenia Nou track. Turn right to reach the starting point.

K14.2 - Font d'en Quelota	30min
Font - Coll Ciuro	30min
Coll Ciuro - Coll d'es Pinetons	1hr
Coll d'es Pinetons - Coll d'els Ases	1hr
Coll d'els Ases - K14.2	1hr

20. CIRCUIT OF THE PUIG ROIG
Note: at the time of going to press access through Mossa farm is being strongly discouraged. In the hope that this will change in the future this walk, well-known to local walkers and others, is included in its original form. Meanwhile some walkers may prefer to approach this walk from Lluc and Coscona as in Walk 27. In this case either

complete the circuit in reverse, or walk along the cliff path to the Pas d'en Segara and return. This section is in any case the most attractive part of the walk.

The Puig Roig is the lowest of the 1,000m summits of Mallorca, but it is one of the most attractive mountains on the island with its encircling red cliffs. It is especially striking seen in evening light from the Soller-Lluc road and it is well worth stopping at the small *mirador* near Escorca. On this classic circular walk around the mountain, new views are constantly being revealed and give endless pleasure no matter how many times the walk is repeated. There are a number of excellent bivvy sites under overhanging rocks and local walkers like to start the walk in the late afternoon and sleep out there. The route also passes the interesting old cave houses of Coscona, built under overhanging rocks. These are still in occasional use.

The circuit of the mountain is a delightful excursion, far preferable than a climb to the top. The traverse of the mountain from south to north can be done, but is an arduous route over very rough ground.

Type of walk: On good but in places very stony paths. From Coscona to Mossa the path is less used and more difficult to follow.

Starting point:	Mossa gates at K15.7 on C710
Time:	5hr 45min
Distance:	14km
Highest point reached:	c.700m
Total height climbed:	218m
Grade:	B+
Map:	Son Marc 1:25,000

This walk is becoming so popular that finding a place to park near Mossa gate is becoming increasingly difficult. If possible, arrange to be dropped off here and picked up at the end of the day. The road to the farm is private and cars must not be taken there.

Follow the track to the finca, a large sheep farm, and go through the gate at the far side of the house. Cross the clearing straight ahead to find the beginning of the excellent mule track that leads up to the Coll d'els Ases. This path slopes up the side of a very steep cliff and at one time had protective handrails, now disappeared. From the pass follow the path around the northern slopes towards the coast. At the most northerly point the path turns a corner, the Pas d'en Segara, then runs south-west, contouring below the cliffs. There are excellent views here of the old Torre de Lluc and the spectacular headland, the Morro de Sa Vaca. After crossing a stile by a sheepfold the ruined customs house comes into sight below. Go through a gap in the wall above the barracks. The path then traverses to Coscona where it joins the track from the customs house. (Alternatively follow the wall down to the ruined building and pick up the track there. There is a water tank with a spring behind it at this point.)

About two minutes or so after leaving the houses of Coscona, and just before the track bends to the left, look out for a narrow path beginning by a double-trunked olive tree growing at the edge of the road. (Ignore another path a few metres before this one.) This is the key point for finding the way back to Mossa. If you find the road is beginning to descend then you have gone too far and should return to find the start of this path.

At first the path is easy to follow with red paint marks and cairns, but encroaching vegetation sometimes obscures it. When the pinewood is reached, make for the terrace above the fig tree, then climb up onto the next terrace by a red paint mark. The path then contours some way to reach a clearing at the further edge of the woods. A large boulder with three paint marks indicates the place where a short descent is made to a terrace. Turn left along this terrace and go through an opening in a wall. Keep following the path along old olive terraces until the large circular platform of an old threshing floor is reached.

From the threshing floor the path rises slightly to go above an enclosure with an old building. Behind the building there is a spring in an underground tunnel, hidden by brambles. The path then crosses a stream-bed before dropping down by some old terraces and contours along one of these below a wall with a fence on top. Paint marks and cairns are then followed along a rather overgrown section, then down a slope of open ground to a gate at the corner of an oakwood. The path used to go all the way to Mossa inside the wood, but now a new road made for forestry operations is soon picked up and followed through the flat fields to reach Mossa.

Mossa gates - Mossa farm	30min
Mossa farm - Coll d'els Ases	25min
Coll d'els Ases - Pas d'en Segara	55min
Pas d'en Segara - Coscona	1hr 30min
Coscona - Mossa farm	1hr 55min
Mossa farm - Mossa gate	30min

21. PUIG DE MARIA

The Puig de Maria is a small but distinctive hill near Pollensa. There has been a chapel on the top since 1348, and in 1362 this was in charge of three women, the first female hermits in the history of the Baleares. At one time there was accommodation for as many as 70 people, and in recent years this was available to anyone. There was a large refectory and kitchens for the use of day visitors, for use of which a donation was requested. In 1988 the elderly nuns who had run the place for years decided the time had come to retire, and for a while the future was uncertain. However, it is now in private hands and the bar and restaurant services are once again available. (Not always; sometimes found to be closed.)

Outside there are terraces and a natural garden from which there are extensive views. Many local people go up there on Sundays and on Easter Monday it is a place of pilgrimage to all Pollensa.

Type of walk: Very easy, but steadily uphill on a country lane which becomes a narrow but well-made mule track near the top.

Starting point:	Pollensa
Time:	1hr 30min
Distance:	3.5km
Total height climbed:	290m
Grade:	C
Map:	Pollensa 1:25,000

Start at the petrol station in Pollensa, in the wide road parallel to the main Palma road. Follow the signposted road 'Puig de Maria' across the main road and straight up the narrow winding lane ahead. Turn sharp right at the first bend, then left past several terraced gardens and fields. At first the road is surfaced, but very narrow. (There is a turning space at the top but no parking.) From the end of the road a wide path with steps leads in 15 minutes to the walled terrace at the side of the chapel.

22. CUCULLA DE FARTARITX

This impressive peak, although of no great height, dominates the town of Pollensa and the Vall D'en Marc with its spectacular cliffs facing west, north and east. It is approached by a very interesting old mule track as far as a high farm on the Fartaritx plateau. An intermittent and narrow path now skirts the farm and leads to the summit plateau at a natural

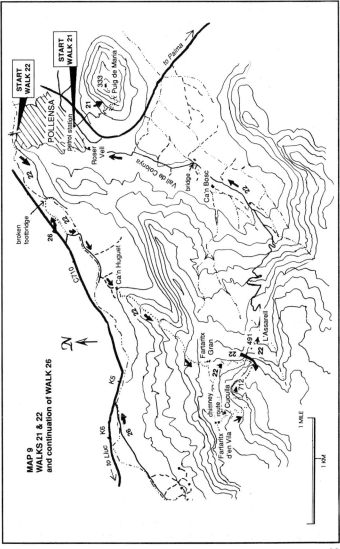

MAP 9
WALKS 21 & 22
and continuation of WALK 26

START WALK 22

START WALK 21

333 Puig de Maria

to Palma

21

POLLENSA

petrol station

Roser Vell

Vall de Colonya

bridge

Ca'n Bosc

22

22

broken footbridge

26

22

C710

Ca'n Huguet

22

N

K5

22

Fartaritx Gran

491 L'Assarell

22

22

to Lluc

K6

26

chimney route

Fartaritx d'en Vila

712 Cuculla

1 MILE

1 KM

99

break in the cliffs. (An alternative walk involving a steep scramble up an interesting little chimney is also described.)

Type of walk: Level easy walking as far as Ca'n Huguet, then uphill steadily along a well-made mule track to the high plateau. After this the mountain path is less well-defined but not difficult.

Starting point:	Pollensa
Time:	6hr 30min
Distance:	14km
Highest point reached:	712m
Total height climbed:	662m
Grade:	B+
Map:	Pollensa 1:50,000 or
	Pollensa 1:25,000 and
	Son Marc 1:25,000

Leave Pollensa by the Calle de la Huerta and turn left at the old unnamed road just before the bridge. After 1km a ruined footbridge will be seen on the right. Cross the stream-bed which is usually dry and go straight on along an old track passing a large house on the left. When a good track is reached, turn left and follow this over a bridge, after which it swings sharp right. Keep straight on with the stream on your right. After about 700m the road turns sharp left. Almost immediately the main track bends left again, but at this point leave it and follow the minor track which forks right. Follow this track along until it turns right in front of a barn. It is important not to turn right here but to go straight on along a grassy track between a house and a water tank, to find the mule track which doubles back right behind the house (Ca'n Huguet).

At the old deserted house, above Ca'n Huguet, go up the steps, passing an old well on the right. Keep straight on, outside a wall, and into the oakwood by a wooden gate. Follow the track up through the woods where there are often several pigs foraging for acorns. The path goes through a gate at the top of the wood, then through a gap in a stone wall. Turn left here and go through a metal gate. After a further five or six minutes there is a sharp turn left along a track which becomes quite wide and appears to have obliterated the original mule track for a short distance. It leads in ten minutes to a gate (new in 1989) where the old mule track is picked up again, winding upwards through an attractive natural garden of flowering shrubs. In about 45 minutes this leads to a high farmhouse, Fartaritx Gran, near a stream.

Turn right alongside the wall enclosing the fields. Where the wall turns left go up several zigzags and very soon leave the main path, which continues along the plateau, by a red paint sign and follow the wall uphill. A narrow trod can be followed up above the enclosed fields contouring towards some large oak trees. In the wood continue to contour along open easy ground with occasional cairns until after passing a sitja and a ruined shelter the path leads uphill towards the Cuculla. Below some pinnacles the path turns left then slopes up to the base of the cliffs. After turning a little corner a sloping rocky ledge, across which is a fence, leads up to reach the top of the cliffs at a natural break. Turn right and go up easy ground for about 400m to reach the top.

Alternative ascent: Grade A+
Instead of going round the outside of the Fartaritx Gran fields, where the wall turns at right angles, follow the main path which continues in the direction of Fartaritx d'en Vila, a ruined house completely hidden in a clump of trees. If you want to look at this, stay on the path which leads to a gate and then a flight of old stone steps. If not, bear left as you approach the trees, then make towards a large palm tree.

From the palm tree, it is easy to choose a way up into the wide upland valley of old neglected terraces backed by high cliffs. There may appear to be no way up these cliffs, but such a way can be found from the obvious corner up on the left. At the foot of the corner there is a large boulder covered with ivy. Go up past this on the right to arrive at the foot of the little chimney. There are no difficulties, although long legs are an advantage in one or two places. It is surmounted in about ten minutes and a further ten minutes of easy walking leads to the summit.

Descent:
It is possible to make a circular walk by descending to a high farm L'Assarell and walking back to Pollensa by the road in the Vall de Colonya, arriving in the town by the old church Roser Vell. To do this, return to the prominent cairn at the cliff-edge some 400m south-east of the top. Follow the twisting path down the cliff, through the fence and past a little gully. Almost at once looking across to the right, a wall will be seen on a col. Descend and cross the intervening valley by any way that seems best and climb over the wall. Make for the farm below, choosing a way among the many animal tracks. Care should be taken not to disturb the many animals here. Once through the gate there is a surfaced road all the way back to Pollensa. At first this goes down quite steeply to the valley floor, then is level most of the way. Keep to the main track, taking a left

101

turn over a bridge opposite a large house. If preferred, return by the same way used for the ascent.

Pollensa - Fartaritx	2hr 30min
Fartaritx - Cuculla	1hr
Cuculla - Assarell	45min
Assarell - Pollensa	2hr

23. PUIG DE CA

The Puig de Ca lies between Tomir and the Cuculla de Fartaritx, these three being the peaks which overlook the town of Pollensa on the south of the Vall d'en Marc. Although not so spectacular as the Cuculla, it has steep cliffs and provides an interesting walk. A particularly unusual feature is the old snow house with the curving roof, also seen on Walk 24(b).

Type of walk: Partly on good tracks and a well-made mule track and partly on pathless ground with some route-finding required. Rocky on the top but not difficult.

Starting point:	Ca'n Huguet
Time:	5hr 45min
Distance:	12km
Highest point reached:	878m
Total height climbed:	800m
Grade:	A
Map:	Pollensa 1:25,000 and Son Marc 1:25,000

Going from Pollensa towards Lluc, turn left at K2.7, cross the bridge and follow the road to the right. Park somewhere along this lane which runs alongside the river. Go up the old mule track from Ca'n Huguet to Fartaritx Gran as for Walk 22.

Cross the stream and walk alongside the wall enclosing the fields. Where the wall turns left, go up a little zigzag and then keep on the path which continues in a westerly direction to the ruined house Fartaritx d'en Vila. There is a gate just before and below the house. Turn left up steps half-hidden among the trees and go between the old buildings. Behind the property turn right and continue along the track in the same direction as before. There is a locked gate to surmount at a boundary fence, after

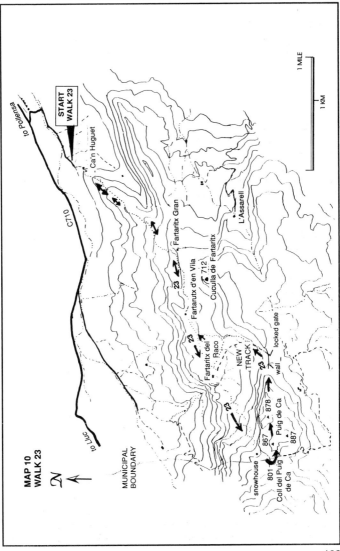

**MAP 10
WALK 23**

to Pollensa

START WALK 23

Ca'n Huguet

C710

to LLUC

MUNICIPAL
BOUNDARY

Fartaritx Gran

23

Fartarutx d'en Vila

712
Cucuia de Fartaritx

L'Assarell

Fartaritx del
Raco

23

NEW
TRACK

23

locked gate

wall

23

snowhouse

801

867

878

887

Puig de Ca

Coll del Puig
de Ca

1 MILE

1 KM

103

which it is better to avoid going too close to the next house, Fartaritx del Raco, where walkers are not welcome. It can be by-passed on the right.

Once this is passed, make towards the Coll del Puig de Ca, using traces of the old path where found. This must once have been an excellent mule track serving the snow house, but unfortunately it has fallen into almost total disrepair. Above the snow house the ground becomes steeper but the remains of the path are more evident. Go through the hole in the fence to reach the col, where a wide track leading south commences.

Follow the track to the boundary wall and then turn left into a shallow gully, making for a low crag at the top. There is an easy way up a sloping ledge and the west top is reached in a further few minutes. Double back to continue over the main top and along the ridge down to the Coll de Miner. Cross the wall across the col near the crag as there is a high locked gate on the col itself. Follow the new track (not shown on the published maps), but leave it where it bends left towards Fartaritx del Raco. Cut across the corner towards the ruined house, finding your own way rather than looking for the defunct path shown on the map. From Fartaritx d'en Vila, follow the path to Fartaritx Gran and return by the mule track to Ca'n Huguet.

Ca'n Huguet - Fartaritx Gran	1hr 15min
Fartaritx Gran - Coll del Puig de Ca	1hr 30min
Coll del Puig de Ca - Puig de Ca	45min
Puig de Ca - Coll de Miner	30min
Coll de Miner - Ca'n Huguet	1hr 45min

24. PUIG TOMIR

Tomir is a well-known and popular mountain, owing to its commanding position at the head of the Pollensa valley and its accessibility. It can be reached in one hour and thirty minutes from the road end by a well-defined path and is one of the places where Black Vultures are sometimes sighted. For these reasons it is a mountain where other walkers are likely to be met, especially at weekends. Most people go up and down from Binifaldo, a short but enjoyable excursion. The views from the top are extensive and it is an interesting summit with a deep circular snow-pit. All the summit area is bare and rocky and there are steep crags on the northern side. Two different and longer walks are described here.

24(a). Binifaldo, Tomir and Aucanella

Type of walk: Mainly on rough and stony paths and including a short but very easy scramble. There are some route finding problems, especially at Aucanella where trees and scrub obscure the way.

Starting point:	Binifaldo
Time:	5hr
Distance:	7km
Highest point reached:	1,103m
Total height climbed:	638m
Grade:	A
Map:	Son Marc 1:25,000 and Selva 1:25,000.

To reach Binifaldo turn left (east) at K17.4 on the Pollensa-Lluc road, through an open gateway. Take the furthest left fork when three green gates are reached at Menut. (At weekends this gate is closed to traffic and this adds about 2km to the walk.)

The road ends at the Binifaldo bottling plant where there is a parking place. The walk starts between the gate to the plant and the forest fence. Follow the boundary fence up until a painted arrow marks a sharp right turn and the path begins to wind up through the trees. After leaving the woods there is a level section and then a rising traverse above a scree. After crossing a second and wider scree the path rises steeply to a little col. On the other side of this col it continues to rise steeply, keeping close against the rocks on the right. In the main the path is a good one with rock steps built up in the steeper places. It leads in a further 15 minutes from the col to a little rock slab about 4m high. Although this is very easily surmounted by means of a groove sloping up diagonally from right to left and well supplied with hand and footholds, it comes as a surprise to those unused to using their hands on a walk.

Above the slab the path continues upwards in a shallow valley which leads directly to the summit ridge. However, it is easier, being less loose and stony, to leave this valley in a few minutes by a cairned path on the right, only turning left towards the head of the valley when another line of cairns is reached. On arriving at a small col between two tops of the main ridge, turn left and follow the cairns up gently rising ground to the summit.

From the top go down east to reach the *casa de nieve* in ten minutes, then continue down towards the Coll del Puig de Ca. In places the remains of the old track used by the snow-workers can be picked out. Aim

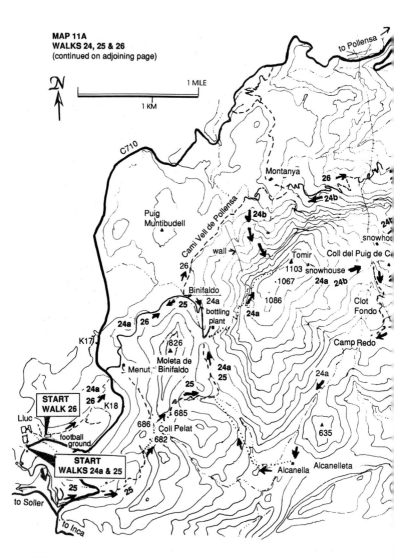

N

1 MILE

1 KM

to Pollensa

C710

Montanya

26

24b

Puig
Muntibudell

24b

wall

26

snowhou

Tomir
1103 snowhouse

Coll del Puig de C

Binifaldo

25   24a

1067

24a   24b

bottling
plant

1086

24a

Clot
Fondo

24a   26

25   26

826

24a

Camp Redo

Moleta de
Menut   Binifaldo

24a
25

K17

START
WALK 26

24a

26   K18

25

685

25

682   Coll Pelat

24a

635

Lluc

football
ground

686

START
WALKS 24a & 25

Alcanella   Alcanelleta

25

25

to Soller

25

to Inca

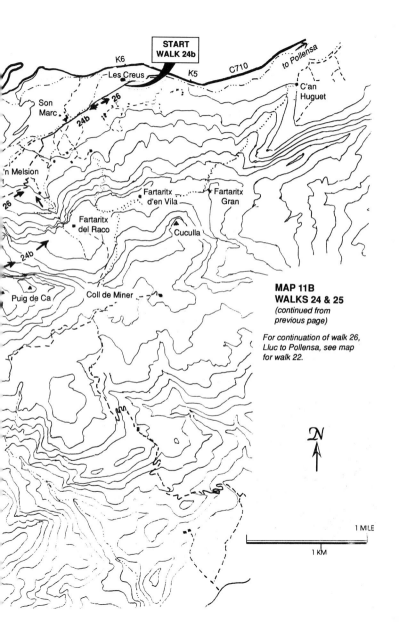

START
WALK 24b

K6

Les Creus

C710

K5

to Pollensa

C'an
Huguet

Son
Marc

26

24b

'n Melsion

26

Fartaritx
d'en Vila

Fartaritx
Gran

Fartaritx
del Raco

Cuculla

24b

Puig de Ca

Coll de Miner

MAP 11B
WALKS 24 & 25
(continued from
previous page)

For continuation of walk 26,
Lluc to Pollensa, see map
for walk 22.

𝒩

1 MILE

1 KM

slightly to the right of the col at first to avoid some steep ground, then towards the centre where a Land-Rover track will be found. Turn right along this and follow it down past a small hollow, the Clot Fondo, on the right. When another track is met turn right again to reach a flat plain known as the Camp Redo. From the turning circle at the end of the track a narrow path leads to a gap in a boundary wall and on through a narrow valley which skirts the south-east slopes of Tomir.

There are occasional cairns on this path which leads to a sizable flat area containing the ruined house Aucanella. This was once a cultivated clearing but is now so overgrown with large trees and dense shrubs that it is difficult to find the way through. The best way is to turn left at the boundary fence and follow the path right to the house. Then follow the vestigial remains of the track which runs almost west for about 500m. Look out for the place where it turns north towards the Coll d'es Pedregaret. Once on this path it is easy to follow. After crossing the stream-bed it rises high on the left side of the valley where it is well-marked by cairns. Higher up it goes into the forest, then crosses the stream to join a cart-track. This rises steadily to reach the col by the forest gate at Binifaldo.

Binifaldo - Tomir	1hr 30min
Tomir - Coll del Puig de Ca	45min
Coll - Camp Redo	30min
Camp Redo - Aucanella	1hr
Aucanella - Binifaldo	1hr 15min

24(b). Tomir from the Pollensa valley

This alternative way up Tomir is a long and strenuous one involving a scramble up one of the northern ridges and a pathless descent. It is a satisfying way up because Tomir lies at the head of the valley, and it will please those who regard it as 'cheating' to start the climb of Tomir from Binifaldo. The route begins from the Cami Vell de Pollensa; the old road, in use before the construction of the current main road the C710. The descent goes past the most fascinating of the old snow-houses on the island, one that has a curved tile roof.

The start of the route is not easy to find. Before attempting it, it is a good idea to study the northern aspect of Tomir in late afternoon light from the C710. At this time of day the ridges stand out clearly. The ridge described is not the one with a wall running down it but the one to the left of this and it forms the boundary of a well-defined gully. This gully is the Torrent Son Marc and the ridge forms a water-shed between this and the

Torrent de Mortitx further west.

Type of walk: Very strenuous and with difficult route-finding. For experienced walkers only.

Starting point:	Pollensa-Binifaldo road
Time:	7hr
Distance:	11km
Highest point reached:	1,103m
Total height climbed:	970m
Grade:	A+
Map:	Son Marc 1:25,000

Turn left from the Pollensa-Lluc road C710 at K5.5. This junction is a fork with a large tree in the angle between the two roads, until recently signposted 'Las Creus'. A place can be found to leave a car at the side of this road after about 1km. Walk up the valley towards Tomir. At Ca'n Melsion the road turns sharp left, then bends right, after which there is an unlocked gate across the road. Soon the road swings sharp right; note the track on the left which is the return route for this walk. The gravel surface now ends by the locked gate to Ca'n Cuñat. The old road continues to be well-defined and rises through the forest in a series of hairpin bends. It then crosses a plateau of cultivated ground before reaching the edge of the woods below the northern cliffs of Tomir.

Ignore a new track on the right not shown on the map and continue along the old road which crosses a stream near the farm 'Montanya'. Take the left turn after this and after several bends look out for an old cairn on the left of the track, just below a *sitja*. This is less than 0.5km from the left turn. Do not waste too much time looking for this cairn as there is no real path anyway and it is a question of struggling through the trees and vegetation for a short distance to reach the open ground of the ridge above. The ridge is quite obvious, bounded on the left by a deeply cut gully.

The line of the ridge is easy to follow, with any difficulties being avoided on the right. There is nothing very difficult, although some loose rock may be met with in the upper part shortly before the summit ridge is reached. The summit ridge is then followed left along the edge of the crags, or slightly to the right of it where cairns show the easiest walking. (This coincides with the ordinary route up from Binifaldo.)

From the top, descend to the Coll del Puig de Ca, passing a snow pit and making use of the remains of an old path. At the col, turn left and go through the hole in the fence. A path will be found leading down to the snow-house. This is steep at first, but there are traces of an old built-up path. (Note that the descent begins quite near the foot of the impressive cliffs of the Puig de Ca and the direction is a little east of north.)

From the snow-house the old path has almost completely disappeared, but the ground is not too rough. Keep going down in a north-easterly direction towards the farm Fartaritx del Raco. Before reaching this farm go through a gap in the wall on the left, on the other side of which a narrow path can be found. This traverses to the west and crosses a stream at the head of a steep grassy valley, then leads down into this valley before becoming lost above the forest. After entering the forest the way is a little confused, but try to keep fairly near the stream to avoid some steep ground. Pick up the old track which leads past a deserted farm and eventually rejoins the route of ascent near Ca'n Cuñat.

Ascent:	4hr 15min
Descent:	2hr 45min

25. BINIFALDO AND MENUT

Binifaldo and Menut are two publicly-owned fincas in the mountains not far from the monastery of Lluc. They are managed and conserved by the Govern Balear in association with the Ministry of Agriculture and Fisheries. The houses at Binifaldo have been restored and are used for educational purposes. The house at Menut has a defensive tower and is used as a centre for forestry. The main road C710 passes through the Menut area and some excellent picnic areas have been provided, near to K17. There is also an area where camping is permitted, on application to the Conselleria in Palma.

This walk explores the area of the two fincas which is very typical of the mountains of Mallorca. There are large areas of oak woodlands, formerly exploited for the production of charcoal, and pines growing higher up the slopes here and there, replacing the oaks. The bedrock here is a very permeable limestone with karstic erosion producing some very curious rock formations. The well-known 'Camel' rock is in the recreation area west of the C710 opposite Menut. A path leads to it, shown on a map on the noticeboard. The high rainfall combined with the rock type has produced a series of springs, of which one, the Font des Pedregaret is exploited commercially at Binifaldo. One spring, La Font Ufana, is different from the others in that rain water and melting snow from Tomir and Sa Moleta drain into a phreatic tube. This emerges in the woods at the side of the track in the Bosc Gran. It is said to flow all the year round.

Type of walk: Easy on good tracks all the way. Some ups and downs, but nothing very steep.

Starting point:	Lluc car park
Time:	3hr 10min
Distance:	8km
Highest point reached:	687m
Total height climbed:	345m
Grade:	C
Map:	Selva 1:25,000 and
	Son Marc 1:25,000

From the monastery car park go south to the Restaurant de la Font Coberta. Turn left and follow the minor road up to join the C710 just below the road junction near the petrol station. Turn left and walk along the main road for about 500m to a hairpin bend. Just before this bend go through a gate with a private hunting sign. (If this is locked, access is made at the side of another gate about 50m further on.) Follow the main track up towards the Coll de Sa Font at 687m, ignoring branch tracks. High up, look out for a cairn on the right which shows the narrow path leading to the col. Go through a gap in the wall across the pass and follow the cairns across a large flat area (due north) until a new wide track is met at the Coll Pelat.

Ignore the left turn which goes downhill and keep straight on, still on level ground. (This area can be confusing as there are three cols very close together and the tracks are either not on the map at all or are not shown correctly.) The level track leads to the third and unnamed col at 685m. Go through the opening in the wall and follow the forest track down into the Bosc Gran and the Alcanella valley.

When the valley floor is reached, the track turns left and goes uphill to the Coll de Pedregaret, near the bottling plant. Go through the forest gate and follow the surfaced road down to the Binifaldo finca. There is a shelter here and a water supply. Continue down the road to meet a green metal gate that may be locked but has pedestrian access. Five minutes later turn left on the C710 and in 100m turn right on a wide track, by a gate which is sometimes fastened up and has to be climbed. This leads to Lluc and is part of the old road from Lluc to Pollensa. After passing a camping site the path goes across a football pitch to arrive at Lluc. Turn left and then right along the road to reach the starting point.

Lluc - Binifaldo	2hr
Binifaldo - Lluc	1hr 10min

26. LLUC TO POLLENSA BY THE OLD ROAD

The new road between Pollensa and Soller has resulted in the old road becoming a quiet and attractive byway through delightful countryside, making a pleasant and easy walk. The only snag is that some walking has to be done along the main road, the C710, from the junction at K5.4 to K2.7.

A party that can have the use of two cars might prefer to leave one at K5.4 before catching the Inca bus which leaves Pollensa at 09.15. A bus leaves Inca for Lluc at about 10.00 am from outside the railway station, where it waits for the train to arrive from Palma. The bus journey from the flat plain up through the mountains to Lluc is worth every peseta, the scenery being most impressive.

Type of walk: Easy, along tracks, and mainly downhill. In midwinter it can be mainly in the shade.

Starting point:	Lluc monastery
Time:	4hr 45min
Distance:	20km
Highest point reached:	610m
Total height climbed:	100m
Grade:	C+
Map:	Inca 1:50,000 and Pollensa 1:50,000

From the monastery go out of the main entrance and turn left along the road. After about 200m turn left again between two stone gateposts, then almost immediately right through an iron gate. Go through the football ground and cross over to a stile at the far end on the left. The old road begins here and is at first horizontal, then rises in a series of bends to reach the C710 at a double gate which occasionally has to be climbed. Turn left along the main road and first right after c.100m at an open gateway with blue paint signs at K17.4. After a few minutes the road forks left, at the furthest left of three green gates. This road gently rises up to

610m, the highest point of the walk, before dropping down to Binifaldo. In about 30 minutes look out for a left turn, about 20m before reaching a large restored building which is the headquarters of ICONA.

At this point we leave the tarmac road which services the Binifaldo bottling plant and return to the old unsurfaced road, crossing a little stream and going through a wooden gate. Twenty minutes later there is a double gate with a pedestrian access in a boundary wall. In a further 15 minutes take a right turn at a place where the main track goes sharp left, near a *finca* called La Montaña. The old road we are following contours towards a stream-bed, then drops down fairly steeply to join another track from La Montaña.

About 30 minutes later the track goes through a metal gate into a fairly level cultivated area, with carobs and almond trees, then descends gradually to another metal gate in a boundary wall with a 'private hunting' sign. Once through here it descends through a wooded area in a series of zigzags. In about half an hour Ca'n Cuñat is reached at a green metal gate with round stone gateposts. Just past here the track swings sharp left opposite a wooden gate and in a further ten minutes arrives at Ca'n Melsion. The old track then becomes much wider and continues to join the new road at an angle. This is at about K5.4 and there is a large tree in the angle between the two roads. (There used to be a sign on the tree, saying Las Creus.)

From the Las Creus junction it is unfortunately necessary to walk along the main road to K2.7 (a very small marker stone partially obscured by grass). Turn right here and in a couple of minutes or so turn left along an overgrown grassy path at a point where the main track turns right. Ten minutes later, after passing a house with vociferous barking dogs, cross a stream-bed (usually dry) and turn left along a good road to reach Pollensa near the Roman Bridge. Turn right along the Calle de la Huerta, then left at the Banca Central to the square with the cockerel fountain, then right, left, and right and left again to get to the main square.

Lluc - Binifaldo	1 hr
Binifaldo - Montaña	35min
Montana - Ca'n Cunat	1hr 20min
Ca'n Cuñat - K2.7	1hr 25min
K2.7 - Pollensa	25min

27. LLUC TO COSCONA AND THE TORRE DE LLUC

Coscona is a fascinating place with a number of 'cave houses' built under a huge overhanging rock. They face south and have a very impressive view of the Puig Mayor. These houses can also be seen on the round of the Puig Roig, but the walk described here, although slightly longer, is a very much easier one. Before rising to Coscona the route crosses an absolutely flat plain which looks as though it once held a lake. Now there are cereal crops, olive trees and sheep with tinkling bells grazing among them. Impressive cliffs dominate this plain at the beginning of the walk, with the red walls of the Puig Roig in full view straight ahead. Further on the ruined barracks of an old customs house stand in a prominent position overlooking the deep cleft of the Torrente de Pareis. Although this makes a worthwhile objective in itself, the walk can be extended further on towards the old Torre de Lluc, perched on a headland overlooking the sea.

Type of walk: Very easy walking on a track which is level at first, then rises steadily up to Coscona. The surface is a kind of cinder track which is quite pleasant to walk on, but becomes stonier after Coscona. After the ruined customs house there is only a narrow and partially lost path, but the old Torre de Lluc is in sight all the way.

Starting point:	Locked gate c.3 km from Lluc
Time:	4hr 35min
Distance:	15km
Highest point reached:	560m
Total height climbed:	420m
Grade:	C (to Customs House), B beyond
Map:	Inca 1:50,000 and
	Pollensa 1:50,000

Cave house at Coscona

The start of the walk is found by driving right up to the front entrance of the monastery and turning left along a road at the side of a restaurant. Go through a gate (which must be reclosed) then take the first turn right. The road descends in a series of bends and leads to a heavily padlocked gate. There is parking space for several cars here.

Go through the pedestrian access gate and follow the level road to a large *finca* called Ca'n Pontico. (The barking dogs are chained.) The surfaced road becomes a cinder track at the back of the house and it is simply a matter of following it all the way to Coscona. There are several gates. Soon after passing a shallow covered water tank the track begins to rise in zigzags and occasional shortcuts are worthwhile. About 1hr 15min from the start of the walk there is an open gateway with the word COSCONA chiselled out of a wooden board, but it is a further 25 minutes from this gateway to the cave houses.

After the cave houses, continue along the track which descends a little then doubles back to a spring in a shallow valley before arriving at the ruined barracks. The ruins themselves are not exactly attractive, but the situation is a magnificent one. However, it is well worth the extra effort to follow the vestigial remains of the path which goes on to the old watch-tower near the sea. To do so, look for the red paint sign 'Morro Vaca' by

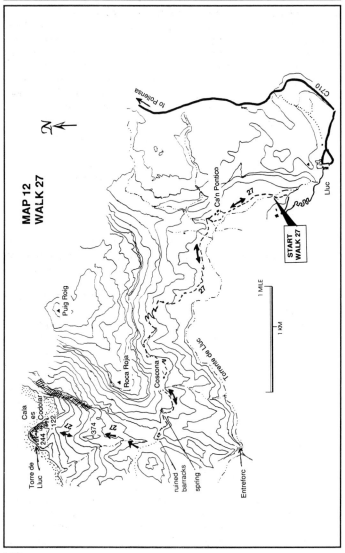

the gap in the wall as you arrive at the barracks. Follow the line of the old path parallel to the wall, passing a pair of olive trees. Before the next large tree, turn right to find the traces of the old path, built up at the edges and marked by a few cairns. Keep to the left of the low hill ahead, then bear right to a small col and descend slightly to cross a stream bed. Continue on fairly level ground and make towards a fence near two pine trees. Here will be found a gap in the fence with a red paint mark on one of the fence posts. A few yards to the left it is possible to pick up the old path marked by cairns as far as a little knoll which is a really excellent viewpoint.

Locked gate - Coscona cave house	1hr 40min
Coscona - Customs house	20min
Customs house - Viewpoint	20min
Viewpoint - Locked gate	2hr 15min

28. TORRENTE DE PAREIS

Pareis means 'twin' and this gorge has been cut by the action of the two streams Lluc and La Fosca, which meet at a place known as the Entreforc and continue as the Torrente de Pareis, the twin stream, to the sea at Sa Calobra.

The route is one of the most popular on the island, going through a narrow gorge between cliffs over 300m high. The scenery is wild and spectacular and the stream disgorges into the sea at a lovely bay with clear turquoise and deep blue water between rocky headlands. It is more of a scramble than a walk and is only recommended to those who are suitably experienced. In places the scrambling becomes more of a rock-climb and many people take a short line to safeguard the ascent or descent of the difficult places. Fixed ropes are sometimes found, but more often than not they have broken or worn out, although the pitons seem to remain in place. Recently some of the smooth boulders have been roughened to give a better grip. Although experienced climbers will have no trouble making a through descent of the whole gorge from Escorca to Sa Calobra, it is suggested that others take two bites at the cherry and make approaches from both top and bottom.

Logistics can be a problem for the through route especially in winter. Some leave a car at Escorca and count on getting a lift back. In summer, the bus can be used from Soller to Escorca and a boat taken back to Puerto Soller from Sa Calobra. (Last boat 4.45 pm) The whole descent takes from 3¹/2 to 5 hours, depending on conditions and the fitness and

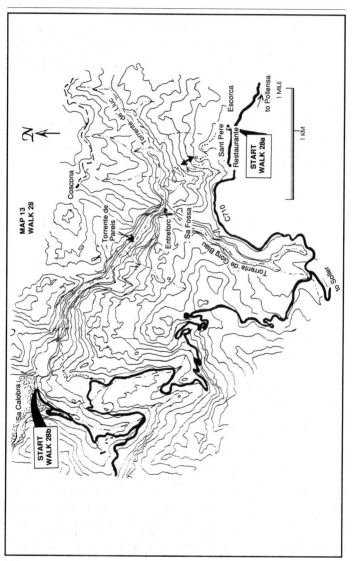

ability of the party.

It is essential to choose a day during a period of dry weather. After rain the rocks will be wet and slippery and there are deep pools which have to be waded or even swum across. Although high summer is usually recommended for this excursion, we have found that most winters provide suitable conditions most of the time.

28(a). Escorca to the Entreforc and return

This section is the easiest part of the gorge, but still takes you into very impressive places. It also allows time for a diversion to the entrance of the La Fosca cave system and to go beyond the Entreforc to the top of a large boulder section which is one of the more difficult places.

Starting point:	Restaurante de Escorca
Time:	3-4 hr
Distance:	c.6km
Total height climbed:	Descent from 650m to 180m and return
Grade:	B.
	Map: Pollensa 1:50,000 and Inca 1:50,000

From the car park opposite the Restaurante Escorca, go through the gates of the small thirteenth century church of Sant Pere. Pass to the right of the church then turn left up some steps by an old olive tree. At the top of the steps turn right along the path towards the farm. When two gates are reached, go through the one on the left and a minute or two later turn left by a large litter bin. Sometimes there is a signpost, but the bin is always there. Follow the path down through the wood and climb over an iron gate. Continue along the path in the same direction for five minutes, looking out for a sharp left turn. The old paint mark on an olive tree at this point is barely discernible, but there should be a cairn. If you come to a spectacular rock arch, you have gone too far and must go back. It might be considered worthwhile to miss this turn deliberately to enjoy the view.

From the sharp left turn the path goes down some steep rock, turning first left then right, after which it is easy to follow right down into the gorge in a series of bends. Low down, look out for a right turn some 20m after passing a fig tree. A narrow path leads through clumps of *carritx* into the bed of the Lluc stream. Note this point which otherwise may be missed on the way back. Once in the stream-bed turn left and look out for another narrow path on the left which avoids some boulders and leads to the

Entreforc. At the Entreforc is a stone marked as a crossroads, and pointing the way to Lluc, to Sa Calobra, to Sa Fosca and 'Millor no entri'. This latter points to the vertical rock wall and means 'better not go' in Mallorquin.

For the diversion to Sa Fosca, keep near the rock wall on the left where there is a trace of a path. After about 20 minutes the rock walls meet overhead and increasing darkness makes a return to the Entreforc advisable. (This is the entrance to a large and complex cave system requiring caving experience and equipment.)

From the Entreforc follow a narrow path on the right, indicated by red paint marks. This leads down into the gorge towards Sa Calobra. Twenty minutes later the top of some enormous blocks will be reached and it is recommended that a return is made from this point.

28(b). Sa Calobra to Entreforc and return

Sa Calobra is a tiny cove with a shingle beach between rocky cliffs and a small harbour where boats from Puerto Soller ply in the summer. It is a deservedly popular place but an early start will avoid the crowds who arrive by coach and boat. The drive down is spectacular with one hairpin bend after another and even a 'knot' where the road passes under itself. However, it is a wide, well-maintained road and the coaches are normally concentrated in the middle of the day.

All the difficulties of the gorge are in this section and it should only be attempted after a dry period. Sometimes bad flooding can occur after heavy rain and flash floods are not unknown. It is possible for the tunnel to be waist-deep in water, providing quite an alarming experience. Normally, the vast amphitheatre at the exit only has a trickle of water going out to sea and is even used for open-air concerts in the summer. The original way into the amphitheatre before the tunnel was constructed provides an 'escape route' should the tunnel be found in flood. Some old steps on the south side lead up a steep and narrow gully to a col. Going down, the left-hand branch leads down to the path near the car park. There are some stone steps still in place but with time and lack of maintenance these are likely to disappear.

Starting point:	Sa Calobra
Time:	5-6hr
Distance:	7km
Total height climbed:	180m
Grade:	A+
Map:	Pollensa 1:50,000 and
	Inca 1:50,000

(N.B. All lefts and rights in the following description are for anyone looking up the gorge.)

Go through the tunnel from the path at the end of the car park into the wide amphitheatre hidden behind the rocks. If the conditions are right for the walk there will be very little water disgorging onto the shingle beach. Start walking into the gorge and in about ten minutes some easy boulders are surmounted on the left. Few of the many visitors venture beyond this point. Next, after stretches of easy walking interspersed with clambering over boulders, there is a narrow section leading to the first little difficulty. This is a large boulder with a pool at the bottom. The way up is by rather greasy holds on the right, finishing over a small chockstone. About ten minutes later an enormous block almost fills the gorge, with a small boulder in front. The best way to tackle this is by the groove on the left wall.

An easier section of boulders and scree comes next, passing a side gully on the right, after which there is a varied stretch with two pitches easily climbed by sloping shelves on the left. The gorge then narrows again and is filled with a chaotic mass of huge blocks. On the right a red arrow indicates a fascinating through route between a giant block and the right-hand wall. After this only one more boulder gives a trifling difficulty before a path on the left avoids further problems and leads to the Entreforc.

If you are intending to continue up to Escorca, there are no further difficulties, but you need to look out for the exit from the Lluc stream on the right, leading up to the path.

Ascent:	2½-3hr
Descent:	2-2½hr.

29. CALA TUENT AND SA COSTERA

Cala Tuent is a small bay which was the objective of an abortive 'urbanisation' project, of which there is little to be seen except a few isolated houses. Thankfully it seems the plans for a four-storey hotel and other out of place projects have been abandoned, and although the bulldozed road has destroyed a traditional old mule track, it has its uses in leading to the start of this attractive walk. This road branches off from the spectacular La Calobra road and goes over a pass on which is the thirteenth century chapel of San Lorenzo. The path is part of a long established route from Soller to Sa Calobra, which is not easy to do unless transport can be organised at the beginning and end of the walk.

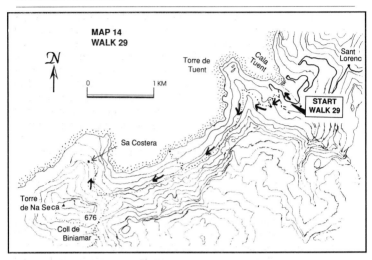

The walk described here goes along a very pleasant corniche path overlooking the sea between two rocky headlands. The destination is a large ruined house called 'Sa Costera' where several large terraces make perfect picnic places and there is a spring hidden in a tunnel behind the house.

Type of walk: There is a rise up to 200m by a good path followed by the corniche path which has a few minor ups and downs before finally rising up to about 300m near the Coll de Biniamar. This path was originally a well-made mule track and is still in good condition, although the vegetation is encroaching in places. The branch path out to Sa Costera is much more overgrown and rather rougher going. Although the measured map distance is only 10km, the actual distance must be rather more. There is a surprisng amount of ascent involved too for a coastal contouring path.

Starting point:	Cala Tuent
Time:	4hr 40min
Distance:	10km
Highest point reached:	320m
Total height climbed:	370m
Grade:	C+
Map:	Soller 1:50,000 and Pollensa 1:50,000

Park at the side of a wide road immediately after crossing the bridge where the road swings round towards the sea. Walk along this road towards the restaurant (closed in winter) and take the first turn left, waymarked by a blue arrow painted on a rock and the words 'A La Costera'. The path leaves this track on the right after passing a concrete driveway and is marked by a cairn and another blue painted arrow. The old cobbled mule track is picked up behind a new building and leads to a large deserted house. In front of this is a sloping grassy terrace dotted with olive trees. The house itself is an interesting place with all sorts of old machinery such as olive presses. On arriving here, turn right across the terrace in front of the house, taking particular note of this point as it is easy to miss the left turn in descent.

Follow the path up to a gap in a stone wall, at which point a splendid view of the coast and the way ahead opens up. The corniche path begins here, descending at first then keeping fairly level for quite long stretches. At one point a flattish green field near a water tank and a small building will be noticed down by the sea. A cairn and a blue arrow marks the descent path to this spot, which could make an alternative walk.

When the path begins to rise up towards the Biniamar col, look out for a small cairn on the right just below a red arrow on a boulder. Turn right into a clearing, then leave the wide and obvious track to turn left up a narrow and rather overgrown path which cuts off a corner and an unnecessary ascent. It joins the main path from Biniamar by a wall with a red paint spot. Follow this path, mainly descending, to the Sa Costera house, passing a branch path left which is signposted 'Torre' in red paint. Return the same way; the views are worth looking at in both directions.

Cala Tuent - Sa Costera	2hr 25min
Sa Costera - Cala Tuent	2hr 15min

30(a). MASSANELLA, NORMAL WAY

Massanella is the highest accessible peak in Mallorca since the Puig Mayor is prohibited. As such it is very popular and other walkers are often met, especially on Sundays when many local walkers take to the hills. Because of its height and situation the views are outstanding, so if possible choose a fine clear day for the ascent. The twin peaks at the top are visible from many places and make the mountain instantly recognisable. The old iron cross which used to mark the top has been replaced by a concrete trig point. Sometimes a summit book may be

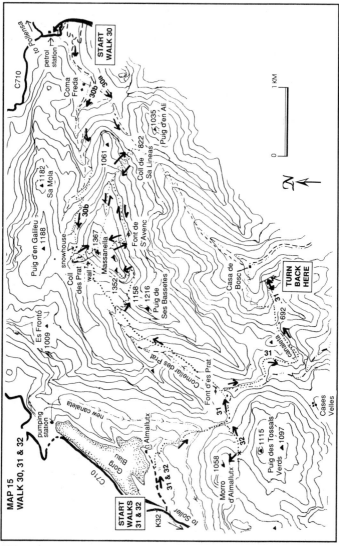

MAP 15
WALK 30, 31 & 32

found in a sheltered place a few metres below the top. A freshwater spring, the Font de S'Avenc, not far below the summit, is approached by stone steps leading down into two caves. Water dripping down the rocks collects in a series of stone troughs in the lower cave. This is a very attractive place on a hot day.

Park near the petrol station on the Lluc-Inca road, avoiding the centre of the lay-by which is used by coaches stopping at the restaurant.

Type of walk: Quite strenuous, but mainly on reasonably good paths. In the upper part the paths are very stony in places and not always easy to follow.

Starting point:	Petrol station, Lluc
Time:	5hr 15min
Distance:	11km
Highest point reached:	1,352m
Total height climbed:	795m
Grade:	B+
Map:	Selva 1:25,000

Walk towards Inca and go through the green gates on the right immediately after crossing the bridge over the Torrent des Guix. Follow the unsurfaced track up to the finca Comafreda, doubling back up to the right about 250m from the start (where the road straight ahead leads to the farm of Es Guix). Short cuts can be taken on the first section, but these are steep and can be muddy. They start just inside the entrance gate. After levelling out, the Comafreda track passes a locked gate with pedestrian access on the right. Beyond this is the cultivated area with the farmhouse set back on the right.

From here, bear left and take the path on the left-hand side of the wall which bounds the fields. The path follows the wall at first and then rises through the woods (paint marks renewed in winter 1991) to join a wide cross track at a large painted boulder. (This point may also be reached from the beginning of the cultivated area by following the blue arrows through the open gateway and along a wide track, ignoring right turns.)

Follow this track up left to the Coll de Sa Linea at 822m, where there is a large clearing. Turn sharp right at the two indication stones. A good path leads up fairly steeply in zigzags, arriving at an engraved stone marking a bifurcation in the path. The left-hand path is signposted 'Font y Puig' and the right-hand path 'Puig y Font'. Either route may be taken to the top by good well-marked paths, although the one to the right is the easiest to follow.

If the left-hand route is taken, a keen eye must be kept for paint marks and cairns as it is easy to wander off the route on one of the many natural ledges that look like paths. There is a large cairn marking a place where the path begins to rise towards an isolated alzine or evergreen oak. Marker stones have been cemented to the slabs to show the way. Above this a roughly horizontal section leads to the spring. From the spring the path continues horizontally for about 20m before leading up a rocky staircase to the sloping shelf that lies below the summit. On this shelf another indication stone points the way to the top, near which is a very large snow-pit.

To descend, go down on to the shelf below the top and follow the path which is well-marked and rejoins the route of ascent at the bifurcation with the engraved stone. In mist the direction from the top is south-east.

Lluc petrol station	- Coll de Sa Linea	1hr
Coll de Sa Linea	- Font de S'Avenc	1hr
Font de S'Avenc	- Massanella summit	45min
Massanella summit	- petrol station	2hr 30min

30(b). MASSANELLA BY THE COLL DES PRAT

The Coll des Prat is a high pass, 1,126m, to the north of Massanella. There used to be a very good track all the way up but it has fallen into disrepair since the old snow-houses on the pass were abandoned. The pass was also used by pilgrims on the way from Soller to Lluc.

Type of walk: Quite strenuous. The scramble from the Coll des Prat to the summit is steep and exposed, requiring experience and a head for heights. (Note that this has been upgraded to A++ as several readers have found this route to be very difficult.)

Starting point:	Lluc petrol station
Time:	5hr 15min
Distance:	12km
Highest point reached:	1,352m
Total height climbed:	795m
Grade:	A++
Map:	Selva 1:25,000

Follow the normal way up for about 40 minutes until the wide track is met by a large boulder with a red paint mark. Turn right here, passing a *sitja* on the left. Climb over a low wall at a barrier across the track and turn left to pass a spring. A good forest road leads up through the trees. When the trees thin out the old trail continues right up to the top of the pass. There is a little confusion around the ruined buildings and snow houses but it is very easy to reach the pass, across which is a wall. Turn left and go up to the foot of the crags on the left-hand side of the wall, looking for a gully which can be ascended fairly easily at first. Where this becomes steep traverse right until a way can be found up a steep but easy chimney, reaching the summit ridge about 70m to the right of the top. (People have also been observed ascending a gully on the right-hand side of the wall, but this appears to be rather loose.)

Descent can be made either by the direct route or by way of the Font de S'Avenc, which is recommended. From the top follow the path slightly east of south to the lip of the sloping shelf below the summit. An engraved stone points to the rocky staircase that leads down to the spring. The path from the spring is quite well-marked, but surprisingly easy to lose, so keep looking for cairns and paint marks. This path leads to a junction with the more direct route from the summit, at a marker stone just above the 'Avenc de Cami'. The path down to the Coll de Sa Linea is now obvious. At this col turn left and in about 15 minutes turn right at a painted boulder and follow the path down through the woods to Comafreda.

Petrol station	- Coll d'es Prat	2hr 15min
Coll d'es Prat	- Massanella	50min
Massanella	- Font de S'Avenc	30min
Font de S'Avenc	- Coll de Sa Linea	50min
Coll de Sa Linea	- petrol station	50min

30(c). MASSANELLA FROM ALMALLUTX

This interesting route makes use of an old track which is another part of the ancient Pilgrim's Way from Soller to Lluc. (This old route can be followed almost completely, except for a short distance near Cuber where the new canaleta must be used: Soller - Biniaraix - Coll de L'Ofre - Cuber - new canaleta - Coll des Coloms - Font des Prat - Coll des Prat - Comafreda - Coll de Sa Bataia - Lluc.) The first part over the Coll des Coloms is also used on several other walks and as far as the covered spring, the Font des Massanella, with its crystal-clear water is well-known. The continuation of the route up the long Comellar des Prat, although a popular route for Mallorquins, is unknown to most British walkers.

If transport can be arranged from Lluc at the end of the day it makes an enjoyable excursion to descend Massanella by the normal way. Otherwise it is necessary to return by the same route. There is a point of difficulty on the way up to the col between Massanella and the Puig de Ses Bassetes which some walkers may find too great. In this case a good alternative is to make for the Coll des Prat from which it is not much further to reach the 1,258m top of Sa Mola, opposite Massanella to the north and west. Then either return to Almallutx or descend to Comafreda and Lluc by the way described for the ascent in 30(b), depending on transport arangements.

Type of walk: A good path, well-marked with red paint and cairns and at a reaonable gradient leads all the way up to the Col des Prat. Paint signs and cairns on pathless ground lead to the col at 1,188m referred to above. The little rock step which must be surmounted here might be regarded as an easy rock climb. After that the route is rough and rocky but not difficult.

Starting point:	K32 on the C710
Time:	6hr 20min
Distance:	12km
Highest point reached:	1,352m
Total height climbed:	800m
Grade:	A++
Map:	Selva 1:25,000

From K32 go over the Coll des Coloms as for Walk 31 and continue to the Font de Massanella (marked as Font des Prat on the map). Just before reaching this a branch path right is marked with a red M for Massanella. This immediately crosses the stream-bed and continues away from it for 100m or so, rising slightly to the east side of the valley. It then bends left through the trees to follow the valley well above the stream-bed. (Alternatively go first to the spring, then cross the stream-bed immediately opposite and bear slightly right to join the path there.) The path is well-defined and liberally endowed with paint marks and cairns. Higher up the path divides into two and then rejoins. Take the right branch which passes below some large rocky outcrops of a coarse conglomerate. Look out for the painted boulder with the words 'Lluc' and 'Massanella', the latter pointing up to the pass between the latter and the Puig de Ses Bassetes. The rock step to the col is surmounted by stepping up on adequate but sloping footholds for two or three moves until a large and

The Canaleta de Massanella (Walk 34)

Cornadors from near Coll de L'Offre (Walk 44) (Author)
Descent from the Portell de sa Costa (Walk 45) (Author)

comforting 'jug-handle' can be gripped with the right hand. A few easier moves and it is done. Once on the col the only difficulty is in deciding the way through the rocky wilderness ahead. There are no more paint marks and few cairns which in any case are difficult to see amongst the rocks.

Rock-climbers may like to turn left and go straight up the steep ridge leading to the top. Walkers should make a very slightly rising traverse across easy ground to the foot of a rocky spur about 300m away. Look out for the easiest ways up various sloping ledges and gullies until it is possible to go back left to join the ridge above the steep section. Follow the ridge up to the top. There is quite a prominent cairn on the first top, then the twin top can be visited before crossing over easy ground to the main top with the trig point.

K32 - Font des Massanella	1hr 10min
Font des Massanella - col	1hr 20min
Col - top	1hr 30min
Descent to Lluc	2hr 20 min

31. CANALETA DE MASSANELLA FROM THE GORG BLAU

This old *canaleta* carries water from the Font des Prat, high up in the mountains, to the village of Mancor de la Vall, on the edge of the plain to the north of Inca. The project was carried out by a local man Montserrat Fontanet, after it had been declared an impossible feat by various prestigious foreign engineers. It still functions as well as it did when it was built 240 years ago. Before modernisation in 1983 when the water was piped, it used to flow in an open channel and was even more attractive. One of the snags of the pipeline being buried is that wild pigs which forage in the woods keep digging up the earth, making walking more difficult. Access to the water is provided by taps at intervals along the pipeline, signposted 'Agua potabile'. In dry weather when the reservoirs are low, hardly a trickle comes out of the taps, so don't count on being able to quench your thirst here.

Type of walk: Not strenuous, but somewhat exposed on the aqueduct.

Starting point:	K32, on C710
Time:	4hr 20min
Distance:	12km
Highest point reached:	795m
Total height climbed:	315m

Grade:	B
Map:	Selva 1:25,000 and
	Soller 1:25,000

Park on the grass verge opposite K32 and follow the route up to the Coll des Coloms as in Walk 32. Follow the path down over the pass and after about ten minutes go through a gateway. Go straight on to reach the Font des Prat, or Font de Massanella, in a further five minutes. Alternatively, take the first narrow path on the left by a *sitja* to the old Es Prat farmhouse, from where there are good views, then bear right to reach the spring. The spring, situated in an open glade, is covered over and gated. Cross the stream and follow down the left bank for about 300m to an open meadow. Large clumps of the summer snowflake, *Leucojum aestivum*, flourish here in late winter and early spring, in pools of water fed by the stream.

The canaleta begins here, with the pipeline buried by earth and stones in between the stone walls that used to bound the open channel. In about five minutes an arched aqueduct carries it across a ravine, then it continues along the side of a wooded hill. Soon it goes round a corner by means of a tunnel, then drops down slightly to a wooded col at 692m, between Es Castellot and Mitjana. After this it falls, gently at first then more rapidly to the long and narrow Massanella valley. Continue following the pipeline as far as the place where it is crossed by a wall and begins to plunge steeply down the hillside. Return by the same route to the starting point. (Before reaching this turning point several cairns may be noticed, marking a path which goes down into the forest on the left. This can be followed on a longer walk starting at Mancor de la Vall, Walk No.34.)

K32 - Coll des Coloms	50min
Coll des Coloms - Font des Prat	15min
Font des Prat - wall	1hr 10min
Wall - Coll des Coloms	1hr 15min
Coll des Coloms - K32	50min

N.B. 1. The Coll des Coloms is shown wrongly on the IGN maps as being between Morro de Almallutx and the Tossals Verds.

2. Mancor de la Vall is also known as Mancor del Valle.

32. MORRO D'ALMALLUTX

The Morro d'Almallutx is one of the peaks of the Tossals group which lies south of the Gorg Blau and east of Cuber. It is the easiest top to reach and has splendid views of Massanella and the east side of the Puig Mayor with its impressive cliffs. One of the other tops, the Puig des Tossals Verds at 1,115m may also be climbed from the col between the two peaks.

On this col at 954m are the remains of an old *casa de sa neu* and a hut where the snow collectors lived.

Type of walk: Some route-finding because of trees limiting vision. Pathless and rough at the top, but not difficult ground.

Starting point:	K32 on C710
Time:	3hr 20min
Distance:	8km
Highest point reached:	1,058m
Total height climbed:	433m
Grade:	B
Map:	Selva 1:25,000 and Soller 1:25,000

Park on the wide grass verge opposite K32 on the Pollensa-Soller road. Walk up the road towards Soller to the first gate on the left: this is the entry to the *finca* Almallutx and there is a 'no entry' sign on the gate. The track leads down to the valley floor and makes a sharp bend to the right before going through a gateway. A cairn on the right marks the beginning of a good path leading up through the woods, a little indistinct at first. This path passes several *sitjes* before leaving the woods for more open ground. Turn right to re-enter the woods almost opposite to an old bread-oven, which at first sight looks like a very large cairn.

Soon the path crosses a modern aqueduct along which water is pumped from the Gorg Blau to Cuber in a deep open channel. The path now goes through a narrow valley, rising slightly to the Coll des Coloms, reached shortly after passing the second of two gateways. Where the path starts to level out, an enormous pointed rock can be glimpsed through the trees high up on the right. Keep the position of this in mind, in case you lose the path in the trees, which is very easily done. About 20m after the main path starts to descend, turn right at a marker stone bearing the numbers 802,092.

This path used to be a good one as it once served the needs of the snowhouse on the col above, but is now partly obscured by fallen trees. There are some cairns and some red paint marks. An old lime kiln is passed. After passing a large boulder, the path crosses the valley to the left. Make for the left-hand side of the large rock pinnacle noted from below, after which the col is easily reached. Turn right and go up by easy rocks, almost bare of vegetation to the top of the Morro.

K32 - Coll des Coloms	50min
Coll des Coloms - Morro d'Almallutx	1hr
Morro d'Almallutx - K32	1hr 30min

(N.B. the Coll des Coloms is shown wrongly on the IGN maps as being between Morro d'Almallutx and the Tossals Verd.)

33. PENYAL DE MITX DIA

The Penyal de Mitx Dia is the highest point on Mallorca after the Puig Mayor. It is in fact a subsidiary summit of Puig Mayor and as it is outside the military zone it is possible to go there. Being advised to apply for permission in writing, this was done, but when no reply was received we decided to go there anyway. No one stopped us, but as a precaution we left our cameras behind. (Do not attempt to go along the ridge towards the true summit: walkers approaching this from the north have been warned off by armed soldiers.) Local walkers say the authorities have no objection to small groups going up there but large parties would not be welcome.

The route is an interesting one, making use of an old mule track which passes the deep and impressive *cases de nieve* of the Puig Mayor and which was probably the original way to the summit before the radar station was built. On a good day the views are outstanding, covering virtually the whole island.

There is a parking place near the tunnel, or the bus from Soller can be used very conveniently for this walk.

Type of walk: At first on a well made but disused path, then up very steep and difficult ground with exposed rock slabs. Some scrambling is involved. The descent is also rough and steep with loose scree.

Starting point:	C710, 600m from tunnel
Time:	3hr 40min
Distance:	7km
Highest point reached:	1,401m

Total height climbed:	512m
Grade:	A+
Map:	1:25,000 Soller

The path, which is not very obvious, starts on the right hand side of the road bridge crossing the Torrent Mayor, looking up-stream. In 20 minutes there is a small waterfall below two rock pinnacles, where the path swings right then back left. An old ivy-covered *casa de nieve* is passed, near a ruined shelter. Further up is another large snow pit with curved walls. At one time this path was an excellent well-built mule track and it can still be followed with ease in spite of having collapsed here and there. Follow it almost up to the Coll de N'Arbona, but before reaching the fence (which is the military boundary) cross over left to the foot of a low crag and go up the gully on the far side of it.

Now choose any line up to the ridge above. The rocks are quite steep in places and although small loose stones are sometimes a nuisance there is plenty of solid rock. The angle eases off just before the ridge, then some slabs slope up into an obvious gully. One of us reached the ridge by means of an easy chimney, about 15 feet in height, the other found an easier way

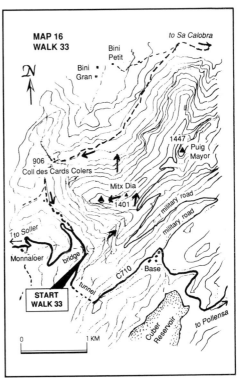

MAP 16
WALK 33

to Sa Calobra

Bini Petit

Bini Gran

1447

Puig Mayor

906
Coll des Cards Colers

Mitx Dia

1401

military road

military road

to Soller

Monnaloer

bridge

START WALK 33

tunnel

C710

Base

Cuber Reservoir

to Pollensa

0   1 KM

to the left of this. Once on the ridge turn left towards the top where there are three small stone shelters with low walls.

Continue along the narrow and delightful rocky ridge to the south-west top. From here it is only another ten minutes down to a col, where the descent to the Bini valley begins on the right. There is no path, but the going is quite reasonable at first. Eventually, about 40 minutes from the col, a cairn on a U-shaped lip is reached. This shows the way down into a gully with rather loose stones.

From the foot of this gully keep going downhill, picking the best way through the vegetation and tumbled rocks until a wide cart-track is met. Once on the track, turn left and walk over the Coll des Cards-Colers, taking a left fork to reach the C710 and the starting point of the walk.

Bridge on C710	- Coll de N'Arbona	1hr
Coll de N'Arbona	- Mitx Dia	50min
Mitx Dia	- Bini valley	1hr 30min
Bini valley	- Bridge on C710	20min

34. CANALETA DE MASSANELLA FROM MANCOR DE LA VALL

This very interesting circular walk makes use of country roads, old mule paths, the *canaleta* path, and forest paths and tracks. The scenery is very varied and it is a good walk for seeing wild flowers. The descent down the Massanella valley goes through a very narrow and wild gorge between vertical rock walls, gradually giving way to olive terraces and almond orchards. The walk starts from the small village of Mancor de la Vall (aka Mancor del Valle) which is 5km north-east of Inca.

Type of walk: A very varied walk including easy walking on surfaced roads, good tracks, overgrown paths and easy but spectacular walking along the *canaleta* with some exposure. Descent is by a well-graded forest path to the Massanella valley and the wide easy track downwards. The ascent is nowhere very steep, but there are some route-finding problems especially on the overgrown part. This section would be improved by greater usage.

Starting point:	Mancor de la Vall
Time:	6hr 35min
Distance:	16km
Highest point reached:	approx. 750m
Total height climbed:	510m

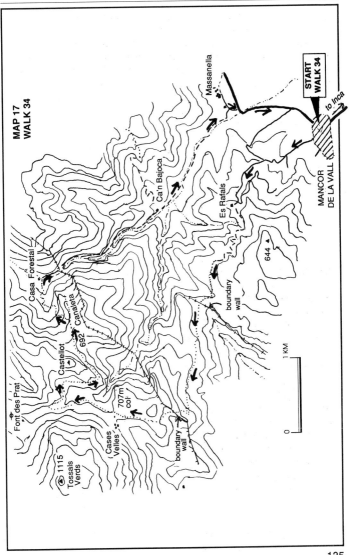

MAP 17
WALK 34

START
WALK 34

to Inca

MANCOR
DE LA VALL

Massanella

Can Bajoca

Es Rafals

644

boundary
wall

Casa Forestal

Canaleta

692

Castellot

Font des Prat

Tossals
Verds
1115

Cases
Velles

707m
col

boundary
wall

1 KM

0

Grade: A
Map: Selva 1:25,000

There are some wide roads where a car can be left on the east side of
Mancor. Follow the Carrer Mayor to the Placa de Dalt and turn right into
the Carrer Bartolomeu Reus. This road bends sharp left at a restaurant
and begins to go uphill. After crossing a stream-bed there is a branch
track left. Ignore this and go straight ahead on the main right-hand
branch. Five minutes further on the road swings right and there is a
camino particular notice (which applies to cars). A footpath misses out
the first bend on this road. In a further five minutes there is an unlocked
gate across the road. Continuing uphill a large *finca*, Es Rafal, comes into
view. Before reaching it there is a covered well on the left of the road. The
surfaced road ends at the house, but a good track continues through a
gate on the left of the house.

    Keep following this track until it turns right through a wall. Go straight
on at this point on a less well-used track which descends slightly to an
oakwood. In a few minutes this track approaches an obvious boundary
wall, very high and with a fence on top. The old 1:25,000 map (1962)
shows two tracks continuing on the other side of this wall which don't
appear to exist, and the new map shows no paths beyond this point. The
way to continue is to keep on the main track as it swings right until after
about 20m a narrow inconspicuous path with occasional white paint
marks is found on the left. This path rises up roughly parallel to the wall
and leads to a gateway with a broken down gate.

    On the other side of the wall an excellently made path continues,
sometimes contouring and sometimes rising gently. Occasional cairns
and red paint marks are useful as vegetation has obscured the way in
places. After almost 2km this path turns a corner and rises in a few bends
to a gap in another boundary wall. The next objective is a low col across
an intervening valley. There is a path marked on the old map and there
are some red paint marks at first, but then it becomes lost and provides
a struggle through giant *carritx* grasses and some thorny broom.

    When the col is reached make for a gap in the wall and on the other
side follow a faint path down slightly to join a better path rising up from
the Tossals Verds house. Turn right and follow this path up to the 707m
col. This is a large flat area with a rough shelter on the left, and an old well,
the Font de Sa Basola, up on the right. Keep straight on roughly in the
centre of the flat area. The path keeps to the right of a line of bushes and
then enters the wood on the left through a gateway. This path is now a

well-built one contouring into the valley head below a pipeline. When the stream is reached, find a way to cross it and turn left until it is possible to scramble up the bank to find the canaleta path.

Follow the canaleta to the right along the viaduct and round the head of a side valley, through the tunnel, then round another corner and on to a wooded col at 692m. Approximately 20 minutes after the tunnel and shortly after the canaleta begins to descend from the col look out for a narrow path leading into the oak forest on the left. This is a key point and it is well cairned. (It is possible, but not recommended, to follow the canaleta itself down to the valley. It becomes extremely steep at the bottom and after a rock step of about 4m is even more difficult to follow.)

The excellent path beginning here can be followed easily down through the trees, being very well constructed as well as marked by blue painted arrows and a number of cairns. It is narrow at first but becomes wider after passing two *sitjes* and leads down to a clearing with a forest house. At this point it joins another track coming down from the Pas de N'Arbona. Turn right and follow the main track down the Massanella valley, passing a house called Ca'n Bajoca, where there is a wooden stile at the side of a locked gate. Lower down the track bends sharp left, then goes through a gate near the property of Massanella. Turn sharp right here, as indicated by a white arrow painted on a tree. The road then bends left to arrive at a T-junction. Turn right here and walk the short distance along the road to Mancor and the starting point of the walk.

Mancor - Es Rafal	40min
Es Rafal - Boundary wall	35min
Boundary wall - 707m col	2hr
707m col - canaleta	30min
Canaleta - descent path	40min
Descent path - Casa Forestal	40min
Casa Forestal - Massanella	1hr 10min
Massanella - Mancor	20min.

35. CIRCUIT OF THE TOSSALS GROUP

The four peaks of the Tossals group are in the reservoir area south of the Gorg Blau and east of the Embalse de Cuber. This walk follows various pipelines and goes through some very interesting country. A torch is advisable for some of the tunnel sections.

Type of walk: Fairly rough walking most of the way, especially the downhill section from Cuber. An easy middle section on a surfaced road up to the Tossals Verds house, then an old path, not always easy to follow.

Starting point:	Cuber reservoir
Time:	5hr 40min
Distance:	12km
Highest point reached:	822m
Total height climbed:	467m
Grade:	B
Map:	Soller 1:25,000 &
	Selva 1:25,000

From the parking place at the entrance to the Cuber reservoir walk through the access gate and along the road towards the dam. Just before reaching the dam take the stony track descending into the gorge below. In five minutes either go straight on along the main track, or branch right by a large boulder with a paint sign to go through the first tunnel. At first it is very rough and stony but the walking becomes easier after crossing the stream. Later there is another rough section where the path has been washed away and is badly overgrown with brambles and other vegetation.

The path then accompanies the waterpipe through several tunnels where the old *canaleta* or open water channel can be seen, still with water flowing along it.

After the last tunnel the wide track gives easy walking and leads down to an upland plateau above Almedrà. Follow the main track downwards, ignoring an apparent left turn which leads only to a pipeline. About five minutes after this, take a left fork which leads in another five minutes to a yellow gate with a green stile on the left. There is a tarmac road from Almedrà on the other side. Turn left here and follow this road up through olive terraces to a house called 'Tossals Verds'. The tarmac road ends here. Go up through the house gates and another gate at the left hand side of the house. A well laid mule track marked with blue paint signs will now be found leading by twists and turns up to a shallow valley, almost a plateau. Some ruins marked as 'Cases Velles' on the map, will be seen high up on the left. The path then follows a new pipeline which lies in the old *canaleta*, to arrive at a col at 707m, quite near the ruined house. There is a rough shelter on the left here, made of tree branches and tarpaulins and also an old well, the Font de sa Basola, on the right.

Keep straight on roughly in the centre of the flat area. The path keeps

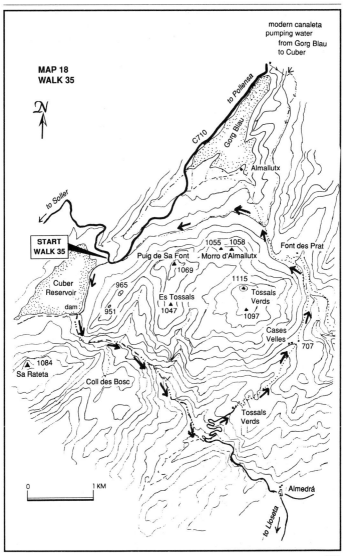

MAP 18
WALK 35

N

to Pollensa

modern canaleta
pumping water
from Gorg Blau
to Cuber

C710

Gorg Blau

Almallutx

to Soller

START
WALK 35

Puig de Sa Font

1055 1058
Morro d'Almallutx

Font des Prat

1069

965

1115

Cuber
Reservoir

dam

951

Es Tossals

Tossals
Verds

1047

1097

Cases
Velles

707

1084
Sa Rateta

Coll des Bosc

Tossals
Verds

Almedrá

0   1 KM

to Lloseta

to the right of a line of bushes at first and then enters the wood through a gateway on the left. This is a good path keeping below a pipeline. Before the stream is reached the old Canaleta de Massanella will be seen on the other side of the valley, being carried round the hillside on an arched aqueduct. Just before reaching the stream, scramble up a dark smooth slab to reach the pipeline and follow this along, crossing the stream near a *sitja*. Follow the track up to the Coll d'es Coloms and down the other side. When the new aqueduct is reached turn left and follow it all the way back to Cuber. It joins the main road about five minutes before the reservoir.

Cuber - yellow gates	2hr 5min
Yellow gates- Tossals Verds	35min
Tossals Verds - Cases Velles	55min
Cases Velles - Coll d'es Coloms	55min
Coll d'es Coloms - Cuber	1hr 10min

36. SA RATETA AND L'OFRE

L'Ofre is best seen from Soller, from where it is usually climbed, as a distinctive triangular peak. The walk described here starts and finishes at the Embalse de Cuber (pronounced em-bal-say day coo-bair), a large reservoir where sometimes ospreys may be seen fishing. Many other birds too may be seen, including Red Kites and Black Vultures. This route is a high ridge walk from Sa Rateta to L'Ofre, returning by the Cuber valley.

Type of walk: Not too strenuous, thanks to the high starting point at Cuber, but rough rocky ground and quite difficult route-finding on the ascent of Sa Rateta. Easy return route along a cart-track.

Starting point:	Cuber gates at K34 on C710
Time:	4hr 20min
Distance:	8km
Highest point reached:	1,091m
Total height climbed:	561m
Grade:	B+
Map:	Soller 1:25,000

Park by the locked entrance gate to Cuber. Go through the pedestrian access gate and walk along the road to the dam. It is best to study the next part of the route while approaching the dam. Looking straight ahead a

Massanella from Sa Rateta

narrow scree-filled gully with a sharp right-angled bend in it can be seen, falling away into the gorge below the dam. The aim is to reach this gully at the 'elbow'. The easiest way is to continue along the road past the dam for some 50m or so, then turn off left. Cross over a rocky spur and then contour round the shallow valley, rising towards a cluster of evergreen oaks. When the 'elbow' is reached, a broken wall and fence is crossed and from this point a series of cairns leading up the gully will be found. This ascent is quite easy but steepens a little higher up. Exit from the gully is by a conspicuous pine tree seen on the skyline. On the other side of this skyline ridge is a hidden valley. Cairns continue to mark the route which progresses upwards at an easy angle, making use of natural ledges of rock and scree. It emerges finally on a plateau at the head of the valley.

Swing round to the right and make for the top of Sa Rateta, across rocky but easy ground. There is a summit book started by a group of Mallorquin walkers in 1983. (This was missing in 1990.) From the top the ridge continues horizontally at first towards the south-west and then drops down quite steeply to the Coll des Gats at 996m with traces of a path. There is an unusual and conspicuous patch of short grass on this col, rare in Mallorca. Going up the next ridge from here, the steep crag ahead is avoided by making for an obvious shelf on the left. Then easy rocks lead round behind the steep ground to re-join the ridge. Continue over the double top of the Puig de na Franquesa (1,063m, 1,067m) and descend to the 965m col before L'Ofre. (There is a way down into the Cuber valley from this col if a shorter walk is wanted.) The L'Ofre ridge is gained by easy slabs to the left of the pylon, and a cairned path followed to the top.

To descend, go back along the ridge for about 50m to a small shoulder and find the path down to the south, towards the Coll d'en Poma, marked by red paint. This path has many variations, but the main one arrives on flattish ground about 50m east of the wall which runs south from the foot of the rocks. Turn right along the cart-track and go through the gap in the wall. Follow this track round to the Coll de L'Ofre where there is a large cairn. The wide track leads back along the Cuber valley to the starting point. A short cut through the trees can be taken on the left quite near the beginning of the descent from the col.

Cuber entrance - Sa Rateta	1hr 30min
Sa Rateta - L'Ofre	1hr 15min
L'Ofre - Coll de L'Ofre	35min
Coll de L'Ofre - Cuber entrance	1hr

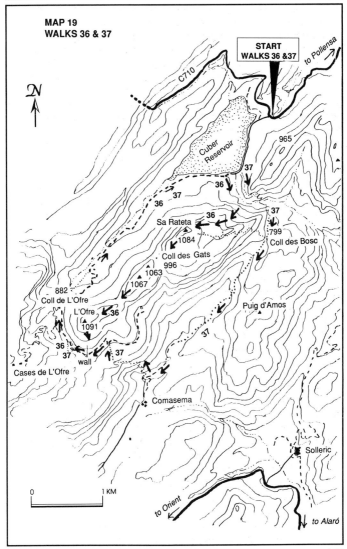

MAP 19
WALKS 36 & 37

37. CUBER AND COMASEMA CIRCULAR WALK

The Cuber reservoir is the starting point for several walks, and the wide track leading past it to the Coll de L'Ofre is well-known. The Comasema valley on the other side of the Sa Rateta - L'Ofre ridge is less well-known and this circular walk links the two by little-used paths, giving an interesting round with splendid views. There are two telescopes at two viewpoints along this walk, slightly off the track but worth the short detours. One is just before going through the gap in the wall on the wide track south of L'Ofre. The other is on a gently sloping shelf overlooking Soller, 200m or so south of the Coll de L'Ofre.

Type of walk: Mainly easy on fairly level wide tracks, but some ups and downs on rough and stony paths.

Starting point:	Cuber
Time:	5hr 40min
Distance:	12km
Highest point reached:	888m
Total height climbed:	530m
Grade:	B
Map:	Soller 1:25,000

Walk along to the reservoir and just before the dam turn left and follow the track down the valley with the pipeline. Five minutes later either turn right opposite a paint sign on a boulder and go through the tunnel or keep straight on along the upper track which goes over a shoulder and then zigzags down. Cross the stream-bed and turn left, following the concrete wall of the pipeline on the right. In a little under ten minutes look out for a cairn and a painted red arrow showing the way up onto a cobbled track which goes up parallel to the pipeline at first. This old track, once part of the ancient Pilgrim's way to Lluc, twists and turns and eventually turns right up a rock slope to the Coll des Bosc, at the head of the Comasema valley. The Coll des Bosc can be a slightly confusing place because visibility is hampered by the trees. First of all a false col is reached, then the path rises again. When the true col is reached there are several prominent cairns, and the more obvious path turns right to go up Sa Rateta. At this point turn left through trees and shrubs to find a broad clearing.

The easy but rather stony old track beginning at the clearing leads down through the woods into the Comasema valley, passing after 15 minutes an old spring on the right, the Font de sa Cisternata. (Not good

Comasema. A typical old Mallorquin manor house

water.) The path continues down through the woods passing signs of charcoal-burning activities and an animal shelter before reaching a gateway at the edge of the woods.

Some 20 minutes after the gateway and about 200m before reaching the large buildings of Comasema turn right between two stone walls into a dry stream-bed. Paint signs on the right-hand wall include a blue arrow showing the way to Soller, and a yellow one pointing back to Cuber. It is quite likely that these are completely obscured by brambles, but there is only one such stream-bed.

This is the beginning of an ancient track, again part of the Pilgrim's way, which leads up a steep hillside, Es Barrancons, by a winding route on the right of the gully. Well-graded, but partly obscured by vegetation, this emerges onto a flat shelf below a wood, a good viewpoint. Go through a metal gate into the woodland and turn left to follow the main path, with some blue paint signs and cairns. Turn sharp right after going through a broken down wall and follow the path at the side of this wall up towards a flat circular area. Look out for occasional cairns, but in general keep straight on up a kind of ridge to reach a wide forest track at a bend. Turn left and follow this along to the south side of L'Ofre. After going through a gap in a wall, near where a path goes up to L'Ofre's summit, the track

145

swings round and arrives at the Coll de L'Ofre.

From here there is an easy walk back to Cuber and the start of the walk. A short cut can be taken on the left of the track on the way down from the col.

Cuber - Coll des Bosc	1hr 10min
Coll des Bosc - Es Barrancons	1hr 15min
Es Barrancons - Coll de L'Ofre	1hr 45min
Coll de L'Ofre - Cuber	1hr 30min

38. LLOSETA, S'ESTORELL AND BINIAMAR

This very attractive circular walk through varied scenery begins in the village of Lloseta, 3km west of Inca. The route goes around several small hills, crosses a col at 508m and returns to Lloseta through the hamlet of Biniamar. The views of the mountains are outstanding, especially of S'Alcadena with its encircling vertical cliffs and of the ridge from L'Ofre to Sa Rateta. The walk is particularly beautiful in February when the almond trees on the Estorell estate are in blossom.

Type of walk: Mainly on wide tracks and country roads giving very easy walking and partly on a narrow well-made path in woodland where some attention to route-finding must be paid to avoid being led astray by minor paths.

Starting point:	Plaza des Isglesia, Lloseta
Time:	4hr 45min
Distance:	14km
Highest point reached:	508m
Total height climbed:	341m
Grade:	C+
Map:	Inca 1:25,000

From the parking place in front of the church, the Plaza des Isglesia, go down the steps to the long street of Guillermo Santandreu and turn right. Keep straight on to arrive in about ten minutes at the edge of the town, where the main road turns left to Alaró. Take the right fork here, then at a road junction where there is a well turn right again. After passing a large cemetery on the left there is a long straight stretch passing several smallholdings and going straight towards S'Alcadena through many fields of almond trees.

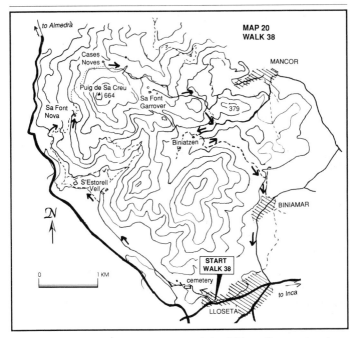

MAP 20
WALK 38

The track goes through the gates of the S'Estorell property where there is a notice prohibiting the picking of mushrooms and snails (*setas y caracoles*). Ahead lies the old abandoned house of Estorell, in a prominent position on the lower slopes of the Puig de Sa Creu. As you approach this, turn left through a gateway and follow the track round to the left of S'Estorell. (A diversion may be made to look at this if you are interested.) The track continues through a metal gate, then bends right to meet a T-junction where the left turn is taken. (The track on the right comes from the house.) After going through another metal gate, between a large rock on the left and a wall on the right, the track begins to climb up quite steeply in zigzags. (At a bend to the left, note a minor track coming in from the right. This is an alternative route described later.) About five minutes further on, after passing a small ruined building, there is an excellent lunch spot in a clearing next to a spring, Sa Font Nova, on the right of the track.

Continue up the main track rising in bends until a small cairn is seen on the left at a point where there is a sharp swing to the right. This indicates the beginning of a good but narrow path which rises steadily through the woods. At one point, after climbing a wooden rail type of stile and going through a wire mesh gate, there is a bifurcation which is not very obvious. Take the right branch here and on the way up a number of places used for *caza a coll* (thrush-hunting) will be noticed. After the path has levelled out, it descends slightly and at this point is easily lost. Look out for the cairns which show the way down to a field in the corner of which and on the right will be found a gate.

This gate leads to a high cultivated plateau and a path contours along the edge of one of the wide terraces to reach a track by a new house. Turn right along the track and after passing between an open water tank and a covered spring, the Font de Sa Barbara, go through a metal gate where there is an extensive view down towards Inca, the central plain, and the coast. Continue down this road which eventually leads to Mancor de la Vall. However, to return to the starting point of the walk, it is necessary to look out for an old track not on the map. This will be found on the right at a wide place on the road and just before a sharp bend to the left. There is a red spot on an old olive tree, hardly noticeable unless you are looking for it. This track, gated at the top and the bottom, leads down to join the road from Mancor to Biniatzent. Turn right towards Biniatzent where there is a sharp turn left. The road now descends at the side of a stream bed. Turn right when a cross track is reached to reach the hamlet of Biniamar at a large impressive house. Turn left along the Carrer des Comte to reach the main road, then right to reach the start of the walk by the church in Lloseta.

Lloseta - S'Estorell	1hr
S'Estorell - Sa Font Nova	40min
Sa Font Nova - New house	1hr
New house - Biniamar	1hr 45min
Biniamar - Lloseta	20min

Alternative route from Estorell to Sa Font Nova
From the track in front of the main entrance to the house, turn right, and in 20m go up left by an old water tank. Follow, not without difficulty, a partially and sometimes completely buried pipeline, up though old terraces in a roughly northerly direction. After getting into a wood the pipeline is a bit easier to follow. Near an old lime oven an overgrown but wider track can be picked up. This leads slightly downhill to join the main track up the valley some five minutes before the Font Nova.

39. PUIG DE S'ALCADENA

The massif of S'Alcadena is on the east of the Alaró-Orient road, opposite the Castell d'Alaró, Walk 40. Quite different in character from the walk up to the castle, which is easy and popular, this walk is rough and does not attract many people. It is a striking mountain from all directions, being defended on all sides by vertical cliffs. These cliffs are in places 200m high and extend for several kilometers, although so far only six recognised rock climbs have been recorded. This walk utilises the one line of weakness on the east side. The approach is by a private road through the grounds of the *finca* Son Cadena where the owner is likely to be met tending his fields. A few minutes conversation is customary, however rudimentary your Spanish. He will most certainly want to know where you are going and will helpfully point out the way.

Type of walk: Although a good path is used most of the way, this has fallen away at one point in a fairly steep gully. Some walkers have been forced to retreat at this point.

Starting point:	K18, Alaró-Orient road
Time:	4hr 10min
Distance:	8km
Highest point reached:	813m
Total height climbed	607m
Grade:	B+
Map:	Alaro 1:25,000 and
	Inca 1:25,000

A car may be left on the grass verge near the K18 stone. Walk towards Orient and almost immediately take a right fork where the main road bends left. Take the second right down a narrow lane with a stone barn on the corner and then cross the Sollerich stream by a ford. (No water, normally.) The gates of the *finca* Son Cadena are soon reached and the track followed up to the farm buildings. At the house turn right through a gate, then left round the back of the house. Turn right up a well-laid cobbled track which leads through olive terraces to the east side of the mountain and eventually through a gate.

Go through the gate, turn left and then almost immediately right. This path continues to contour along the eastern slopes through cultivated terraces and then into a wood of evergreen oaks and pines. After going through another gateway with a boulder at the right-hand side the path begins to rise more steeply and there are some cairns. Soon a very old

149

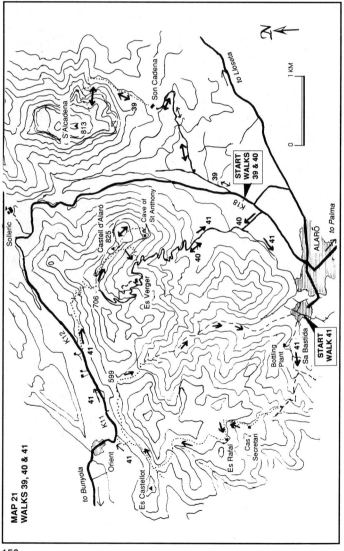

MAP 21
WALKS 39, 40 & 41

S'Alcadena

gate between high stone gateposts topped with wooden beams is reached; this is the only access to the normal way up the mountain.

The route now goes up a wide gully by a well-constructed path. The only difficulty is at the point where this has collapsed and steep ground has to be crossed with some care. After emerging on a shoulder the path ascends gradually to the south to end at a *sitja*. From this *sitja* go straight on along a continuing and waymarked path which slowly contours round the top of the cliffs until it turns up fairly steeply towards the top. A shorter way is to go straight up from the *sitja* but this is rough, vegetated and steep and not recommended.

K18 - Son Cadena	40min
Son Cadena - path end	1hr 10min
Path end - summit	40min
Summit - Son Cadena	1hr
Son Cadena - K18	40min

40. CASTELL D'ALARO

The Puig d'Alaró is one of the two 'sugar loaf' mountains seen on the west side of the Palma-Inca road. The other is Alacdena, Walk 39. The castle formerly covered almost all the top of the mountain and the approaches to it are well-defended by steep cliffs. The only way up is by a steep cobbled path with steps and ramps leading to the gated entrance. The remains are still very impressive and the views extensive. On the topmost point of the hill is a small bar-restaurant in the style of an alpine hut, offering coffee, food, wine and accommodation at reasonable prices. (Closed on Tuesdays.)

An optional extension to the walk is a visit to the Cave of Saint Anthony, a large cave with a sloping floor reached in about thirty minutes from the top. This lies out at the end of a ridge running south-east then south and culminating in an old defensive tower with steep drops almost all round.

A narrow road runs up to a col at 706m, passing the restaurant Es Pouet on the way. Good traditional food is served here and it is very popular at weekends, which are best avoided.

Type of walk: Easy walking up a narrow road and a good path. The extension to the cave is over more difficult terrain; the path is not very easy to follow and the going is quite rough at the end.

Starting point:	K18 on the Alaró-Orient road.
Time:	3hr 30min (Add 1hr for the cave)
Distance:	9km
Highest point reached:	825m
Total height climbed:	600m
Grade:	C (B to the cave)
Map:	Alaró 1:25,000

A car may be left on the wide grassy verge near the K18 stone on the road from Alaró to Orient. Turn back towards Alaró and take the road signposted 'Castillo, Es Pouet' which is about 200m from K18. (Alternatively drive up this road for a short distance to park on waste ground on the left.) Walk up the road, taking advantage of the short cuts. The first one begins by an enormous boulder after going through a gateway. There are three short cuts which make use of an old mule-track, winding up through terraces of olive trees. The third short cut bypasses an alternative path used on the descent.

After passing the restaurant Es Pouet the main track keeps to the left,

152

Approaching the Castell d'Alaró

153

or an alternative on the right with more bends can be used. Both lead to the col where there is a large open space used as a car park. The path to the castle goes up on the left of a wall and is signposted with a yellow painted arrow. This well-built path joins another path used on the descent and the gatehouse of the castle is reached five minutes later. Allow a few minutes for looking round here before continuing to the top.

To find the cave, go past the outbuildings and follow a rather confusing path through the woodlands, looking out for cairns and paintmarks. A descent of the order of 100m or more is called for, but this is fairly gradual. The entrance to the cave is well-hidden and unlikely to be seen until the old tower perched on the end of the ridge is reached. From the tower, look back along the path and the dark hole that leads into the cave will be seen. Go inside, and light shining through another hole shows the way. If the floor is dry it is safe to explore thoroughly, but remember there is a steep drop below. This is not a place to take small children.

Retrace your steps back to the top and continue down past the castle to the path-junction met on the way up. Turn left and follow the path down to join the road. It is signposted 'Alaró a pie'. On the way down a branch path leads back to Es Pouet if you are in need of refreshment. If you are going straight down, there are two short cuts to find.

K18 - summit	2hr
Summit - cave, and return	1hr
Summit - K18	1hr 30min

41(a). ALARO-ORIENT CIRCULAR WALK

The walk to the Castell d'Alaró from Alaró is well-known and deservedly popular. Less well known is the approach from Orient, a very attractive old village situated in a peaceful valley. The 'surprise view' of Orient on this circular walk is really outstanding and the whole walk is full of interest. Alaró is an old town with narrow streets, many of them one way. Approaching from the Palma or the Inca direction, follow the town centre signs until a way out on the west side of the town can be found. There is a place to park by some new houses just outside the old quarter of Sa Bastida.

Type of walk: All the walking is easy on lanes, tracks and good paths, except for a short distance between Cas Secretari and Rafal. The pull up to the Coll de S'Era is quite steep but on a surfaced road.

Starting point:	Sa Bastida, Alaró
Time:	5hr 20min.
Distance:	13km
Highest point reached:	825m
Total height climbed:	626m
Grade:	C+
Map:	Alaró 1:25,000

Leave Sa Bastida by the Carrer de Son Borras. In ten minutes the road passes the bottling plant of the Bastida spring. Follow the narrow but surfaced road up through the woods to the Coll de S'Era, ignoring a number of branch tracks on both sides. On the far side of the col is a valley filled with olive terraces, the Clot des Guix (483m). Go to the side of a new metal gate, then take the first turning right about two minutes further on, bypassing another locked metal gate. The track ends at a house, Cas Secretari, but a path continues at the right-hand side of it, passing a spring. A rough path now leads upwards to the top of the terraces, keeping near the right side. On the top terrace it turns left and leads easily to a ruined house, Es Rafal, going through a metal gate with a sign saying it is to be kept closed. Before reaching the house and less than 20m from this gate turn right at the far side of a low wall. Follow the path alongside this wall and go through another metal gate into a wood. When the path bifurcates take the left hand branch which runs parallel to the wall. Go through a gap in a wall and keep following the woodland path which is well-marked.

In due course the path arrives at a pass at 572m to the east of Es Castellot. On this pass the path turns at right angles between two rock walls which frame an outstanding view of Orient and the hills beyond. Follow the wide track down and after ten minutes turn down left at a fork. Continue along this track until a gate is seen on the left and painted signs indicate that this is the way to Orient. The path joins the tarmac road slightly to the east of the village. Turn right and follow the road past the Hermitage hotel. Less than 300m from here turn right through a gate into the olive terraces. Turn left and follow the path, at first parallel to the road, then sloping uphill towards a wooded gully. The path enters the wood and rises up in zigzags to reach a large sloping area used as a picnic place and, regrettably, as a car park, the Pla d'es Pouet. From here the descent can be made either by the narrow road on the right via the Es Verger restaurant, or preferably by following the path to the castle and the footpath down from there. (See walk 40). If you have left a car at Sa

Bastida, then keep following the road which hugs the bottom of the hill and leads into the old part of Alaró and Sa Bastida.

Alaró - Cas Secretari	1hr
Cas Secretari - Pas de S'Estalot	50min
Pas de S'Estalot - Orient	15min
Orient - Castle	1hr 30min
Castle - Alaró	1hr 45min

41(b). ALARO-ORIENT CIRCULAR WALK: SHORT VERSION

This route does not include the Castell d'Alaró, but is a very pleasant excursion in quiet and little-known countryside.

Starting point:	Sa Bastida
Time:	3hr 15min
Distance:	10km
Highest point reached:	599m
Total height climbed:	422m
Grade:	C+
Map:	Alaró 1:25,000

Follow route 41(a) as far as the gate where the path descends to Orient. Very faint red paint marks may be seen here with arrows and the words 'Orient' and 'Alaró', on rocks on the right hand side of the path. Continue along the track which rises in zigzags through the woodlands until there is a sudden view of the Orient valley, near a hunters' shelter. The track turns right here and keeps to the right of flattish ground, before going into woodlands again and descending into a narrow valley. Keep following the cairns and paintmarks.

The path joins a cart-track which goes steadily downhill to reach the houses of Sa Bastida where the walk begins.

42. NAMARICH

Namarich is also called Sa Puig de Na Marit. This interesting walk goes through varied and quite spectacular scenery in a very quiet area. Although much of it is wooded there are also open areas with panoramic views and impressive rock walls towering over the trees. The Coma Gran used for the descent is very beautiful, with oak woods in the upper part, leading to an almond orchard, a wonderful sight in February when the blossom is fully out. Below this the valley narrows between steep rock walls where there is a cave house built under a rock recalling those at Coscona. (See Walks 24 and 27.)

Type of walk: Easy walking on country lanes, paths and tracks, except for the last little path to the top which at the time of writing is very overgrown and not easy to follow.

Starting point:	Bunyola
Time:	5hr 20min
Distance:	14km
Highest point reached:	671m
Total height climbed:	476m
Grade:	B
Map:	Soller 1:50,000 or
	Alaró 1:25,000

Park at the town cemetery which is about 1km from Bunyola along the Santa Maria road. Walk towards Santa Maria and take the signposted left turn to Es Cocons, at a place where there is a large electricity sub-station in the angle between the two roads. The road then passes in front of the houses of Es Cocons. A few minutes further on ignore a left turn to some other houses. In a further few minutes a house called Ca Na Moragues is reached. Turn right at this corner, noting that the track straight ahead is the one used in the descent.

Follow the narrow surfaced road up through a gateway with pedestrian access to a large house called Cas Bergantet. From the semicircular platform below the house go through a little gate which leads to a path along an old terrace. In five minutes this reaches the Coma d'en Buscante where a track goes up left, passing a cross track and continuing straight up the valley bottom, quite steeply in places. A small house built under a rock will be noticed and further up a ruined house with a well. Beyond this point the track becomes narrower and rather overgrown, but after another ten minutes or so it enters a mature oakwood which gives delightful soft walking on a bed of oak leaves. When the wood thins out the path becomes somewhat overgrown with *carritx* but is still easy to follow as it clings to the very narrow valley floor.

Eventually the path arrives at a high wooded plateau where it swings round to the right to reach a wide track about 10m from a clearing. Turn right along this track and in a short distance (30-40m) take the first turn right along quite a wide track. This almost horizontal track runs parallel to the ascent path up the Coma d'en Buscante and is attractively

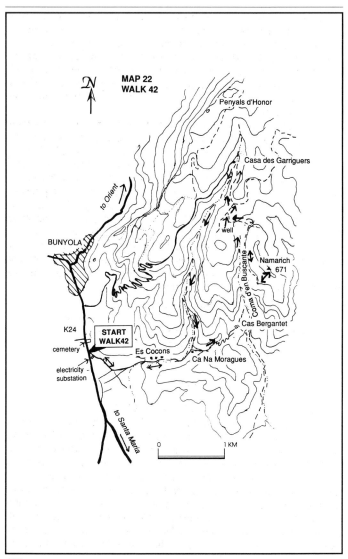

MAP 22
WALK 42

Penyals d'Honor

Casa des Garriguers

well

Namarich
671

to Orient

BUNYOLA

Coma d'en Buscante

Cas Bergantet

K24

**START
WALK42**

cemetery

Es Cocons

Ca Na Moragues

electricity
substation

to Santa Maria

0   1 KM

overgrown with various flowering shrubs such as cistus, rosemary and St. John's wort. The path contours above crags similar to those seen on the other side of the valley and then rises to end at a clearing.

From this point a narrow and very overgrown path can be followed, not without difficulty, to reach the summit ridge of Namarich in about 20 minutes. Turn left to reach the trig point. Unless this path is found to have been more used and easier to follow it is recommended that markers be left to aid the descent.

Return down the narrow path to the clearing at the track end, then back along the cart track to the large clearing just past the junction with the ascent path. Go straight on through this open space following the wide track which runs north-west. In ten minutes it reaches a T-junction where there is a well. Turn right and in a further five minutes join another track and turn left. Follow this horizontal track overlooking the forested valley of Sa Coma Gran. In ten minutes a large clearing will be reached, where there is an ICONA shelter, the Casa des Garriguer. (A minor road from Bunyola ends here; this place may be crowded on Sundays.)

The return route descends directly from this clearing and is easy walking down a good track, full of interest. The route of ascent is met at the corner by Ca Na Moragues. Continue down the hill to Es Cocons and then along the road to the starting point.

Bunyola cemetery - Cas Bergantet	1hr
Cas Bergantet - Namarich	1hr 50min
Namarich - Casa des Garriguer	1hr
Casa des Garriguer - Ca Na Moragues	1hr
Ca Na Moragues - Bunyola cemetery	30min

43. L'OFRE AND SA RATETA FROM ORIENT

L'Ofre is often climbed from Soller, from where its triangular shape is a familiar sight. The walk up the Pilgrim Steps from Biniaraix to the Coll de L'Ofre is a classic. This point can also be easily reached from Cuber and the track followed round to the south where a marked path leads to the top. (The walk along the ridge to Sa Rateta has been described in the reverse direction from Cuber, see Walk 36.) The views are outstanding. The route described here from Orient is less well-known and has the advantage of a beautiful approach by the Comasema valley from Orient. Orient itself is an old and lovely village in the mountains, reached by driving through Alaró from Consell on the main Palma - Inca road. There

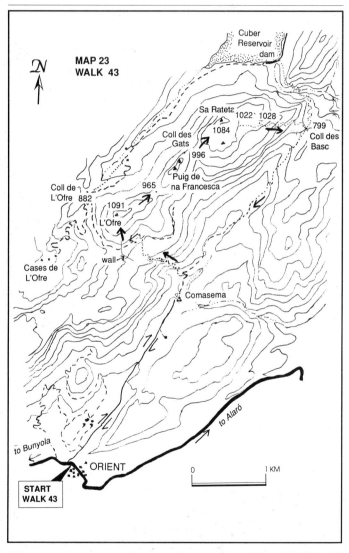

Fornalutx. (Walk 50)

Stone steps and water irrigation channel at La Trapa
(Walk 61) (Author)
Typical flowers of Mallorca: below left - Bermuda Buttercups
below right - Cistus Albidus

is room to park in the village where refreshments are available. The narrow road to Comasema is strictly private and no attempt should be made to drive there.

Type of walk: Easy walking in the Comasema valley, but a rough path up to L'Ofre and stony, largely pathless ground along the ridge. The descent to the col at the head of the Comasema valley is by an old stone track, partly vegetated or destroyed but easy to follow.

Starting point:	Orient
Time:	6hr
Distance:	15km
Highest point reached:	1,091m
Total height climbed:	516m
Grade:	A
Map:	Soller 1:25,000

Go out of Orient towards Bunyola and take the first sharp turn to the right. Follow this narrow road through the cultivated fields of Comasema and through the large and beautiful old farmhouse buildings. About 200m after going through the buildings the main track bends right. Leave it here to turn left into a dry stream-bed between two walls. On the right-hand wall there are some painted signs, partly or totally obscured by brambles. A yellow arrow points right to Cuber and a blue arrow points left to Soller.

The path goes to the right out of the stream-bed and rises in zigzags. It is well-marked with paint signs and cairns, but a little rough and overgrown in places. After arriving at a little rocky platform offering a splendid view over the valley the path goes through a metal gate into woodland. Follow the path left at first, then turn right along a broken-down wall. The path has some blue markers and some cairns but is a little confused. It then joins a wide forest track at a bend. Turn left here and follow it until shortly before it reaches a gap in a wall. A marked path from here now leads to the summit of L'Ofre.

Returning to Orient by the same route provides a satisfying walk, but a more strenuous and very interesting alternative is to walk along the ridge north-east to Sa Rateta. Follow the cairned path along the ridge down to a col at 965m, then up to the Puig de na Franquesa whose highest point is 1,067m. After this there is a short descent to the Coll des Gats (also known as the Coll des Planet) at 996m. There is a flat grassy area on this col that would be a tempting campsite in good weather. Going up to Sa Rateta from here the ridge rises steeply, then flattens out.

Leave the summit slightly south of east, looking out for a rectangular enclosure, and passing on the way an old snow hole partly blocked by a very big boulder. The path down begins by the enclosure and is marked by some red paint signs. Follow this stony path down into a hollow filled with clumps of *carritx*, approximately at the spot marked 1002 on the 1:25,000 map. From the hollow the stony path continues to the east, below a subsidiary rocky top at 1,028m. It was once a well-made path, now badly deteriorated in this area. Once the cairns marking the way are picked up it is then easy to follow all the way down to the Coll des Bosc, in spite of being overgrown by incredibly tough trees and shrubs in places.

At the col, marked by several cairns, the more obvious path turns left towards the Almedrá valley. At this point go straight on through the bushes to reach a large open clearing where a wide forest track begins to descend to Comasema. There are several short cuts on the way down, usually marked by cairns.

There is a spring, the Font de sa Cisterneta, on the right of the track after about 15 minutes of descent. The path zigzags through the woods with numerous *sitjes* and other signs of the charcoal burners activities. A large animal shelter is passed on the right. After about 40 minutes it emerges through a gateway into the open and almost level fields above the Comasema farmhouse. Follow the road back to the starting point in Orient.

Orient - Comasema	30min
Comasema - L'Ofre	1hr 30min
L'Ofre - Sa Rateta	1hr 15min
Sa Rateta - Coll des Bosc	1hr 15min
Coll des Bosc - Comasema	1hr
Comasema - Orient	30min

44. CUBER AND ES BARRANC

Mallorca has no natural lakes, but the two reservoirs built to augment Palma's water supplies provide satisfactory alternatives. The largest of them, Cuber, occupies a natural basin below the steep buttresses of the highest mountain, Puig Mayor, looking doubly impressive reflected in the still water. This can be a good place for birds, Red Kites for example.

This easy, classic walk through the mountains, mainly downhill, is carried out with the aid of the C710 bus which runs from Soller over to Pollensa.

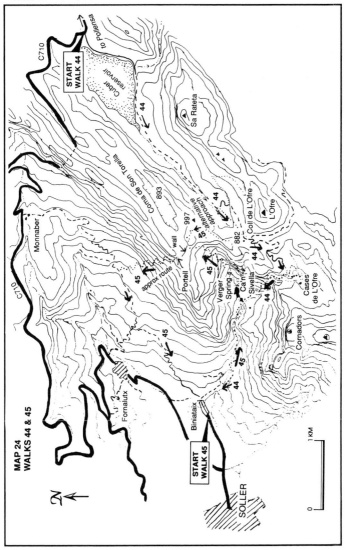

MAP 24
WALKS 44 & 45

N

START WALK 44

C710

to Pollensa

Cuber reservoir

44

Sa Rateta

893

Coma de Son Torella

wall

alternative approach

44

Coll de L'Ofre

L'Ofre

997

882

44

approx route

45

Portell

45

Verger

Spring

Can't

Sivella

44

Cases de L'Ofre

Monnaber

C710

45

45

Comadors

44

45

Fornalutx

Biniaraix

START WALK 45

SOLLER

0   1 KM

There is a natural picnic place on a gently sloping grassy shelf overlooking the Soller valley, very near the Coll de L'Ofre. The descent by the Pilgrim Steps goes down an impressive gorge below the steep rock walls of Cornadors, with typical Mallorquin terraces growing ancient olive trees.

Type of walk: Very easy, along a wide track at first, over the Coll de L'Ofre, then down the excellent built up mule track known as the Pilgrim Steps down to the hamlet of Biniaraix.

Starting point:	Cuber gates, C710
Time:	3hr 45min
Distance:	13km
Highest point reached:	882m
Total height climbed:	Ascent 130m, descent c.800m
Grade:	C+
Map:	Soller 1:25,000

Go through the entrance gate and follow the road along past the dam. Just at the end of the lake there is a mountain shelter with a fireplace in one corner, but no other comforts. There are locked gates along this road, which is used by the people who work at the L'Ofre farm and drive up from Soller each day, but pedestrian access is provided for walkers.

Where the track bends left near some trees, an obvious short cut will be found on the right hand side, leading up to the Coll de L'Ofre where there is a large cairn. On the other side of the col turn right at a junction and follow the descending track to the Cases de L'Ofre, where there are several buildings and a freshwater spring. Opposite a barn not far past the spring, turn right by a wall where there is a painted sign to Soller. Walking down the *barranc* is like walking down a stone staircase but with spectacular views at every turn. About half-way down you will notice a path junction by a house with a walled garden, which is the way up to the Verger spring and the Portell de Sa Costa, Walk 45.

Once in Biniaraix turn left through the village and follow the road back to Soller.

Cuber - Coll de L'Ofre	1hr 10min
Coll de L'Ofre - Cases de L'Ofre	25min
Cases de L'Ofre - Biniaraix	1hr 40min
Biniaraix - Soller	30 min

45. ES PORTELL DE SA COSTA

The 'Portell' is a gateway on the high ridge of the Serra de Torrelles where there is a sudden and magnificent view of the Soller valley and the coast with its circular harbour. The Verger spring is an attractive place to visit, especially after recent rain when little waterfalls cascade over mossy rocks, but this is a difficult route. An easier approach to the Portell is from the Coll de L'Ofre, either from Cuber (see Walk 44) or by the *barranc*. If the *barranc* is used, then take the right fork at the junction described below and at the Cases de L'Ofre turn left and follow the track to the col.

Type of walk: A steep and stony descent. Ascent by the Verger spring is very strenuous with loose scree.

Starting point:	Soller
Time:	6hr 20min
Distance:	11km
Highest point reached:	c.900m
Total height climbed:	c.860m
Grade:	A+
Map	Soller 1:25,000

Leave the main square in Soller, the Plaza de la Constitució, by the road to Biniaraix. Go through this village to the public wash place at the end and there turn right on the narrow track signposted to the 'Barranc'. The path crosses the stream, which is usually dry, and then goes up by the old stepped path, part of a centuries old Pilgrim's route to the monastery at Lluc. After going through a narrow section of the gorge and passing a small house, a path junction will be reached at the corner of another house. (Both the left and right-hand ways from here look impossible, although the path on the right, leading to the Cases de L'Ofre, is actually very easy all the way up and can be used as an alternative approach.)

To go up by the Verger spring route turn left here and in ten minutes Ca'n Sivella will be reached. This is a house in a most attractive situation having a terrace with a round stone table. From the terrace there is a marvellous view of Soller framed by the walls of the *barranc*. With your back to the house, the path goes up straight ahead and crosses the stream. Keep following the path which goes up through old terraces, watching out for a right turn indicated by a faint silver arrow and the words 'Es Verger'. Soon after this fork right along a horizontal path, indicated by another painted arrow. The Verger spring will be reached about 20 minutes after leaving Ca'n Sivella.

The difficult part begins after this, with only traces of paths up loose stones and scree and several patches of brambles and other thorny vegetation. The best way is mainly on the right-hand side, although sometimes clambering up large boulders in the centre makes a good alternative. Eventually easier ground is reached after passing some pine trees, although before this you may well wish you had opted for the easier way up the *barranc*. When a wall is seen across the top of the slope ahead, make for a gap near the middle. A few yards on the other side of the gap there is a view down the Torrella valley and on the left the Portell de Sa Costa will be seen.

Turn left to reach the portal. Just through the opening is another gateway below which is a rather fine rock pinnacle. Here is a good place to rest and admire the view before starting the descent, because although there is an excellent and well-graded path all the way down, it is rather stony and care is needed. At first there are some tight bends, then wider sweeps. There are a few places where a fallen tree or minor rock fall has blocked the way. If the path is lost, it is best to backtrack and find it again. After about one hour of descent, the path goes left and slightly uphill to reach a small knoll. Continue over this in the same direction and in two or three minutes a green paint sign saying SOLLER with an arrow will be seen.

After about another half hour the path arrives at an old stepped track between walls, but there is a little confusion here and it may be necessary to cast about to find it. There are some weekend houses in the woods here, fenced off both from the mountainside and a dirt road. If this dirt road is accidentally reached, turn left and the stepped path will be found by the entrance gate to Ca'n Xarpa. Follow the old path down past a spring to reach the Monaber road, and then turn left to return to Biniaraix by the public washplace at the top end of the village.

Soller- Biniaraix	30min
Biniaraix - Ca'n Sivella	1hr
Ca'n Sivella - Verger spring	20min
Verger spring - Portell	1hr 50min
Portell - road	1hr 30min
Road - Biniaraix	40min
Biniaraix - Soller	30min

Alternative starts
From the Coll de L'Ofre pick up a narrow path on the west side which leads slightly east of north towards an unnamed top with spot heights of

966m and 997m overlooking the high Torelles valley and almost 1km from the col. (This top is named as Loma, 966m on the older maps.) The path veers round this on the east side and then turns towards the west to reach the Portell de Sa Costa. It crosses some flattish ground between the upper slopes of the Verger spring route to the south-west and the Torelles valley on the north-east. Allow about 40 minutes from the Coll de L'Ofre to the Portell de Sa Costa. If using the bus from Soller along the C710, from the Cuber entrance gate to the col it is about 1hr 10min. From Biniaraix to the col allow about 2hr 50min.

46. CORNADORS

Cornadors overlooks the *barranc* of Biniaraix, up which go the well-known Pilgrim Steps, a wonderful old cobbled track originally going all the way from Soller to Lluc. There is a viewpoint near the top, the Mirador de L'Ofre, from which the mountain of L'Ofre is seen to great advantage. The view of the almost vertical face of Cornadors from the path is possibly even more striking than the view from the *mirador* itself. The walk up the *barranc* contends for the most popular walk on the island, so weekends are best avoided. The gorge itself is outstandingly attractive with hundreds of tiny terraces accommodating olives and oranges, flanked by steep rock walls on either side. It may be useful to know there is a freshwater spring at the Cases de L'Ofre, the Font de Sa Teula. This is a short way along the track towards Cuber, from the path junction at the top of the *barranc.*

There is some confusion about the height of Cornadors on the maps and in various books. The mirador is undoubtedly on the 957m top, which has a precipitous north face towering over the barranc. The name 'Cornadors' means horns, and there is another steep-sided top at 809m which also overlooks the barranc and must be the other horn. However, the name Cornadors on the map is nowhere near either of these. The 1,014 top on the Alfàbia ridge is now named as Sementer Gran, so is not the other top of Cornadors as previously assumed.

The Mirador is maintained by the Fomento del Turismo, as is the mountain hut near the top of Cornadors on its southern side. This has a sound roof and stone benches.

It is a moot point whether this walk is better done as described or in the reverse direction. For those who elect for the latter, some notes are included in the text to indicate key points. The attraction of ending at Biniaraix is that you can look forward to a glass of freshly squeezed

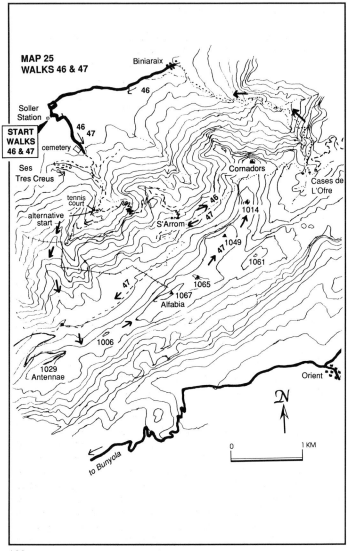

MAP 25
WALKS 46 & 47

Biniaraix

46

Soller
Station

46   47

START
WALKS
46 & 47

cemetery

Ses
Tres Creus

Cornadors

Cases de
L'Ofre

tennis
court

46

alternative
start

47

S'Arrom

1014

1049

47

1061

1065

47

1067
Alfabia

1006

1029
Antennae

Orient

N

to Bunyola

0   1 KM

orange juice at a bar on the main street.

Type of walk: Almost entirely on cart-tracks and well-made paths. No difficulties, but quite a long and strenuous ascent.

Starting point:	Soller railway station
Time:	5hr 40min
Distance:	16km
Highest point reached:	957m
Total height climbed:	900m
Grade:	C+
Map:	Soller 1:25,000

From the railway station, face downhill towards the church and turn first right along a narrow street, passing the hotel Guia. Take the first right again, second left, then first right again. Keep along this road, the Calle de Pablo Noguerra, until the cemetery is passed on the right. After passing the cemetery take a left fork, then in two minutes a right fork which crosses the stream by a bridge. One minute or so later take a sharp left turn. After this it is a question of keeping to the main track, marked here and there with small red paint marks. The track is well-maintained and leads up through an area of old olive terraces and some weekend houses. Higher up it enters a forest of evergreen oaks where *sitjes* and lime-ovens abound.

After about an hour and a half go through a gate to meet another track at a T-junction and turn right. (There is a blue painted sign here pointing down to Soller, useful if reversing the walk.) After five minutes or so go through a metal gate and take a right fork. The farmhouse S'Arrom is now in sight on a plateau high above. The track swings left, then goes up a narrow gully in a series of tight bends. Watch out for the steps leading to a pedestrian access gate, as the double gates across the track are locked. When S'Arrom is reached, follow the track round to the left, then right again past the house to the south. An engraved stone sign with the word 'MIRADOR' and an arrow points to some stone steps. These and the path ahead lead to an old well in a tunnel, the 'Font de Ses Piquetes', with some badly polluted water. After reaching the well, scramble up the hillside above to regain the cart-track. (There is another engraved stone at this point, marking the beginning of this short cut if you are descending this way. Look out for it as it saves quite a distance.) About ten minutes further on the track does a sharp bend to the right, where there is yet another stone. After this it becomes a narrow path which climbs in

169

zigzags up a sloping shelf to a col, where a high fence is crossed by a stile. The *rifugio* is in sight here and is reached in a further 15 minutes, turning left at the 917m col due south of the top of Cornadors.

From the shelter it is only a few minutes to the top and over the other side to reach the impressively situated mirador. To continue the walk, return past the shelter to the col. Turn left here and follow the path down to the houses on the tiny green plateau of L'Ofre. Go through the field gate and follow the path to a large barn with painted signs on the walls. These point right to 'L'Ofre Mirador. Soller 8km' and left '27km Lluc. Por favor, no acampar, TOROS'. (No camping please. BULLS.) Just past the barn turn left off the main track, indicated by a sign to Soller, and begin the descent of the gorge. In reverse, the directions are all quite clear here. About 50 minutes after leaving the Cases de L'Ofre the path arrives at a corner of a wall, where there is a painted arrow pointing up. In reverse, look out for this junction as the other branch goes up to the Verger spring (see Walk 45).

Continue down the main track which goes through a narrow and shady section and crosses the stream several times by bridges and stepping-stones. Not that there is much need for these as there is rarely any water in the stream-bed. Near Biniaraix the path joins another track at a gate with a 'No entry' sign and another sign which reads 'L'Ofre, Lluc a peu' (L'Ofre, Lluc on foot.). Turn left to arrive at the small village by the old public washplace. Follow the road through or take the stepped street on the right, re-join the road and follow it back to Soller. To return to the station from the main square, go up the hill to the right of the church.

Soller station - S'Arrom	2hr
S'Arrom - Cornadors	1hr
Cornadors - Cases de L'Ofre	35min
Cases de L'Ofre - Biniaraix	1hr 35min
Biniaraix - Soller station	30min

47. THE ALFÀBIA RIDGE

The long high ridge of Alfàbia dominates the Soller valley and represents a constant challenge to walkers based in the area. The ridge is over 4km long with several tops over 1,000m, the highest being 1,067m. Although the southernmost top is despoiled by TV and radio masts, all the rest of the ridge is wild and pathless, and being difficult ground to walk on is rarely visited. The views are extensive and the glimpses down into the quiet Orient valley on the east are especially charming.

Type of walk: Steep but easy at first, then rough and slow along the ridge over tilted and dissected limestone pavement.

Starting point:	Soller railway station
Time:	8hr
Distance:	20km
Highest point reached:	1,067m
Total height climbed:	1,076m
Grade:	A+
Map:	Soller 1:25,000 and
	Alaró 1:25.000

Follow Walk 46 as far as S'Arrom. Instead of taking the short cut by the well continue along the cart-track past the farm towards the south-west until, shortly after a sharp hairpin bend to the left, a red arrow is seen, pointing to a path leading up into the oak woods. Follow the path with the aid of red and orange paint marks, over a wall by a ladder stile and on until you come to a *sitja*. Turn right along a track just above it, then right again along another wider track where there is an orange arrow painted on a rock. This track bends left at a junction, then curves back right below a steep rock wall. A few minutes later the track arrives at a broad shelf with few trees. The main track descends, but a branch leads along the plateau towards the radio masts and the road leading up to them.

At a bend, where the track crosses a stream-bed and just before reaching the access road to the masts, turn up left towards the lowest point on the ridge. The stone walls seen on the way up are the remains of an old snow house. Progress along the crest of the ridge is difficult and slow, so it is recommended that the new bulldozed track on the Orient side is followed until it peters out after crossing a col. After this natural ledges may be found leading easily up towards a gap in a wall on the way up to the main Alfàbia top. There is a trig point on the first top and about 15 minutes later a wooden cross on a secondary top. Although the broad rock ridge is easier than the southern part, the going is still quite hard and it may be quite a relief to reach the final top of the ridge, Sementer Gran at 1,014m. After this it is 20 minutes or less to join the path near the *Rifugio* on the Cornadors walk.

Turn left here and return to S'Arrom using the short cut by the well, indicated by an engraved stone about 25 minutes after leaving the col. (Alternatively descend by the barranc to Biniaraix.)

Soller - S'Arrom	2hr
S'Arrom - 978m col below masts	1hr 15min
978m col - Alfàbia	1hr
Alfàbia - Cornadors col	1hr 15min
Cornadors col - S'Arrom	45min
S'Arrom - Soller	1hr 45min

Alternative start

Follow the S'Arrom track until it turns left by a large house on the left with a tennis court on the right. Take the narrow track on the right through an open gateway and passing above the tennis court. Follow this lane up into a sloping valley, the Coma des Negret, passing several small houses. When the last house is passed the track becomes narrower and old steps in zigzags lead high up into a corner below an impressive steep wall. Ignore the left turn into the wood and follow the path making a rising taverse to the right. This leads to a restored *caseta* in a magnificent situation looking across the Soller valley to Mitx Dia, the western outpost of the Puig Mayor.

The path continues up to a small col bounded by a wall with a fence, which can be surmounted without too much difficulty. On the other side of the wall turn left and follow a pleasant woodland path up for about ten minutes and go through or over an old gate. A continuous but sometimes overgrown path twists and turns up towards the Alfàbia ridge, the antennae on the southernmost top being visible from time to time. Occasional cairns are a help where the path is obscured by vegetation or falling trees. This path leads to the plateau below the ridge quite near a farm building shown on the map. At this point refer to the main description for the continuation of the route up to the ridge.

48. CIRCUIT OF BALITX

A long and interesting walk with varied scenery. From the Coll d'es Figueral there is an excellent corniche track about 200m above the sea, with panoramic views of the coast, the rocky islet S'Illeta and an impressive overhanging tower, the Penyal Bernat.

The return route goes inland with views of the Torre de Na Seca, Coll de Biniamar, Puig Mayor, the Torrent des Llores and the farmlands of Balitx in the valley below. From Balitx part of a very old path, which was the original way from Soller to Sa Calobra, is used for the return to Soller.

Type of walk: Easy at first along a corniche track, followed by rough descents and ascents involving some scrambling and route-finding.

Starting point:	Puerto Soller
Time:	6hr 15min
Distance:	13km
Highest point reached:	407m
Total height climbed:	c.490m
Grade:	A+
Map:	1:25,000 Soller

From the quay walk south to the Sa Figuera road and turn left at this double street on the left (true right) side of the river. Follow it up to the Carrer de Belgique. At the first sharp bend in this new road go straight on through an open gateway and continue on up a narrow and fairly steep lane which leads directly to the Coll d'es Figueral. At the col follow a narrow lane which makes a sharp bend to the right and winds slightly uphill before beginning to contour in a north-easterly direction above the coast. Some height is gained in a series of bends and some steps make a short cut at one point.

Shortly after passing a new concrete road on the right, leading to the property of S'Illeta de Ca'n Cordo, a high locked gate is met. Twenty metres before the gate go through a gap in the wall on the left then along to the wall next to the gate and over it by a half stile. Do not continue along the main track, but instead go down left at the side of the wall to reach the terrace below by a couple of stone steps. Cross this terrace to go through a gap in another wall. A few metres after the gap ignore a branch path on the left and continue horizontally along the terrace. The path is not obvious at the beginning but soon becomes a wide well-made path, very easy to follow although a few trees have fallen across it.

This excellent path gives good views of the S'Illeta island, and after sweeping round a corner even more dramatic views of the cliffs. Although this path ends at a *sitja*, a continuation marked by cairns leads up to the crags below the Coll de Cordellina. The route which is cairned has been built up in places to aid the crossing of a steep rock wall. This is not difficult but quite steep and requires some care. After this it rises in zigzags to the Coll de Cordellina, between Balitx and an unnamed 277m top.

Climb over the stile on the col and then turn left as indicated by red paint marks on the rock. The next objective is a small col, the Pas de H'Eura (the Pass of the Ivy) at c.350m, seen on the opposite ridge across a small intervening valley. Two sticks to the right of a big tree mark the spot. One way to get there is to follow the narrow path down to the valley

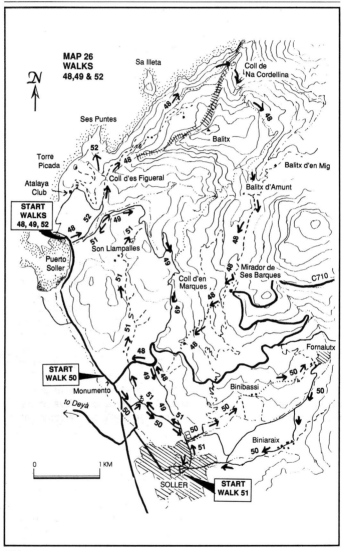

MAP 26
WALKS
48, 49 & 52

N

Sa Illeta

Coll de
Na Cordellina

Ses Puntes

48

49

Torre
Picada

Balitx

Balitx d'en Mig

Atalaya
Club

52

Coll d'es Figueral

48

Balitx d'Amunt

START
WALKS
48, 49, 52

48

52

49

51

51

48

Mirador de
Ses Barques

C710

Son Llampalles

51

49

Puerto
Soller

51

Coll d'en
Marques

48

49

START
WALK 50

48

Fornalutx

50

Monumento

49

48

Binibassi

50

to Deyà

51

49

51

50

50

50

Biniaraix

50

50

51

0   1 KM

SOLLER

START
WALK 51

floor, then up again on the other side with the aid of cairns and paint marks. A larger cairn marks the place where the route goes up a diagonal rake across a prominent yellow wall, at first sloping from right to left and then back from left to right. It is a great help to pick out this cairn from the Coll de Cordellina with the aid of binoculars. It may be shorter, but no easier, to go straight down bearing slightly right from the Cordellina pass to the bottom of a little rocky outcrop and then contour round to reach the vital cairn at the foot of the yellow wall. Whichever way is chosen, this is difficult ground with loose stones and prickly vegetation. After scrambling up to the 'pass', which is really just a step on the ridge, cairns continue to mark the way for another 50m when a real path will be found among some olive terraces. An old threshing floor is reached just before a barn. The path goes between the barn on the right and two large boulders making natural shelters on the left. After this it rises slightly before continuing along the slopes of Balitx in a roughly south-westerly direction.

About 15 minutes further on the path goes through a gateway, just above Balitx d'en Mig. Turn right and follow the path up towards some broad terraces, all the while contouring round towards the valley head. The valley head is a col at 388m with a wall across the top. (There is a fenced gap in the wall, with a track down to Puerto Soller on the other side, which can be followed as an alternative to the descent described.) On the Balitx side of the col a path leads round to join the road just below the property of Balitx d'Amunt. Turn right here and follow the road through a gate and on towards the Mirador de ses Barques.

Shortly before reaching the Mirador, take a right turn at a painted boulder, then immediately turn right down a narrow path at the side of a fence. This path is not easy to follow at first although there are several paint marks, but in a few minutes a small house will be noticed and the descending track found just below this, at the side of a wall with a fence on top. There are blue arrows painted on the wall and the path descends at the side of some olive terraces. Go through two gates and in a few more minutes arrive at a road, where there is a red arrow on the wall pointing to the right and the word 'Port'. Ignore this, as it leads down to the Coll d'en Marques road near the rubbish dumps from where it is a long walk back uphill to the port.

Instead, turn left and then immediately right to pick up the continuation of the old track. Some ten minutes later a small spring of drinkable water is passed and in a further five minutes a cart-track is joined, by a yellow painted arrrow. After a further few minutes the track passes a large house, and starts to bend right. Turn left along a footpath at this point and follow it down until it is cut by the C710. Find it again by turning left, then immediately right, at a sign which says 'Ca'n Bisbal'. The track is surfaced as far as this house, then the old path continues down towards Soller. In ten minutes or less turn right at another road junction, where the sign on the path you have just left says 'Camino Viejo de Balitx - Tuent - Sa Calobra'. Go down to a T-junction and turn right. Follow this road to join the C710 at Sa Taulera and turn left to the Monumento, where the tram or bus can be picked up to either Soller or Puerto Soller.

Puerto Soller - Coll D'es Figueral	25min
Figueral - Cordellina	1hr 30min
Cordellina - Balitx de Dalt	2hr 30min
Balitx de Dalt - Ses Barques	20min
Ses Barques - Monumento	1hr 30min

49. COLL D'EN MARQUES

A very attractive and easy walk, along a quiet country road between Puerto Soller and Soller. All the way the road goes through orange groves and terraces of olives and carobs. Hundreds of small birds feed among these trees, although many more will be heard than seen. The most common one is likely to be the Sardinian Warbler, a small grey bird with a black head and an orange eye-ring.

Type of walk: Very easy, along surfaced roads all the way.

Starting point:	Puerto Soller, bus terminus
Time:	2hr
Distance:	8km
Highest point reached:	187m
Total height climbed:	187m
Grade:	C
Map:	Soller 1:25,000

From the bus and tram terminus by the quay walk south along the sea front and turn left along the Sa Figuera road, on the south side of the river. (This is a double street with a canopy in the middle, over the river bed.) At the hamlet of Sa Figuera the road bends round to the right and passes a large house with a sign on the gate advertising fresh oranges for sale. (These are more expensive than those in the shops, but every one still has stalks and leaves attached and they are delicious.) After a few minutes go straight on at the junction with the Son Llampais road on the right. After a fairly level section the road climbs steadily uphill to the Coll d'en Marques.

Now follow the road downhill until it meets the C710, unfortunately passing the eyesore of Soller's rubbish tips on the way. The new road has destroyed the old lane so badly that it is best to walk down the main road now as far as the Sa Taulera restaurant at K51. Turn left opposite the restaurant and follow this winding lane, until it meets another road and turn left here to pass the football field. Go straight on over the bridge, and along the Avenue des Asturias, bending left along the Avenue de la Victoria to join the Calle de Sa Lluna. Turn right to reach the main square, the Plaza de la Constitució.

Puerto Soller - Coll d'en Marques	55min
Coll d'en Marques - Sa Taulera	30min
Sa Taulera - Soller, main square	40min

(An alternative is to return to Puerto Soller by the Son Llampalles road, Walk 51. In this case turn right along the C710 at Sa Teulera, then the next turn right at a crossroads.)

50. FORNALUTX

The village of Fornalutx is one of the most attractive in Mallorca. It is very old, with picturesque buildings in narrow stepped streets and well worth allowing several hours to look round.

The excursion begins among typical Soller houses, then follows a narrow path up to Binibassi with its splendid 14th century mansion and where the oranges are reputed to be the best in Spain. The path leads through olive terraces to Fornalutx, in the centre of which is a small square with a fountain. One of the shops in the square sells a small booklet in English describing the old customs and way of life as remembered by one of the older inhabitants.

The *Monumento*, where the walk begins, is a prominent landmark between Soller and Puerto Soller, at the junction of the C710 with the road linking the port and the town. The tram (or bus) stops here.

Type of walk: Easy, on country lanes and easy paths.

Starting point:	Monumento
Time:	2hr
Distance:	8km
Highest point reached:	150m

177

Total height climbed:	130m
Grade:	C
Map:	Soller 1:25,000

From the *Monumento* walk towards Soller on the old road and turn left along Calle Rvdo. Miguel Rosello, towards the church of Nuestra Senora de la Victoria. Turn right at the church, then continue straight on at an off-set crossroads where the road bends to the left. Bend right a little further on and continue to the far corner of the football field. Turn left here along the narrow road between the football field and the river. When the bridge is reached, don't cross it but continue to follow the track which bends left then right. At the next junction, go straight on, ignoring both the left fork and the path turning sharp right.

Ten minutes later turn left up a narrow path which begins by a large carob tree at a bend in the road. A blue painted arrow points the way. After a few minutes take a right turn at a path junction and in a further few minutes Binibassi will be reached. A stepped path begins on the left, between two of the buildings and by a channel of water flowing from the Binibassi spring. Blue and red arrows are painted on the wall and the way goes through a gate with a 'no dogs' sign. After about ten minutes turn right and go through a wall at a place marked by cairns. This path descends through olive terraces to arrive in Fornalutx by the cemetery. Continue into the centre of the village past the sports field to reach the main square.

Leave Fornalutx by the main road towards Soller but after a few minutes turn left along a narrow lane signposted to Biniaraix. This leads to the top end of the little village near the public washplace. There are two ways through Biniaraix, one a road and the other a stepped lane, where unsuspecting tourists sometimes get into difficulties with cars. Return to Soller by the road.

Monumento - Binibassi	50min
Binibassi - Fornalutx	20min
Fornalutx - Biniaraix	20min
Biniaraix - Soller	30min

51. SON LLAMPALLES AND SA FIGUERA

This is a short easy walk between the town and the port of Soller, through typical Mallorquin countryside and with attractive views over to the sea. It can be shortened by starting from the *Monumento*, reached by public transport, or combined with Walk 49 to make a longer circular walk.

Type of walk: Easy, all on country lanes.

Starting point:	Soller, main square
Time:	2hr 10min
Distance:	6.5km
Highest point reached:	115m
Total height climbed:	100m
Grade:	C
Map:	Soller 1:25,000

From the main square take the Biniaraix road, the Calle de Sa Lluna, and turn left along the Calle de Sa Victoria. Fork right just before a bridge and continue along the Avenue des Astorias to the football field. Just past the field take the left fork and follow this rather winding road. Where it takes a sharp bend left, keep straight on past the church to meet the main road, the C710.

Cross the C710 and start walking along the narrow country lane towards some houses. Fork right along a minor track by a small house. This bends to the left where another track signposted to the Bar Estar goes off on the right. Fork left by another signpost to an artists' studio on the right. The track now begins to climb gently up a wooded hill at the top of which is a junction. Take the left fork, which begins to go downhill and through a gate. This very pleasant track goes past the houses of Son Llampalles where the view down to the sea opens up. It is only a short distance down to the port at this point, but there is no way down. Instead the road winds along through olive terraces to join the Coll d'en Marques road at K3.2. Turn left here to reach Sa Figuera, where there is a farm selling freshly picked oranges. Continue along the country road to arrive at the seafront, where the bus and tram stop will be found a short distance to the right.

Soller - C710	40min
C710 - Son Llampalles	40min
Son Llampalles - Puerto Soller	50min

52. SES PUNTES AND TORRE PICADA

Ses Puntes are two rocky points jutting out into the sea on the wild coastline north of Soller. There are views of some impressive cliffs and the small island of S'Illeta. An idyllic place for picnics or fishing, regrettably somewhat spoilt by litter. The Torre Picada is one of the old coastal watch towers, at present closed to visitors. The area surrounding it is a natural rock garden on the edge of the cliffs, with beautiful pink flowers of sage-leaved cistus, rosemary, asphodels and many other plants.

This walk may easily be extended by continuing along the road from the Coll d'es Figueral towards the small island S'Illeta and returning the same way.

Type of walk: Short and easy, mainly on lanes and tracks, but the narrow path from the the Coll d'es Figueral down to the sea is a little steep and stony.

Starting point:	Tram terminus, Puerto Soller
Time:	1hr 50min
Distance:	5km
Highest point reached:	151m
Total height climbed:	255m
Grade:	C
Map:	Soller 1:25,000

From the bus and tram stop walk south along the sea front as far as the Sa Figuera road, a double street with the river in the centre. Turn left here, on the left (or true right) side of the river and follow the road up to the Carrer de Belgique. At the first very sharp bend of this new road go straight on through an open gateway and up a narrow lane which leads directly to the Coll d'es Figueral.

At the col go through a gateway and take the track directly in front descending through woodland towards the sea. It leads in ten minutes to an old lime oven by a stream-bed. Either follow the stream down, or turn right and then first left down a narrow path marked by a cairn. This way leads to a little col behind the Grossa Punta.

To reach the Torre, retrace your steps up to the Coll d'es Figueral and turn right to follow the wide track which leads directly to it. If preferred there is a short cut up through the woods from here which rejoins the main track at a junction with an olive tree in the middle of the road.

The return route to Puerto Soller can be varied. One way is to go back down the track to the junction with the olive tree and turn right. This wide track descends very gradually in big bends. A cairn marks the place where a short cut can be taken to avoid a long descent and re-ascent. When the bottom stretch of road is reached turn right, passing a locked gate which keeps traffic out but allows walkers through. (In 1990 the pedestrian access had been bricked off, but it was still possible to squeeze round the outside edge.)

Another way to reach this point is to go directly south from the tower, following a red earth path that meets the wide track 200m from the locked gate. Keep straight on past a conspicuous round building and the Atalaya Club. Follow this road down through the built up area and past the restaurant 'El Pescador' to the sea front, then turn left to reach the starting point.

Tram stop - Coll d'es Figueral	30min
Col - Ses Puntes	15min
Ses Puntes - Torre Picada	35min
Torre - Tram stop	30min

53. THE LIGHTHOUSE AND PUNTA DE SOLLER

The aim of this excursion is to reach two spectacular viewpoints on the very edge of the cliffs. There are excellent views of mountains and sea. Although only a short distance from the busy resort of Puerto Soller, this area is tranquil and quite wild. In early spring there are hundreds of bright yellow-green euphorbias, with white and pink cistus and blue rosemary flowers scattered among them.

Type of walk: Short and easy. Tarmac road to the lighthouse; then a broad track and finally a short distance on a rough and rocky path.

Starting point:	Tram terminus, Puerto Soller
Time:	3hr
Distance:	6km
Highest point reached:	124m
Total height gained:	224m
Grade:	C+
Map:	Soller 1:25,000

Walk south along the sea front and cross the river by the footbridge. Follow the road which climbs steadily uphill right round the harbour to the lighthouse, overlooking the sea all the way. The track begins between the lighthouse on the right and an abandoned military building on the left.

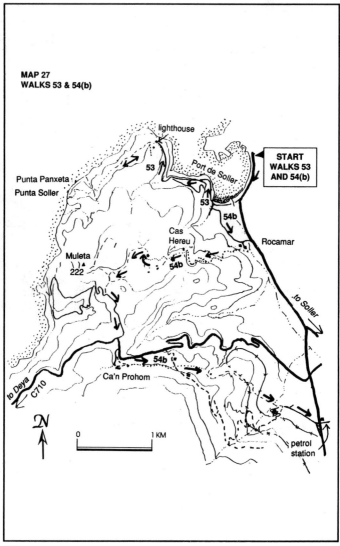

MAP 27
WALKS 53 & 54(b)

lighthouse

53

Punta Panxeta
Punta Soller

Port de Soller

START
WALKS 53
AND 54(b)

53

54b

Rocamar

Cas
Hereu

54b

Muleta
222

to Soller

54b

Ca'n Prohom

to Deya
C710

𝒩

0   1 KM

petrol
station

Punta Panxeta (Kevin Parker)

Two locked chains prevent the gate being opened and access is by ducking between them. Ignore two forks to the left and after 20 minutes a ruined lime-oven will be reached. At this point there is a large fallen tree across the track, which has now become a narrow path. Continue along this for several minutes, horizontally at first and then beginning to descend slightly. Here numerous fallen trees have obscured the way and there are several variations marked by small cairns. Leave the path and cross this area diagonally to the right, where a little search will reveal a very ruinous lime-oven overgrown by trees. The path may be picked up again before it descends in zigzags to a dry stream bed, which is reached only ten minutes after passing the first kiln.

Ten minutes further on the path goes through a gap in a low wall, then rises to a viewpoint on the cliff edge near an impressive overhanging rock. The continuation, marked by cairns, goes up from here, partly on rocky slabs, to reach a higher viewpoint with good views both north and south along the coast. The end of the route is marked by a small red paint sign on a rock, a cross surrounded by a circle.

Return is by the same way.

Puerto Soller - Lighthouse	45min
Lighthouse - Punta de Soller	45min
Punta de Soller - Puerto Soller	1hr 30 min

54(a). SOLLER TO DEYA BY THE CAMI DEL CASTELLO

Between Soller and Deyà some of the high tops of the Tramuntana are only about 2km from the sea. This linear walk explores the delightful area between the mountains and the sea, using old tracks and paths, not all of which are shown on the maps. There are some lovely views of the coast and there is time to look round the attractive village of Deyà.

In winter an early start is recommended as the bus returns from Deyà at 3.45 pm and the next one is at 7.45. In summer the times are 5.00 pm and 8.15 pm.

Type of walk: Fairly easy, mainly on good paths. There is a fairly steep uphill section towards the end, and attention to route-finding is necessary in places. For an alternative start for this walk see 54(b).

Starting point:	Soller, petrol station on by-pass road
Time:	3hr 30min

Distance:	11km
Highest point reached:	c.400m
Total height climbed:	400m
Grade:	B
Map:	Soller 1:25,000

Begin by the petrol station on the Soller - Puerto Soller by-pass road. Go up the road opposite which bends right and in a few minutes go straight on along a narrow path at a point where the main track bends sharp left. The path crosses a stream-bed then rises up an impressive flight of old steps that crosses over the rail track near a tunnel. A few minutes later a branch path will be noticed on the left, but keep straight on here. Ten minutes later the path inexplicably becomes a surfaced road for a few metres, then reverts to a path. Five minutes later go through a gate, and another five minutes after that ignore a right turn. Five minutes later still go through another gate to arrive at a crossroads. An engraved stone here shows the way to Deyà is straight on, and another points back to Soller. The path now bends right and after about 80m there is a right fork onto another path. This path traverses along terraces just outside the boundary wall of the Ca'n Carabasseta estate. There are several gates, which must all be closed. When the Castello is reached there are some large signs explaining that the path has been restored by the Govern Balear and the School of Stonemasons. Go straight on through the gate following the newly engraved signs past the old hermitage to the large farm Ca'n Prohom.

A signpost on a corner of the building points the way to Deyà. The track curves round a large threshing floor and leads to a field gate. Do not go through this gate, and do not turn into the field just before it, but carefully open up the fence on the right of the gate to gain access to a narrow path next to the wall. After about 200m the path goes through a gate to enter a wood and continues in the same direction. Half an hour later the path is cut by a new road near some houses but continues on the other side. (Shortly after crossing this road a short diversion on the right can be made to a spring, reached by a signposted path in 25m. The water in this spring is not flowing strongly and may need sterilising tablets.) Continue along the main path and after passing a row of houses look out for a path junction, ignoring the first set of steps leading only to terraces, but taking a sharp left turn up the second flight of stone steps, where there are several cairns. (The path which goes straight on leads down to the main road near Lluc-Alcari and the walk can be shortened

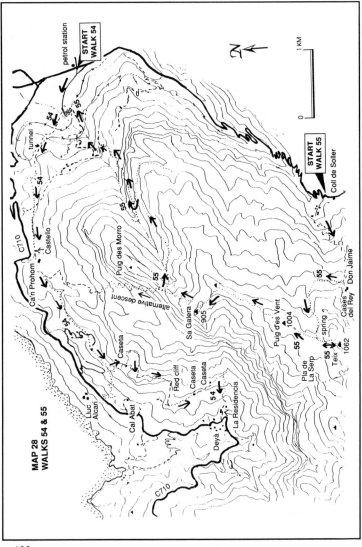

MAP 28
WALKS 54 & 55

in this way.)

This path rises up to about 400m, levelling out after about 15 minutes and passing a *caseta*, or small fieldhouse. Go through a gate here and follow the path up through cultivated terraces in a wide upland valley. At first the path goes straight on at the side of a fence, then sweeps back left and goes up a series of ramps connecting the terraces. Be careful to stick to this path which leads at the top of the terraces to a gate which is fastened up. Do not climb this gate but go down to the right and then back left and under a wooden beam. Cross the terrace ahead and go into the woods through a gap in the wall. After this the track contours to reach a small flat area on a broad shoulder before descending towards a red and crumbling cliff.

After passing this cliff the track makes a left turn and goes through a gateway into an area of open terraces where the rooftops of Deyà are visible ahead. In 1990 this area had been recently levelled, giving rise to speculation about future building development. At this point, although so near the destination, route-finding is quite difficult and it is surprisingly easy to lose the way.

Avoid following the more obvious track which doubles back right to go through a gateway and eventually reaches a private house, Ca'n L'Abat, on the main Soller - Deyà road. Instead, turn left and keep roughly on the same level along a terrace just above a pipeline to reach a *caseta*. Go through the wooden gate and carry on, slightly uphill and still following the pipeline, towards the valley head along a faint path with some cairns. Look out for a cairn indicating a right turn away from the pipeline. There is a confusion of paths here and the main thing is to keep roughly on the same level passing below another *caseta*. The aim is to reach a wooden gate in a stone wall. Follow the path along to reach an old stone track leading to a red dirt road. This descends to pass a large hotel, La Residencia, before arriving in the village by a phone box. (N.B. If reversing this walk, look out for the left fork from the red dirt road onto the old stone track. After reaching the terraces, avoid going straight ahead through the gateway which leads to Ca'n L'Abat, but take the less distinct track which bends back right and climbs up towards the red cliff.)

Soller - Ca'n Prohom	1hr 15min
Ca'n Prohom - Deyà	2hr 15min

54(b). PUERTO SOLLER TO SOLLER BY THE CAMI DE CASTELLO
(See map p182)

This delightful and undemanding walk is ideal for a hot day. It makes use of an old cobbled track not marked on the maps to go up onto the Muleta plateau with excellent sea views. A level easy track leads through fields of olives and joins the Castello track near Ca'n Prohom. The descent by the old Cami De Castello path gives excellent views over Soller to Mitx Dia, L'Ofre, Cornadors and Alfabia. A cold refreshing drink in the square and a return to the port by the old-fashioned tram make an attractive finish to this walk.

Type of walk: Easy, along reasonably well-defined paths and tracks and with no steep gradients.

Starting point:	Tram terminus, Puerto Soller
Time:	3hr 45min
Distance:	10km
Highest point reached:	260m
Total height climbed:	275m
Grade:	C
Map:	Soller 1:25,000

From the tram terminus in Puerto Soller walk south along the sea front and over the footbridge. Turn left at the first road by the Bar Las Delicias and continue along to the Hotel Rocamar, a big place easily seen from the road to the port from Soller. Turn right up to the hotel then left in front of it until the track ends in a rough parking area about 150m past the hotel. On the right will be found an old mule track doubling back up behind the hotel. Follow this up first through woods and then some olive terraces, passing through several gates which need to be kept closed because of livestock. Some red and green painted arrows and yellow paint marks show the way. A little stream is crossed by a bridge and the path then contours back into a gully.

After about 35 minutes a small farm is reached. There is a huge olive tree in the middle of the track and a blue arrow on the wall to the right of the tree shows the continuation of the track. Five minutes later bear right, go through a gate and cross a stream-bed. The track now goes up through olive terraces, and becomes a little indistinct. In fact there are two ways here. Either go right then back left parallel to a wall, or straight on across rocky ground.

A wooden signpost to Deyà on one of the trees points to a gate. Go through this gate and keep close to the wall to reach a group of buildings, one of them very large and with a tower. The path curves right behind the end house and then goes through a double wooden gate. There is a sign on the pigsty here pointing back to Puerto Soller. A blue arrow on the corner of the tower points towards a green metal gate. Go through this gate and turn left at a cross roads, through a gateway marked with a red arrow.

The track now winds between olive terraces, making several sharp bends, to reach a T-junction at an open gateway. Turn left here and follow the road round to reach the main Deyà road. Turn left towards Soller and in about 100m turn right again up a cart track signposted to Ca'n Prohom. This is a private road but at the second bend on the left is a public footpath marked by an engraved stone. A second engraved stone shows the way up to an old hermitage, the Castello, where the path joins one coming up from Soller. At this point there are notices explaining that this old path has been restored by the Govern Balear and the School of Stonemasons.

If this approach is being used as an alternative start to the Soller-Deyà walk, turn right to reach Ca'n Prohom. To continue the walk to Soller, turn left along the path outside the wall of the Ca'n Carabasseta estate. In about 20 minutes go straight on at a cross-track where there are more engraved signs to Soller and Deyà. Five minutes later ignore a left turn and in another five minutes bear left where the track appears to go into a field. The path then goes through a gate outside a boundary wall. Further on the track has been surfaced, but soon reverts to the old cobbled track with steps. It crosses the railway track and then descends to cross a stream-bed. Keep straight on and follow the road round to reach the main road opposite the petrol station. Go down the narrow street ahead and after several twists and turns the main square will be reached.

Puerto Soller - Castello	1hr 45min
Castello - Soller	2hr

55. TEIX AND SA GALERA

Teix is a popular mountain, easily ascended from either Valldemossa or the Coll de Soller, but Sa Galera is rarely visited. The views are extensive and this is a long and interesting walk. From Teix the blue Mediterranean can be seen on both sides of the island, with the main chain of the Tramuntana stretching out on the other side of the col and beyond it the central plain and the hills of the east. Sa Galera itself is an outstanding natural *mirador*, giving almost a birds-eye view of Deyà and the coast between Deyà and Puerto Soller. A high level ridge including the Puig des Vent connects Teix with Sa Galera. There is evidence that this stony, arid area was at one time cultivated and possibly even inhabited during the summer months, with some terracing, buildings that were once roofed and even a threshing floor at an altitude of almost 1,000m.

A taxi or a lift is needed to reach the starting point on the Coll de Soller as there is no bus service over the col. A taxi is not too expensive, especially if four people share; certainly cheaper than hiring a car for the day.

Alternatively, a bus can be taken from Puerto Soller to Valldemossa and the Pla de la Serp reached by one of several possible routes. These are described in a note at the end.

Type of walk: A large part of the route is trackless and it is not recommended in mist. Route-finding on the descent from Sa Galera is not easy, as there only seems to be one way down the line of encircling cliffs.

Starting point:	Coll de Soller
Time:	6hr 30min
Distance:	12km
Highest point reached:	1,062m
Total height climbed:	622m up, 938m down
Grade:	A+
Map:	Alaró 1:25,000 and
	Soller 1:25,000

The walk begins at a bend in the road a little below the col on the Soller side where a surfaced road leads to the Cases d'es Teix and a water bottling plant. After passing in front of the bottling plant bear right and go through an iron gate, behind which are chained dogs. Follow the stony track which leads up through the oakwoods to the Cases del Rey D.Jaime, passing a spring on the right. Many remains of *sitjes* will be noticed in the woods. The three houses lie on a little plateau. Go through the iron gate with a 'please close' notice in five languages and turn sharp right by the fence. The path now contours in a roughly northerly direction for about 600m, when it turns to the west and rises up at the side of a stream. On the whole it is easy to follow, but look out for a place where it doubles back left at a water trough. Oaks give way to pines and open ground is reached before the path leads to a small plateau on the north side of Teix. This is the Pla de la Serp, where there is a spring with good drinking water in a stone trough.

A good path marked by cairns leads from the spring to the top of Teix by way of a small col between Teix and Teixoch. (Teix has the trig point: Teixoch to the north is the same height; older maps had it one metre higher.)

Return to the Font de la Serp by the same path. (The direction is north, should the clouds descend). From the spring cross the little plain and go up on to the ridge beyond. Several ways can be found, starting near a ruined building at the foot of the Puig d'es Vent. Once up on the high ground, which is very stony and arid, the way is marked by paint spots and a few cairns. The route passes a ruined hut, some enclosures and a threshing floor in a very windy spot.

Either go over the top of the Puig d'es Vent, marked as Cañizo on some maps, (1,004m) or keep on the east side of it. A slight descent leads to a gap in a stone wall, after which the ridge narrows a little and the walking becomes easier over solid rocks instead of loose stones. Continue along the ridge until the subsidiary ridge leading out west to Sa Galera is reached. This is almost at a right angle to the main ridge and some cairns will be found marking the way to the white column of the trig point.

A wide tree-filled valley, the Coma de s'Ombra, goes down from Sa Galera in a north-easterly direction. The stream in the centre of this valley is known as the Torrent des Cinc Ponts (five bridges). The descent makes use of some old and rather disused tracks here. Start the descent by first following a narrow path marked by cairns and beginning almost at the summit. This leads down left (north-east) to the col at c.750m between Galera and the Puig d'es Moro. There is a wall running along the col parallel to the ridge, with a fenced-off opening, on the other side of which is a good view down to the coast. This is an alternative way down, to Ca'n Prohom and Soller or Puerto Soller, described later.

To continue the descent turn right at the col and go down in roughly the centre of the valley floor on a poorly defined path with a few cairns. About ten minutes after leaving the col a *sitja* and a ruined building will be reached. From this point a well-made but overgrown cart track leads down the valley on its right hand side. Follow this to the right for about 25 minutes, looking out for a cairn at the end of an uphill section some 200m long. The main track bends to the right at this point. Turn left at this cairn down a track which zigzags down towards the valley floor. Avoid two turnings off this track, the first leading up the valley and the second heading downwards. After a further few minutes the track becomes less well-defined whilst heading up the valley, but continue to follow its line and it soon leads to a broken-down brushwood fence. Step over this and

191

turn immediately right down the valley until another little path is found. This zigzags steeply down to a small enclosure, which has a stile made of branches on the far side. After a further short descent, there is a post in the middle of the path which may once have been an indicator. The track left crosses the stream and leads to some terraces, but we turn right, keeping on the right-hand side of the stream and passing between two small buildings, after which the path improves. Rising slightly the path goes through a gate with an access stile and a 'private hunting' sign.

A very attractive path now leads below an impressive overhanging cliff, the Cingle de Ca'n Canals, then down through terraces of olives. Some curious buildings will be seen further down, built under overhanging rocks. It is now a question of following the main track down towards Soller. This becomes a drivable road from the 'cave houses' and winds back and forth between terraces. Go through a gate by a water tank, turn left and cross a bridge, then turn immediately right. After going under the railway viaduct there is a T-junction. Go through another gate here and turn right. Follow this lane to meet the Soller by-pass road near the petrol station.

Coll de Soller - Cases de Rey D.Jaime	1hr
Cases - Teix	1hr
Teix - Sa Galera	1hr 30min
Sa Galera - Cingle de Ca'n Canals	1hr 40min
Cingle de Ca'n Canals - Soller	1hr 20min

Alternative start from Valldemossa
This is the recommended way because it includes the "Camino del Archiduque", but it adds 4km and c.90m of ascent to the route. (See Walk 57 for Cairats valley approach.)

From the bus stop in Valldemossa walk along the main road towards Palma, turning left just before Son Gual, a large house with a tower. Take the first turn right up through a new housing development. At the top of the hill there is a sign on a lamppost which reads "PUJADA EN ES TEIX, MIRADOR DE SES PUNTES, CAMI D'ES POUET". Follow the red arrow, first left then curving right to reach the start of the path. This goes towards a conspicuous group of umbrella pines, but branches left before reaching them at a rock painted with a yellow 'U'. The track is an old charcoal burners route zigzagging up through the woods of evergreen oaks, going through a couple of ruined gates. Forty-five minutes after the start of the walk a red spot marks a short cut on the right which rejoins the track about ten minutes later. Almost immediately go through a boundary wall to reach a flattish area of fairly open ground, the Pla d'es Pouet. There is a multitude of paths and tracks in this area where it is very easy to take the wrong one.

Ignore the first tracks going both left and right, and keep straight on across the clearing for about 80m until you reach a fork. Take the left fork across a *sitja* and in five minutes reach another clearing at the end of which is the polluted Es Pouet well. Three paths begin near here. One goes left to the Mirador de Ses Puntes (the way of return on Walk 57). One on the right goes to the Pla d'es Aritges and is a shorter way to Teix but misses out the spectacular archduke's path. Take the middle way which leads up to the Coll de S'Estret. There are some stone seats here and some red paint signs to Deyà and Teix. Turn right and follow the path leading steeply up to reach the magnificent wide track built by the archduke. This continues along the very edge of the steep cliffs overlooking Deyà, passing Puig Caragoli, a splendid high viewpoint on the cliff top, and on to the plain of Ses Aritges.

Turn left at a wooden signpost "Al TEIX". The path goes up steeply at first, then in ten minutes crosses a boundary wall with a large ICONA sign. Cross the "Pla de Sa Serp" towards the spring, the "Font de Sa Serp", which is reached on the ascent from the Coll de Soller. Before reaching this point you can look out for sheep tracks to use as short cuts up to the col between Teix and Teixoch.

Alternative descent to Ca'n Prohom and Puerto Soller

At the col between Sa Galera and the Puig des Moro, go over the wooden branches blocking the gateway. Turn right by the wall and in ten metres find the beginning of the descent path on the left, marked by cairns. The path is easy to follow with cairns and paintmarks, except occasionally where a fallen tree has obscured it. There are sections where it contours and others where it zigzags down between impressive cliffs. Eventually it reaches a flat area of the forest and becomes a wide track. Two minutes after passing a 'porxo' or shelter it goes through a wall and meets a wide cross track at an angle. Turn right here and about fifteen minutes later note a rising path on the left at the side of a *sitja*. This branch leads to Deyà. 200m further on go through a gate and follow the wide track down to Ca'n Prohom. Follow Walk 54(a) to Soller, or reverse the first part to arrive at the Port by the Rocamar hotel.

56. PUNTA DE SA FOREDADA

A pleasant coastal walk from near Valldemossa to a spectacular prominent rocky peninsula pierced with a large natural hole, La Foredada. This can easily be seen from the coastal road near Deyà or from the mirador at Son Marroig. Son Marroig was once the property of the archduke Luis Salvador, and is now a museum worth visiting if time is available. (There is a snack bar on the mirador which closes at 5.30 pm.)

If possible, it is best to use a car to Son Marroig, at K66 on the C710, then take the bus to K71.3, which is the junction with the Esporles road just outside Valldemossa, so as not to be limited by the bus time at the end of the day. It is quite feasible to do the walk by taking the 9.30 am bus from Puerto Soller and returning from Son Marroig at about 3.35 pm (3.30 pm bus from Valldemossa). However, this does not leave much time for full enjoyment of the most interesting part of the walk. Taking a taxi from Valldemossa to the Font Figuera gate is well worth considering and also has the advantage of cutting out the road walking section.

Another option would be to drive to the Port of Valldemossa then walk to the last headland where the path disappears. Returning the same way gives a very easy walk of about three hours. Another day or half day could then be spent walking down to La Foredada and back from the mirador. In this case permission should be sought at the house. The way down is over a vertical metal stile at the side of a double gate and thereafter is obvious.

Type of walk: Very easy, except for a 1km stretch near La Foredada. The path has disintegrated here and some care is required, whether clambering over boulders or negotiating the narrow remains of the path. It is this section only which gives the walk a B+ grade.

Starting point:	K71.3 near Valldemossa
Time:	5hr 10min
Distance:	12 km
Total height climbed:	Descent 380m, ascent 300m
Grade:	B+
Map:	Soller 1:50,000

From the Deyà-Esporles road junction walk towards Esporles, then turn first right towards the Port de Valldemossa. This pleasant narrow road descends in zigzags with some entrancing views of the cliffs and the little marina. At K4 turn right along a good cart-track starting at a double bend. There is a double metal gate with pedestrian access on the left and the

194

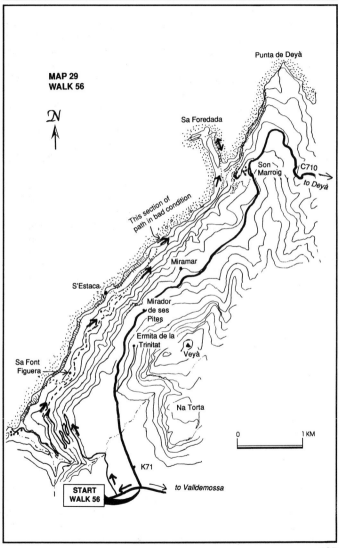

MAP 29
WALK 56

𝒩

Punta de Deyà

Sa Foredada

Son Marroig

C710
to Deyà

This section of
path in bad condition

Miramar

S'Estaca

Mirador
de ses
Pites

Ermita de la
Trinitat

Veyà

Sa Font
Figuera

Na Torta

0   1 KM

K71

START
WALK 56

to Valldemossa

sign on the gate reads 'S'Estaca FONT FIGUERA'. This good level track leads at first through pinewoods and then more open ground with views of the sea. The houses of S'Estaca and Font Figuera are passed, going through another locked gate with pedestrian access.

Further on the road goes down left towards a chained gateway, but the old track continues in the same direction, by a red sign saying 'Fora' and an arrow. The wide track soon ends at a stile, but a narrow path continues, contouring into a re-entrant and then passing a *sitja* and bending left to arrive at a pine-covered headland. There is a picnic place where a stone table has been built between two large rocks. This potentially attractive place has been ruined by an extraordinary amount of litter.

It is at this point that the path deteriorates. Find a way down on to the rocks near sea level, and then make your way along boulders and the remains of the old path until this improves just before the col between the Foredada peninsula and the main coastline. If you are not tied to catching a bus, then you will be able to enjoy the easy walk out to the Foredada. There is a sort of shelter with a roof of pine branches built into the rock near where the track crosses a narrow neck before the final climb to the rock. This is a steep but short little scramble and on the top a path can be found leading to the white column over the hole. (The descent to the hole involves rock climbing and should not be attempted.)

K71.3 - Font Figuera gate	1hr 15min
Font Figuera gate - picnic table	1hr
Picnic table - Foredada path	1hr 15min
Foredada path - Foredada	40min
Foredada - Son Marroig	1hr

57. THE ARCHDUKE'S WALK AND TEIX

The archduke Luis Salvador (Ludwig Salvator is the original form of his name) of Hapsburgo-Lorena came to Mallorca on a visit in 1867 and liked it so much he later came to the island to live, settling at the finca of Miramar near Valldemossa. He was a great benefactor of the island and a very early conservationist; he restored old buildings and did not allow trees and shrubs to be cut down on his properties. He made a marvellous garden at Miramar with native Mallorquin plants and wrote a treatise on the island which dealt with almost every aspect including natural history, economy, language and folklore. One of his properties was Son Moragues, which was bought by ICONA in 1979 and turned over to public use. It is a centre for nature conservation and very carefully managed, with strict

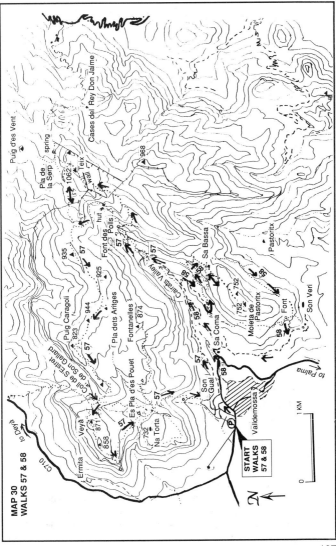

MAP 30
WALKS 57 & 58

START
WALKS
57 & 58

to Deyà

to Palma

Valldemossa

Puig d'es Vent

C710

Càses del Rey Don Jaime

Pla de la Serp

spring

wall

Teix

1062

1106

968

935

925

944

823

Puig Caragoli

Pla dets Aritges

Fontanelles

874

Coll de S'Estret de Son Gallard

Ermita

Veyà

871

858

Es Pla d'es Pouet

Na Torta

732

Font des Polis

hut

Calarts Valley

Sa Bassa

Sa Coma

Son Gual

Pastoritx

Moleta de Pastoritx

752

752

752

Font

Son Veri

57

57

57

57

57

57

57

57

57

58

58

58

58

58

58

58

58

58

58

1 KM

0

N

rules to protect plants and animals and guard against fire.

One of the archduke's achievements of great benefit to walkers was the construction of excellent paths on the Son Moragues estate, in spectacular situations along the edges of high cliffs looking down to Deyà and the coast. Luis Salvador had these built so that he could walk or ride here and enjoy the views without danger or difficulty. To follow in his footsteps is an enjoyable and exhilarating experience and provides one of the best walks on the island. The route described here is quite long and strenuous, but it could easily be split into two or even three shorter walks to allow more time for appreciation of the scenery. One suggestion is to spend a day on the ascent of Teix by the Serra des Cairats, described later, and devote another day to the round walk excluding Teix.

A further interest in this area is the open-air museum provided by ICONA in the Cairats valley, where there is a restored lime kiln, a snow-house and a *sitja* with logs piled up as though ready for charcoaling. All these and more are described in a little booklet with many illustrations. (See reading list.)

ICONA have also provided an attractive picnic place at the Font d'es Poll or Poplars' Well, with wooden tables and seats. A little higher up is a hut where overnight stops can be made. It is equipped with tables and benches and has an enormous fireplace across one corner. The walls are decorated with coloured posters showing plants and animals. This hut was originally the living quarters of the *nevaters* or snow collectors. The *casa de sa neu* nearby is an enormous pit 24m x 8m.

Incidentally the name Teix means yew in Catalan, and there are a number of yew trees, quite rare today in Mallorca, growing on the slopes of the mountain.

Starting point:	Son Gual, Valldemossa
Time:	6hr 10min
Distance:	16km
Highest point reached:	1,062m
Total height climbed:	790m
Grade:	B+
Map:	Esporles 1:25,000 and Alaró 1:25,000

Park in the main carpark on the outskirts of Valldemossa. Walk along the main road towards Palma and take the first wide street on the left and then turn first right. Alternatively continue along the main road for a further

100m and turn left up some old stone steps. From Son Gual, the large house with the tower, walk along a road called Luis Vives, parallel to the main road at first. After passing some new houses the track goes through a gateway into the Cairats valley. It is joined by another track from Sa Coma after crossing a cattle grid in the valley bottom. Further up the Son Moragues estate is entered by a stile next to a locked gate. There is an information board and, higher up, signposts to the points of interest.

The track rises quite steeply before reaching the Font d'es Poll and ten minutes further on arrives at the shelter. The road ends by the snow-pit and the walk then continues along the archduke's path. The signpost for Teix is reached in about 20 minutes. This path leaves the archduke's path on the right and after ten minutes crosses a boundary wall by a stile It leads easily in another ten minutes up to a small plain, the Pla de Sa Serp, where there is a spring. Before reaching the spring a branch path marked by red paint signs slants up right to the col between Teix and Teixoch, then to the top of Teix with its two iron crosses. Return to the archduke's path to continue the walk.

The next point of interest is a *mirador* on the edge of the cliffs overlooking Deià. The path then crosses a flat area, the Pla dets Aritges, where it becomes a little indistinct (Aritges = smilax, the plant with vicious backward-pointing thorns.) The direction here is almost due west. Forty minutes from the junction with the Teix path there is a branch left which can be followed down to Es Pouet to shorten the walk. However, the main path is now especially attractive. It swings towards the Puig Caragoli, a high point with a branch path leading up to it and an excellent viewpoint. After this the path continues along the edge of the cliffs before descending towards a wooded pass, the Coll de S'Estret de Son Gallart. There are some stone seats here in the form of a 'V' and plentiful signs of the thrush-hunter's activities.

There is a path leading down to Deyà here on the right, while on the left a path descends to the Pla d'es Pouet, another way of shortening the walk. It is easy to shorten the walk inadvertently here, so if intending to continue to Veyà, then make sure to cross the col and find the path leading uphill. Keep straight on at another cross-path, looking for the cairns and paint marks leading up to an old stone shelter near the top. This is another of Luis Salvador's buildings. From the top continue along the wooded ridge, passing a trig point. This path is another of the archduke's constructions and easy to follow in spite of being somewhat overgrown by trees. The path leads to the Mirador de Ses Puntes, another impressive viewpoint on the edge of a 400m drop down to the flat plain of Valldemossa.

From the Mirador turn left along a path which passes an old bread-oven and several *sitjes* on the way to Es Pouet. At Es Pouet go straight on past the polluted well and in five minutes a clearing on level ground will be reached. Go straight on again and climb a gate in a stone wall. When a cross-track is met, go straight on down a short cut and rejoin the main track a few minutes later. The whole area is riddled with paths, but the route is now an old charcoal-burners track at a reasonable gradient. Many *sitjes* will be noticed in the forest. Look out for the red paint signs and continue down the track to the forest gate, taking advantage of the short cuts if preferred. At a wider track turn right and continue downhill to Son Gual and Valldemossa.

Son Gual - ICONA shelter	1hr
ICONA shelter - Teix	1hr
Teix - Estret de Son Gallart	2hr
Estret - Veyà	20min
Veyà - Mirador de Ses Puntes	30min
Mirador - Es Pouet	20min
Es Pouet - Son Gual	1hr

Variation: Teix by the Serra des Cairats

This alternative way up Teix is highly recommended. It begins at the Font des Polls and is signposted 'Serra des Cairats'. A wide and well-made track leads to a steep and narrow wooded valley which is surmounted in zigzags. Take a left turn where the main track goes straight on about 15-20 minutes after the start. In a further 20 minutes the track ends at a *sitja*. After this there is no path but cairns show the way up through the wood in a northerly direction to reach a wall. This is crossed by a broken fence at the point where the wall with the fence on top meets a higher wall. The way continues at right angles to the wall up stony ground. When the trees thin out and the angle eases the route continues up the right-hand side of a ridge on bare and solid rock. Cairns show the way to a gap in another wall, and when this is reached the top of Teix with its iron crosses can be seen and is easily reached

To descend, follow the paint marks down towards Teixoch and then down to the Pla de Sa Serp. (To go to the spring, take a right branch before reaching the plain.) Follow the path across the plain and over a slight rise before descending to a wall. This is crossed by a stile constructed from a forked tree. In a further ten minutes the archduke's path is met at a wooden signpost. Turn left to descend the Cairats valley, reaching the snowhouse and then the shelter in about 20 minutes. A further ten minutes and the track arrives at the Font des Polls.

Valldemossa - Font des Polls	1hr 10min
Font des Polls - Teix	1hr 15min
Teix - signpost on path	30min
Signpost on path - Valldemossa	1hr

58. SA MOLETA DE PASTORITX

This steep-sided wooded hill lies to the east of Valldemossa. It is of particular interest for the abundance of sites used by the charcoal burners. These include *sitjes*, some of them very large and prominent by reason of the bright green moss growing in a perfect circle and at least three bread-ovens in excellent repair. Although there are some panoramic views, both of Valldemossa and the peaceful valley of Pastoritx, these are only seen occasionally because of the trees. Another point of interest is the spring, the Font de Sa Predio, passed on the descent. A kind of chapel with a double arch dated 1591 has been built above it. The walk includes a complete circuit of the hill as well as an ascent and is an excellent choice when shelter is required, whether from the hot sun or a cold wind. Park in the main carpark on the west side of Valldemossa.

Type of walk: Terrain very varied, along country lanes and tracks, easy woodland paths, and a descent of a very stony disused cart-track which is quite steep. Attention must be paid to route-finding as trees frequently obscure the next objective.

Starting point:	Valldemossa
Time:	4hr 20min
Distance:	10km
Highest point:	752m
Total height climbed:	460m
Grade:	B
Map:	Esporles 1:25,000.

Walk out of Valldemossa either by the bypass road towards Palma, or by going down the main street past the post office, then bearing left to a road with a no exit sign 'Calle sin salida'. This joins the bypass road by some steps.

Turn left at the first sharp bend and follow the narrow road behind the large house Sa Coma. Turn left through a wooden gate with a pictorial 'no dogs' sign. After 1km turn right along the main Cairats valley track which comes in on the left. Approximately 150m after passing a small building turn right again. Follow this track (south west) for about 15 minutes then turn left at a T-junction. The wide track soon becomes a narrow path leading upwards through terraces. It leads to a stone stile with a gap in the fence on top, then continues to rise in the same direction, keeping below a wall which encloses a wood on the right. Go through a gap in a wall, then enter the wood by climbing steps set into another wall.

Once in the wood the path keeps ascending in the same direction to reach a cairn set on a triangular boulder between two trees. This is a key landmark, indicating a point where there is a gap in the cliffs above, not easy to spot because of the trees. There is not much of a path, but almost directly above the cairn and in a very short distance there are two places where the cliff top can be reached near a broken wall.

Cairns in the wood now show the way across a *sitja*, north-east at first, then bending sharp right to meet a track Turn right again along this track and follow it past a little clearing, then turn left at a bifurcation. Almost immediately a big empty water tank is seen on the left, next to a *sitja*, and after this a small shelter with half a roof. This is Sa Bassa, a significant reference point for the descent. Follow the path from here, rising slightly to reach in ten minutes or so a thrush-hunting structure obstructing the path. About 100m further on there is a large *sitja* and a ruined shelter. Follow the path up left from here to reach the escarpment forming the summit ridge. At this point there is another thrush-hunting station with an impressive view down to Pastoritx. Continue along the ridge to the right to reach the rather indefinite tree-screened top, noting the route carefully so as to be able to retrace your steps.

Return to Sa Bassa. From the *sitja* here go north-east on stony ground to pass yet another *sitja* and join an old cart-track at a hairpin bend. Turn right, noticing another *sitja* and a bread-oven before the track begins to descend a narrow valley in a series of bends. Ignore three turnings left and eventually go through a large opening in a wall which separates the wood from the cultivated terraces of Pastoritx. When another track is met turn right and after a further ten minutes turn right again. Now it is a stiff climb back up to re-enter the wood. A large lime kiln and a bread-oven are then seen on the right and a *sitja* on the left.

Ten minutes later go over a stile consisting of branches across a wire-netting fence with stone steps in the wall below. Descend the pleasant woodland path on the other side in a south-westerly direction. This turns right towards a wall. Go through a gap in the wall near a small stone trough. Turn right to reach the Font de Sa Predio. The path descends through a gateway then through open ground to join a road by the gates of Predio Son Veri. Turn right and follow the road back to Sa Coma and Valldemossa.

Valldemossa - Sa Bassa	1hr 40min
Sa Bassa - Moleta	25min
Moleta - Sa Bassa	20min
Sa Bassa - Son Veri spring	1hr 10min
Son Veri spring - Valldemossa	45min

CYCLAMEN BALEARICUM

59(a). GALATZO BY THE MOLETA RASA

Galatzó is the highest peak in the south-western mountains and the only one over 1,000m in this area. Because of its position it commands some outstanding views. It is seen as a prominent pyramid from many parts of the island. The most usual way up is from Son Fortuny near Estellencs by a good path and it can also be climbed from Puigpuñent or Galilea, or by a long and rather arduous route from the south, starting from the finca of Galatzó. The way described here is not so well-known but is an interesting route when combined with a descent to Son Fortuny to make a circular walk. The only disadvantage is having to walk 3km along the main road at the end of the day. This can be avoided if it is possible to use two cars and leave one in Estellencs.

Type of walk: Strenuous and with quite difficult route-finding.

Starting point:	K97, Estellencs-Andratx road
Time:	5hr 40min
Distance:	11km
Highest point reached:	1,027m
Total height climbed:	916m
Grade:	A
Map:	Sa Vileta 1:25,000 and Andratx 1:50,000

A track leaves the Estellencs-Andratx road on the left by the K97 stone and it is possible to leave a small car a little way up here. Walk up this track and after about 15 minutes another track is met at a T-junction. Turn left (east) here until a path is seen on the right (south-east) leading into a narrow valley. At this point two streams meet. The path leads at first up the right-hand stream-bed. Very soon look out for a way on the left which leads across a scree slope into the other valley. There is another path

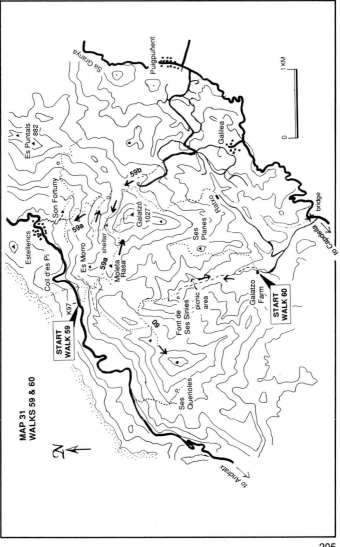

MAP 31
WALKS 59 & 60

N

Estellencs

Coll d'es Pi

K97

START
WALK 59

Es Puntals
882

Son Fortuny

59a

Es Morro

59a shelter

59a

Moleta
Rasa

Galatzó
1027

Sa Granya

59b

Puigpuñent

Galliea

Ses
Planes

Rakax

to Capdella

bridge

Ses
Sinies

Font de
Ses Sinies

picnic
area

Galatzó
Farm

START
WALK 60

60

Ses
Querioles

to Andraix

0   1 KM

here which can be followed up towards the head of the valley. When this steepens, go up obliquely to the right and a short easy scramble leads up onto a small plateau between the Peñal des Morro and the Moleta Rasa. The traces of path now become confused with animal tracks but it is not difficult to pick a way up the gently rising ridge to the top of Moleta Rasa (698m).

From this top, go down the little escarpment by an easy rock groove and continue down to the Coll de Sa Moleta Rasa, where a few pine trees provide welcome shade on hot days. From the col there is a cairned way up some bare rock ribs sloping up first to the left and then back right to regain the ridge by some pines. After this the way goes up a wide valley on the left of the ridge, making for a broad gully on the left of an obvious steep crag. Once in the gully the path becomes better and continues to the top. About five minutes before the top, a summit book is hidden under a large painted boulder. (Missing in 1991.) Paint signs show the way from here up some steepish rocks to the top.

The way down to Son Fortuny is easy to find at first, being a good path well supplied with cairns and red paint signs. It diverges from the ascent route at the bottom of the broad gully and after ten minutes reaches a large white rock with red painted arrows pointing upwards. Going down, turn sharp right here and continue horizontally before descending to a small hut. There are two paths here. Take the left one and after about three minutes turn right at a cairn. A series of zigzags leads down into a gully, part way down which a paint mark indicates another right turn at a T-junction. The path then goes through a rock cutting to enter a wide wooded valley, where it makes a gradual descent to a large *sitja*.

At the *sitja* the path turns sharp left and goes down through the forest with cairns and paint marks showing the route. Unless these are followed assiduously it is easy to wander off on one of the many paths criss-crossing the forest. At one point, well down the valley, a new track crosses the route at an open clearing and the way ahead is unclear. Turn right at a large cairn in the middle of the clearing, then left at a red paint sign where the old track can be picked up again. This old path, laid with cobbles, leads down to the large *finca* of Son Fortuny, from where the farm track can be followed down to the road. Alternatively a short cut can be taken from about half-way down, where a field path leads down the side of the stream and then crosses it to reach the old houses of Estellencs. Unless you have a car waiting for you here, the main road must now be followed back to the starting point.

K97 - Moleta Rasa	1hr 20min
Moleta Rasa - Galatzó	1hr 40min
Galatzó - Son Fortuny	1hr 40min
Son Fortuny - Estellencs	20min
Estellencs - K97	40min

59(b). GALATZO FROM PUIGPUNENT

Puigpuñent is a delightful mountain village to the east of Galatzó. It is reached by very narrow winding roads either from Sa Granja near Esporles to the north or from Capdella and Galilea to the south. Although only short, this is a highly recommended route with splendid distant views and impressive rock scenery nearer at hand. The most difficult part of the route is finding the way to the starting point from the village.

To reach the starting point, take the road west from the village by an advertisement board for the English Rose Bar and Restaurant. This is easily seen if the village is entered from the south. From the north this junction is 200m south of the junction with the Palma-Establiments road and only the back of the noticeboard is seen. Take the first two turns right, quite close together, then after some distance another right turn. Ignore the next right, turning left as indicated by a painted yellow arrow and some purple paint marks. Turn right again at a T-junction with a white house on the left. After passing two more houses on the left go past a quarry and a right fork with a chain across. 200m further on turn right again, and keep climbing steadily, ignoring a left turn, until the surfaced road ends at a rough turning place with two minor roads going off to the right. Park here.

Type of walk: Easy path through woodland at first and then open ground. A traverse path crosses below crags to the north east, then a well marked route goes up steep and rocky ground to the top.

Starting point:	See sketch-map
Time:	2hr 45min
Distance:	6km
Highest point reached:	1,027m
Total height climbed:	530m
Grade:	B+
Map:	Sa Vileta 1:50,000

Purple paint signs, a little faded, and a newly painted red arrow at the road end show the start of the route. A stone arrow and a cairn show a right turn after a few minutes, followed shortly by a left turn. A very good path continues to zigzag upwards with numerous and somewhat superfluous paint signs. There is a marker stone at the point where the east ridge of Galatzó is reached and the traverse path crossing below the impressive north-east face begins here. This rises at the end to reach a small shelter hut, the same one passed on the ascent from or descent to Estellencs.

The way up to the top continues to be well marked. At first up easy ground leading to the foot of a rocky staircase where there is a red arrow painted on a white rock. The angle eases at the top of this but continues to rise up fairly steeply to a natural rock shelter with many paint signs where there may or may not be a hidden summit book. The top is reached in five minutes by a little rock scramble, quite steep but no problems. Return the same way.

Road end - shelter hut	1hr
Hut - summit	30min
Descent	1hr 15min

Notes on other routes up Galatzó

1. There is a way up Galatzó from Galilea marked in yellow paint. The author has not done this route but met a party of German walkers in Estellencs in February 1991, one of whom was still carrying the almost empty tin of paint. This could be a good route for parties who can arrange transport at either end, but it probably joins the route from Puigpuñent described above and will therefore include a long walk on a surfaced road.

2. Galatzó can also be ascended from the south, from the finca of Galatzó. This route is also marked in yellow paint but is not very easy to follow and is rough going in the upper part. It begins to the east of the finca, passing an immense water tank, and going over a broad shoulder west of Ses Planes. After traversing into a side valley it goes steeply up to reach the south ridge slightly north of the Penyal des Ratxo. Continue up the south ridge to the top. If this way is attempted it is essential to park outside the large gates of the property or at the finca itself. The farmer does not mind people parking here, but does not want any parking on the track up to the farm. It is also expected that walkers call at the farmhouse to ask permission and explain where they want to go. (Full details of this route are not included because the author has only descended this way, and that was partly in darkness.)

3. In 1991 the ascent via the finca of Ratxo has been closed by a high

locked gate and dogs on chains across the track. It is possible that this estate may eventually be re-opened as a private park with an admission fee, but this is only speculation.

60. S'ESCLOP

S'Esclop (the name means 'the clog') is at the southernmost end of the Sierra de Tramuntana. Although under 1,000m it is wild and rough and the ascent should not be undertaken lightly. Near the summit are the ruins of a stone hut where the French scientist François Arago lived while making a triangulation to measure the meridian in 1808. The views are extensive and the approach through the estate of Galatzó with its orchards of almond trees is very beautiful. In fact it is a completely different world to the spreading urbanizations of the south coast, only a short distance away. The orchards give way to a track lined with flowering shrubs such as cistus and euphorbia and there is a picnic place with a table and fireplaces. After this it is rough going through a mountain fastness with no sound but the occasional cries of wild goats.

The Galatzó estate is private and permission to make the ascent should be requested at the farmhouse. To reach this drive towards Galilea from Capdella and just after the K2 stone turn left along a narrow unsurfaced road. Go through the impressive gates and drive up to the farm. If permission is given the car can be left in the yard and if not then not so much time will have been wasted. (This is sometimes refused, for safety reasons, if a hunting party has already been given access.) If a short and easy walk is wanted, then going to the picnic area and back is highly recommended.

Type of walk: Easy at first, then a rough path up to a ridge where the going becomes easier. A moderately easy scramble up to the top.

Starting point:	Galatzó farm
Time:	6hr 25m
Distance:	12km
Highest point reached:	916m
Total height climbed:	927m
Grade:	A
Map:	Andratx 1:50,000

The track begins at the side of the farm building opposite the point of entry. At first there are more orchards of almond trees. After about ten minutes take a right fork and follow the easy track along the valley floor. A few minutes after passing the picnic place there is a spring on the left, the Font de Ses Sinies. About 20m before this, the path to S'Esclop branches off on the right. This leads to a ravine at the head of the valley. Just at the moment when it enters the ravine look out for a cairn on the right. This indicates a path which avoids the lowest part of this ravine with its rather dense vegetation. Although this path is marked by yellow paint spots and cairns they are not always easy to see because of the large clumps of *carritx*.

After a short climb up, the route traverses into the ravine, then crosses and re-crosses the torrent bed. Higher up a group of large pine trees on the edge of a hanging valley make a welcome rest stop. From here the path continues to rise towards a rock wall at the head of the valley before veering off to the left. Keep a sharp look out for painted arrows and cairns which mark the easiest way. Eventually the angle eases off and a better path develops, leading to a col near a fenced enclosure. Here the path improves considerably and leads in about 25 minutes to another col, the Coll de Sa Font d'es Quer.

From this col the steep summit rocks can be seen ahead, with several grassy rakes sloping up diagonally from right to left. Follow traces of paths or animal tracks up towards the furthest left of these, which proves to be a reasonable route to the top. (Take note of the point of arrival on the summit ridge so as to find it easily on the way down.) Turn left to reach the top in another ten minutes. Return to the Galatzó farm by the same way.

Galatzó farm - Picnic place	45min
Picnic place - first col	1hr 45min
First col - Esclop summit	1hr 15min
Esclop summit - 1st col	45min
1st col - Picnic place	1hr 20min
Picnic place - farm	35min

61. SA TRAPA BY THE COLL DE SA GREMOLA

The area lying to the north-west of Andratx is wild and unspoilt, being devoid of the encroaching urbanizations elsewhere in the south of the island. There are two high points of interest on this walk. One is a really magnificent viewpoint on the Cap Fabioler overlooking the sea and the isle of Dragonera. The other is Sa Trapa, an abandoned Trappist monastery, now preserved and protected by GOB. There are impressively

Sa Trapa. Abandoned Trappist monastery

built terrace walls, and an old mill still with some of its machinery inside, and parts of an old irrigation system. On the edge of the cliffs is a large circular area, a popular picnic place now, which was probably an old threshing floor.

The walk does not make a complete circle and use is made of the bus which runs between San Telmo and Andratx, on Sundays only (This is time-tabled to leave at 5.15 pm, but quite frequently leaves at 5.0 pm or even earlier!) On days other than Sundays it might be best to do the walk in reverse, beginning with a taxi from Andratx to San Telmo.

Type of walk: Very easy up to Gremola on an old metalled road. Then an easy and wide cart track to Ses Basses, followed by a narrow but well-defined path all the way to Sa Trapa and San Telmo. Between Sa Trapa and the coll de Cala en Basset there is a bit of a scramble down some rock, but it is not difficult.

Starting point:	Andratx, bus station
Time:	5hr 40min
Distance:	14km
Highest point reached:	c.420m

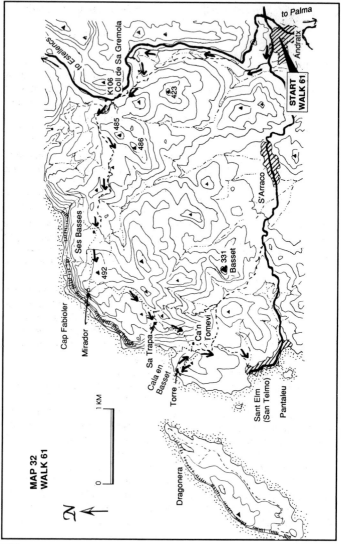

MAP 32
WALK 61

N ←

1 KM

0

to Palma

Andratx

START
WALK 61

S'Arraco

to Estellencs

K106
Coll de Sa Gremola

485
486

423

Ses Basses

492

331
Basset

Cap Fabioler

Mirador

Sa Trapa

Ca'n Tomevi

Cala en
Basset

Torre

Sant Elm
(San Telmo)

Pantaleu

Dragonera

Total height climbed:	c.480m (in reverse, 580m)
Grade:	B
Map:	Andratx 1:50,000

Walk out of Andratx on the road to San Telmo and take the first turn to the right, the Calle de Barcelona. Follow this old road up, ignoring turnings, until it makes a sharp turn right. At this point, where there are painted signs on the wall, turn left on a cart track which goes through several gates before arriving at the Coll de Sa Gremola at K106. From the clearing at the side of the road take the right-hand track, where there is a 'No entry' sign saying 'prohibido el paso, excepto proprietarios'. (This refers to cars, not walkers, so do not be concerned. The route is a well-known and popular walk. Unauthorised cars are in any case prevented from using the track by a padlocked chain a little further on.)

This track is very pleasant walking, on earth rather than stones, and contours with only a few ups and downs at about 400m. Be careful to follow the main track which is drivable to Ses Basses and which runs mainly west. Ses Basses are two houses, probably used intermittently for hunting or tending the small cultivated area below them. From the area behind and above the houses there is an excellent view back along the coast with S'Esclop in the background.

From this point there is only a narrow path which soon begins to climb up to the headland above Cap Fabioler. Do not miss the slight diversion right to the small mirador on the edge of the cliffs. The path from here now turns the corner and goes along an open hillside which in winter is covered with brilliant yellow splashes of thorny broom. Soon it descends through a pinewood to meet a wide cart-track. Turn right and in ten minutes the terraces of Sa Trapa will be reached.

To continue to San Telmo, retrace your steps up behind the large building and at the second bend follow the path off to the right. This climbs up over a bluff, then goes down the steep rocks on the other side, the exact route being quite easy and well-marked by paint signs. The path then descends through the pinewoods to reach the Coll de Cala En Basset. This area is a maze of paths and tracks. There are many short cuts, but for the easiest walking it is best to follow the main path. At a cross-track, signposted right to Cala En Basset and left to Aquamarina, go straight on to reach C'an Tomevi. Go straight on again here to reach a surfaced road, the Avenguda de la Trapa. Follow the main road along the sea front to reach the Plaza de la Caragoler and the bus stop.

Andratx - Coll de Sa Gremola	1hr 40min
Gremola - Cap Fabioler mirador	1hr 40min
Cap Fabioler - Sa Trapa	50min
Sa Trapa - San Telmo	1hr 30min

62. CAPDELLA TO ANDRATX BY THE COLL DE SA COVA

Capdella is a small quiet mountain village in an attractive setting, with almond orchards and mountain views. The old road followed over the Coll de Sa Cova goes through what is still an attractive valley, in spite of an electricity sub-station and various pylons. The track runs below the impressive cliffs of Garrafa, seen to good advantage for most of the way. Capdella is reached by bus from either Palma Nova and Santa Ponsa or from Puerto Andratx and Paguerra. There is only one bus each day so check the timetables locally.

Type of walk: Very easy, along wide tracks and roads.

Starting point:	Capdella bus stop
Time:	2hr 30min
Distance:	8km
Highest point reached:	226m
Total height climbed:	200m
Grade:	C
Map:	Andratx 1:50,000

Walk along the main road towards Andratx for about 700m. Take the third turning left along an old track, shown on the map shortly before the main road makes a 90° bend left. This track soon turns south-west and goes straight on for about 1.5km when it crosses a stream-bed and then reaches a T-junction. Turn right here and in a couple of minutes fork left along a track with a chain across it. Some ten minutes later go through a gate which is closed but not locked. After passing a large building with a guard dog up on the right, the Coll de Sa Cova is reached. There is a fence across the track, a small section of which functions as a gate.

On the other side of the pass turn right at a cross track. Ten minutes further on take a left fork at a place where there is a lime kiln in the angle between the two tracks. Ignore a sharp left turn seen in a further ten minutes. After passing a caseta, or small field house, ignore another left turn after going through a gate. When an old tarmac road is reached turn right to arrive at the Coll Andritxol. Turn right to reach the bus stop by the petrol station on the outskirts of Andratx in about ten minutes.

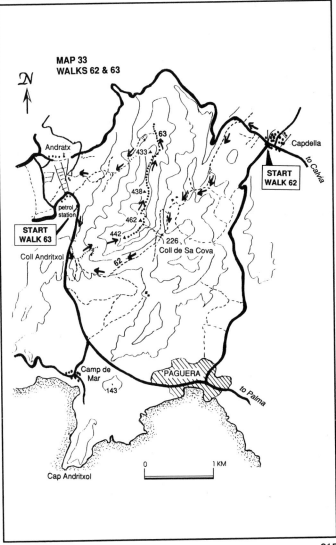

MAP 33
WALKS 62 & 63

𝒩

Andratx

63
433▲

438▲

462▲

442
226
Coll de Sa Cova

62

petrol
station

START
WALK 63

Coll Andritxol

Capdella

to Calvia

START
WALK 62

Camp de
Mar
143

PAGUERA

to Palma

0   1 KM

Cap Andritxol

63. PUIG D'EN GARRAFA

Garrafa is a low hill to the east of Andratx. It consists of a long ridge running almost north-south and has several rocky tops known as 'geps'. There are impressive cliffs on both sides but a path provides an easy walk along the ridge which is partly wooded. The top is clear of trees and is an excellent viewpoint, especially of S'Esclop and Galatzó.

Type of walk: The ascent is quite steep and the path very stony. Easy walking along a well-trodden path along the ridge is followed by an easy descent on a wide track.

Starting point:	Andratx
Time:	3hr 25min
Distance:	7km
Highest point reached:	462m
Total height climbed:	420m
Grade:	B
Map:	Andratx 1:50,000

If arriving in Andratx by car, park near the school and the bus station at the north-eastern side of the town. If by bus, ask for the 'gasolinera'.

From the petrol station, walk back up the road towards Palma and in about 15 minutes turn left along the old road, reached just before the Coll Andritxol. In about two minutes turn left along a path to a locked gate which is easily by-passed on the right. Ignore the wide track running south and take the disused track left which leads into a narrow wooded valley, the Coma de Sa Teva. The track soon narrows and becomes steeper, but is marked with cairns and paint spots. In any case it is easy to follow as it more or less keeps to the centre of the valley floor. (After heavy rain it must also function as a stream-bed.)

The path arrives on a flat top to the south-west of the main summit. This top has a large cairn and a stone with a painted red arrow showing the way back down. Follow the narrow path left to reach the main top in about 15 minutes. There is a small shelter on the top near the trig point.

Continue along the path which first descends to an obvious col with a cairn indicating an alternative way down. This could be used to shorten the excursion if required, but has not been tried personally. The main path then runs almost north along the ridge passing 'geps' of 438 and 433m, largely unseen because of the trees. After about half an hour the path begins to descend the east side of the ridge, then swings back left (west) to go through a gap in a wall and arrive at a small grassy col between pine trees. From this point a cart-track begins to descend a cultivated valley, the Coma de S'Ermita The track used to go through two gates near a small field house, but has now been diverted along a narrow fenced path outside the enclosure. It is well marked by yellow paint signs. Shortly after the diversion the main track swings left.

At the bottom of the hill turn left at a cross track. (In reverse, look out for a right turn by an olive tree with a white house on the right.) A little further another track comes in from the left. Follow the surfaced road into Andratx near a school by the Calle Juan Riera. Turn right into Carrer de Son More to reach the bus terminus.

Andratx - Coll Andritxol	15min
Coll Andritxol - south top	1hr
South top - main top	15min
Main top - end of ridge	45min
End of ridge - Andratx	1hr 10min

64. PORTALS VELLS AND PUNTA CATIUS

Portals Vells is a quiet attractive little bay with a small sandy beach protected by encircling rocks. The most remarkable feature though is the series of caverns on the south where the stone used for building Palma Cathedral was quarried out of the rock. These are best appreciated from within; there is no difficulty. On a tiny peninsula below the quarry is a small square room cut out of the rock. It was used as a fort to protect the stone workers from attack by pirates.

Punta Catius is the southern tip of the Calvia peninsula and has an old watchtower on the edge of the cliffs. On a windy day the sight of huge rolling waves breaking over the rocks below the modern lighthouse is worth seeing. Nearby is an abandoned military installation with four cannons making an interesting object of exploration. Machinery for raising shells up to the gun emplacements is still intact.

The starting point is reached by bus from either the Palma direction or from Santa Ponsa direction.

Type of walk: Easy, along dirt tracks, metalled roads and a marked path. The path requires care and a bit of clambering in one place at Cala Figuera.

Starting point:	Son Ferrer
Time:	3hr 25min
Distance:	10km

Carved rock in marble quarry, Portals Vells

Total height climbed: negligible
Grade: C+
Map: See sketch map

From Son Ferrer take the rough track running towards the wooded hill by the edge of the golf course. When the metalled road is reached follow it to the right. Turn left at the large stone sign for Portals Vells. The quarries are seen on the right as the road makes a left turn to the beach. A narrow path leads to them from the end of the sandy beach.

After visiting the caverns return along the path towards the beach, and look for a way to scramble easily up to the cliff top. Here will be found a path running south to Cala Figuera, marked by yellow paint signs. This leads first to a small headland with a deep inlet on the right. The small path bypassing this may not be noticed at first, but will be found on returning from the headland if you overshoot. This delightful path now leads south again to arrive at Cala Figuera. Here, although the descent appears a little difficult, yellow spots show an easy way along rock ledges down to the head of the cove where there are a few small boats.

The caves noticed in the cliff opposite are said to have been inhabited

218

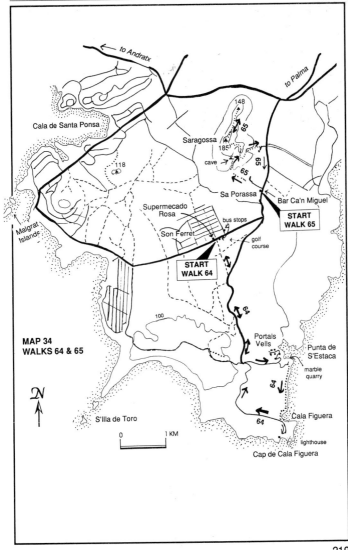

to Andratx

to Palma

148

Cala de Santa Ponsa

Saragossa

185

cave

118

Sa Porassa

Bar Ca'n Miguel

Supermecado Rosa

bus stops

START WALK 65

Malgrat Islands

Son Ferret

golf course

START WALK 64

100

Portals Vells

Punta de S'Estaca

marble quarry

MAP 34 WALKS 64 & 65

N

S'Illa de Toro

Cala Figuera

0   1 KM

lighthouse

Cap de Cala Figuera

2,000 years ago. Cross the narrow shingle beach and yellow marks will be found showing a path up the cliffs, with steps cut out of the rock in places. Turn left along the lighthouse road at the cliff top, which leads past the military establishment. Follow the track on to the old tower on the cliff top.

   To return, follow the quiet lighthouse road through the woods, where hunting is prohibited. The road becomes somewhat busier after passing the Portals Vells and other roads to the sea, but can be avoided eventually by a path in the woods on the right of the road, then later by another path on the left. Return to Son Ferrer by the track at the side of the golf course.

Son Ferrer - Portals Vells	1hr
Portals Vells - Punta Catius	1hr
Punta Catius - Son Ferrer	1hr 25min

65. PUIG D'EN SARAGOSSA

This low hill in the south-west of the island is a natural garden of flowering shrubs. In February there are brilliant yellow splashes of thorny broom and the air is fragrant with dense spikes of lavender. An outstanding viewpoint, with the peaks of Esclop and Galatzó to the north and the sea nearly all round. It is best to shut one's eyes to the unsightly resorts along the coast. It provides a pleasant half day out for anyone finding themselves in this area and is highly recommended botanically. An added interest is a cave, the Cova Forta, described as a Bronze Age dwelling from about 2000 B.C.

Type of walk: A little rough to reach the cave and until the path is reached, easy up to the first top, then a rough intermittent path to the second summit.

Starting point:	Sa Porassa, Bar Ca'n Miguel
Time:	2hr 45min
Distance:	6km
Highest point reached:	187m
Total height climbed:	216m
Grade:	B
Map:	Calvià 1:25,000

Take the dirt road at the side of the bar leading towards the hill. In about

400m clamber over a low wall at the left side of a building at a place where the road makes a bend to the right. A vague path now leads into a shallow valley, keeping to the valley floor and marked here and there with yellow paint. Two lime kilns are passed and after the second one the cave will be seen on the left.

Climb the hill opposite the cave, following yellow paint marks until a wide path is met. Turn left and follow it easily to the top of the hill. On the top is a large gun emplacement dating from the Civil War and also the remains of earlier fortifications. Yellow marks show the way along to a saddle and then up to another top at 149m. There is no path and much spiky vegetation. On this second top is found a ruined talaiot.

Although it is possible to descend northwards to the road, this is not recommended as there is no way through the high fence at the foot of the hill. Better to return the same way. Instead of returning by the cave, the main track can be followed down to the road. This path descends along a ridge and then turns down into a wooded valley on the left. After leaving the woods a dirt road is joined and the main road is reached at a gate with a notice saying 'Don't passing'! This exit is almost opposite a new wide road leading to an undeveloped urbanisation near the Aquapark. Turn right and walk back to the starting point at Ca'n Miguel in about 1km.

(Saragossa is spelt Zaragossa on some maps.)

66. THE MARBLE CAVES OF CALVIA AND THE BURGUESA RIDGE

The marble caves are large natural caverns high up in the steep slopes below the Mirador Alzamora. There is an impressive arch over the gaping mouth of the biggest cavern. Lower down there are a number of galleries and tunnels where the rock was formerly extracted for the making of ornaments. Do not expect to find samples of attractive pieces; they all seem to have gone long ago.

The cultivated Calvià valley is quiet and tranquil and the walk into the narrow Coma de n'Aliga (valley of the eagle) is full of interest. It is almost a ravine in places, narrowing between rock walls, adorned with many plants. The Mirador de Alzamora is an oustanding viewpoint and there is a shelter there. From the Coll des Pastors the path keeps at a high level with splendid views all the way to the Burguesa statue overlooking Palma.

This route is a linear walk making use of public transport and best suited to those staying in Palma or near. The best day to do it is on Monday, as this is market day and there are plenty of buses to Calvià.

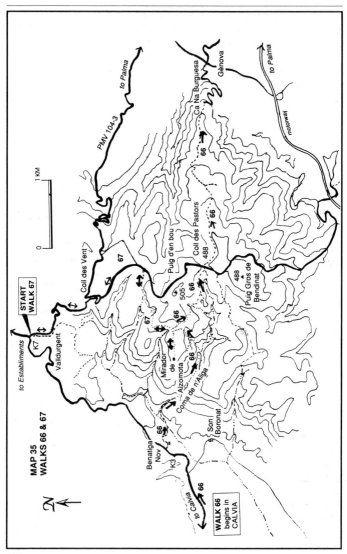

MAP 35
WALKS 66 & 67

Other days a taxi from Portals Nous or elsewhere would be needed. The walk could be extended by descending to Belver Castle and El Terreno instead of taking the bus from Gènova back to Palma.

Type of walk: Varied terrain with country roads, rough paths and stony tracks. Route-finding is somewhat complicated in the area around Alzamora. Not a very strenuous day.

Starting point:	Calvià
Time:	5hr
Distance:	13km
Highest point reached:	448m
Total height climbed:	400m
Grade:	B+
Map:	Calvià 1:25,000

Leave Calvià by the Establiments road to the east of the town. Between K3.2 and 3.3 turn right at the entrance to a farm, Benatiga Nou. Turn left and follow the track round the back of the buildings. There is a low chain across the track, a private hunting sign and a yellow arrow on a post. Follow the main track past an orchard on the right. The track now swings right into the narrow Coma de n'Aliga. Go straight on ignoring a track which doubles back left.

Soon a cluster of old ruined buildings is seen on the left. There is a lime kiln and the others were shelters and storage places used by the miners. One hundred metres beyond this point a sharp turn left, rather overgrown, leads to the abandoned workings. The path zigzags up to several tunnels and a cave. Allow an extra 40 minutes if you want to get right up to this cave, and take great care as the ground is steep and loose in places.

Return to the main track and follow it up to a junction with yellow arrows. Take the left branch marked C for Cova. The good track ends below the big cavern and most people will be content with the views from below. To reach the cave itself requires a steepish rock scramble. Return to the junction on the main track and now go up the narrow path marked M for Mirador. This goes up steeply at first, then levels off. A cairn marks a bend to the left. There are some yellow spots and cairns here and there. A right turn then leads up towards the ridge. Ignore a second right turn. On the ridge a cairn marks the junction with another path coming from the right. Take a careful note of this point. Turn left and walk along the ridge to arrive at the *mirador* in ten minutes.

Return along the same path and look for the cairn that marked the point of arrival on the ridge. Go past this cairn and 10m further on turn right at a second cairn. This path leads along the ridge at first then bends right and descends quite steeply towards a stream-bed. The path almost disappears, but the way is found by keeping a careful lookout for cairns. After crossing the stream-bed the path rises again and joins a good path which leads to a wide track. Turn left to arrive at the Coll des Pastors, a major path junction like a crossroads.

Turn right and follow this wide easy track which keeps to the side of the broad ridge running east. After about 20 or 25 minutes bear left (almost straight on) at a path junction. Keep on the main path which continues eastwards to arrive at the Mirador and the statue Na Burguesa. Follow the road down to Gènova and on to the main Palma road.

Calvià - Benatiga Nou	55min
Benatiga Nou - Marble quarry	35min
Marble quarry - Alzamora	1hr 15min
Alzamora - Coll des Pastors	45min
Coll des Pastors - Na Burguesa	1hr
Na Burguesa - Gènova	30min

N.B. Buses leave Gènova for Palma every 30 minutes. The last bus is normally 20.30. (Line 4.)

67. MIRADOR DE N'ALZAMORA FROM VALLDURGENT

This Mirador lies on the end of a ridge curving round from the Coll d'es Pastors and the Puig d'en Bou; it is not as shown on the new 1:25,000 map but about 800m further south. From the terrace outside the stone shelter there are panoramic views across the cultivated Calvià valley to Esclop and Galatzó. Although so near Palma the area is very quiet and peaceful, but it is an area popular with hunters. Among the luxuriant vegetation there is an abundance of Arbutus unedo, the strawberry tree.

Type of walk: Easy, at first on roads and tracks, then a good path.

Starting point:	K7 on Calvià-Establiments road
Time:	3hr 20min
Distance:	10km
Highest point reached:	c.430m
Total height climbed:	c.200m

Grade:	C
Map:	Calvià 1:25,000

From the bend at K7 two roads lead off to the south. Take the left-hand one (the other road leads to the large finca of Valldurgent). After 2km of steady uphill walking leave the road by a wide track beginning at a U-bend and well indicated by painted arrows. This track sweeps round the head of the valley, rising very slightly to reach a large clearing after another track has joined it from the left. A few minutes later go straight on at another cross track. The track now narrows and begins to descend towards a stream bed. After climbing up again on the other side of the stream it continues to rise to meet a cross path marked by a cairn on the ridge. Turn right and 10m further on notice another cairn marking another path on the left. (Take note of this point in anticipation of your return.) The Mirador is reached in less than ten minutes walking from here.

For an easy walk, return by the same way.

Alternative return by the Puig d'en Bou
The Puig d'en Bou at 503m makes an alternative way back which is a bit more strenuous and somewhat rougher walking. In this case, start walking back along the ridge and take the second path on the right. The top of the Puig d'en Bou is almost due east from here, so leave the path and make for it, picking the best line through the scrub and trees. From the top find a convenient way down to join the broad track a little over 100m to the east. Turn left and follow this track until you join the route of ascent.

A third way back is to keep on the above path and follow it to the Coll d'es Pastors which it reaches after descending into a gully and up again. (It becomes very indefinite until after the gully.) Turn left to reach the col and left again at a major cross track. This contours along the side of the Puig d'en Bou and is followed to join the route of ascent. Another option is to include the ascent of Bendinat from the track leading to the Coll des Pastors.

K7 - Mirador	1hr 40min
Mirador - K7	1hr 40min
Mirador - K7 (by Puig d'en Bou)	2hr
Mirador - K7 (by Coll d'en Pastors)	2hr

Outlying areas

68. BEC DE FERRUTX AND THE ERMITA DE BETLEM

The mountains of Artà are the highest of the Serra de Levant, the discontinuous chain of mountains bounding the central plain of Mallorca on the east. Although only of the order of 500m they have many of the characteristics of the higher Serra de Tramuntana and are certainly wild and unfrequented. The Bec de Ferrutx is not the highest of these hills, Morey being 561m, but it is certainly the most spectacular. The mountain tops are all very stony and arid with a garigue type vegetation; many asphodels, flat-topped thistles, sparse clumps of carritx and some dwarf fan palms. There are wide and dramatic views across the bay of Alcudia to the Sierra de Tramuntana from this walk.

The walk can easily be split into two shorter walks if required. From Betlem to the Ermita and return is short and easy. Allow three hours including Sa Coassa. There is a narrow but adequate driveable road from Artà to the Ermita, (best avoided at weekends) enabling those who think the full walk too strenuous to walk to Ferrutx and back from there. The way through the narrow streets of Artà is now reasonably well signposted.

Type of walk: Not strenuous, and no route-finding difficulties. Mainly tracks and paths and all fairly easy walking. There is some pathless ground, but it is open and not too stony.

Starting point:	Betlem
Time:	6hr 45min
Distance:	12km
Highest point reached:	522m
Total height climbed:	c.580m
Grade:	B+
Map:	Artà 1:50,000 or
	Colonia de Sant Pere 1:25,000
	and Artà 1:25,000

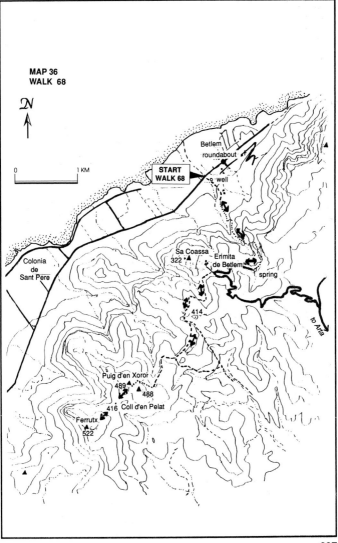

MAP 36
WALK 68

𝒩

0   1 KM

Betlem
roundabout

START
WALK 68

well

Sa Coassa
322

Erimita
de Betlem

spring

Colonia
de
Sant Pere

414

to Artá

Puig d'en Xoroi
489

488

416   Coll d'en Pelat

Ferrutx
522

227

To reach the start of the walk, drive towards Artà on the C712 and turn left at K7.8 towards Colonia de Sant Pere (San Pedro). The best way to identify the start is to continue past San Pedro to the roundabout at the beginning of Betlem and then return the same way for 300m. The path begins by a cross-track on the left and is marked by a cairn. There is a very deep oval well surrounded by a high stone wall quite near the beginning. The track veers right at some old farm buildings and some yellow paint marks show the way. About 15 minutes after passing the farm the path turns uphill by some carob trees on terraces, then goes through a wall and levels out as it enters a deep-cut valley. Follow the well-marked path up this wild valley, devastated higher up by forest fires. (In September 1990 we had to retreat from this walk when we could see a fierce fire raging up near the *ermita* and charred and burning vegetation began to rain round us. A continuous stream of flying boats were dousing the fires with water, but seemed to be having little effect.)

The path rises at a moderate gradient, zigzagging up to the left of a steep headwall to reach a wide upper valley. After going through gaps in two walls, the path continues up towards a field shelter made out of a boulder. Before reaching this, it crosses the stream to join a wide cart-track and rises towards the *ermita*. When a double stone gateway is seen, do not go through it but follow the track left to reach a spring. There is a shrine and a picnic table by the clear water of the *fuente* which is roofed over and provided with a chained iron ladle. Follow the track from here to the gates of the *ermita*, five minutes or less from the spring. It is here that the surfaced road from Artà ends and where there is some parking space for those starting the walk here.

Those making the short walk will have plenty of time to visit the chapel and to go up to the hill behind it, Sa Coassa (322m), where there are panoramic views of land and sea. There is an old semi-roofless building offering some shelter here.

To continue the main walk take the track beginning about 75m from the gates of the *ermita*. This leads west then south into a shallow valley, crossing a stream-bed then swinging back right to a shoulder. The old track descends into another valley and becomes a brash newly bulldozed one which is not very attractive but is easily followed. About 40 minutes from the *ermita* a wire meshed fence across the track can be lowered at the right-hand side and easily stepped over by those on foot. When a T-junction is met, turn right and follow the track through a gently-sloping upper valley with many heaps of stones. Continue until the track ends near the south-east extremity of Xoroi. Ahead is a fence. The easiest way to cross this barrier is to turn right at the track end and follow a level path along a sloping ledge between two rocky escarpments. The low fence can be stepped over, or bypassed at the point where it drops sharply downwards a little way to the right. Walk along the ledge to the far end and then go up towards a large overhanging rock. This is easily passed on either side. Continue over the Xoroi ridge and down (south-west) to the Coll d'en Pelat, on the far side of which is a conspicuous and solitary pine tree. Continue in the same direction to the trig point on the top of Ferrutx. There is no path but the walking is easy on stony ground between clumps of carritx. To fully appreciate this spectacular mountain continue along to the end of the north-west ridge which is the true mountain top.

Betlem - Ermita	1hr 15min
Ermita - Xoroi	1hr 15min
Xoroi - Ferrutx	45min
Ferrutx - Ermita	1hr 45min
Ermita - Betlem	45min

69. CASTELL DE SANTUERI AND SAN SALVADOR

This short easy walk is in the south of the island, south-east of Felanitx. The castle is situated in a very strategic positon on a 408m hill with steep cliffs all round. The curtain walls and towers are very well preserved and can easily be seen by driving up to the end of the approach road. This leaves the Felanitx to Santanyi road on the left about 2km from the town and is clearly signposted. (A key to enter the castle is said to be obtainable from the house below the castle, 3.9km from the turn-off from the main road, but we have always found this unoccupied on several visits.) The view from the car park below the castle is splendid, but must be even better and much more extensive if you are lucky enough to gain entrance. This castle was re-constructed in the 13th century at about the same time as the castles of Alaró and del Rei.

The Santuario de Son Salvador is situated on the top of a 509m hill and dates back to the 14th century. A surfaced road brings many tourists to the top, where an enormous building houses a restaurant and bar. Again, the views are extensive. The paths below the castle go through country which is like a natural garden with many flowering shrubs such as rosemary, cistus, heather, laurel, lentisc and shrubby globularia.

Type of walk: Easy walking along good paths and tracks through attractive countryside. There is a descent of about 50m near the

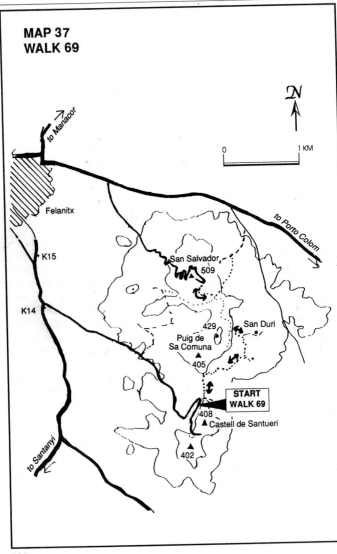

**MAP 37
WALK 69**

to Manacor

Felanitx

K15

K14

to Santanyi

to Porto Colom

San Salvador
509

429

San Duri

Puig de
Sa Comuna
405

START
WALK 69

408
Castell de Santueri

402

0   1 KM

beginning of the walk, then a rise of about 350m in several easy stages, mainly at the end.

Starting point:	180° bend below castle
Time:	2hr 50min
Distance:	8km
Highest point reached:	509m
Total height climbed:	400m
Grade:	C
Map:	Felanitx 1:50,000

From the sharp bend in the road, near which it is possible to park, take a path which leads off in an easterly direction. After about 50m turn left along a narrow overgrown path at the side of a wall with a yellow painted U sign. Other yellow paint marks will be noticed along this path on rocks and pine trees. The wall is a boundary across a col and is most easily crossed where the ground begins to rise and a new forest track can be joined on the other side.

Follow this track downwards into the valley for about ten minutes until a field of carobs and almond trees is reached. Turn left into this field, passing a water trough, where another track will be picked up. About ten minutes further on go through a gateway with paint marks on the gatepost. Almost immediately this track makes a right turn towards a farmhouse. Leave it at this bend and go straight on across the field in the same direction as before. There are faint paint marks on some of the trees. Make a rising traverse and do not worry if the paint marks run out, but make towards a post and wire fence ahead and follow this left to the corner of the field.

Go through the gate in this corner and continue to follow the path uphill, ignoring a minor branch path left and also another cross track. Go through another gateway in a wire fence. Five minutes later a wide cross track is met and crossed, by turning right then immediately left. The path then rises towards a col in the form of a ridge between two small hills. It turns right on the ridge, then contours round another small hill, crossing another track before rising up more steeply towards San Salvador. Go through a metal gate and up the broad track left to reach the top in a further 15 minutes. Return the same way.

Santueri - San Salvador	1hr 30min
San Salvador - Santueri	1hr 20min

70. RANDA

This flat-topped hill in the centre of the Mallorcan plain is known as the Holy Mountain. It has three sanctuaries, the oldest of which, the monastery of Nuestra Señora de Cura, was founded in 1275. The great Mallorcan scholar Ramon Llull lived there for about ten years while writing the first of more than 250 books in Catalan. The library still holds collections of old music books, missals and medieval manuscripts. Cura is right at the top of the hill and the church is open at all times. The museum is opened to visitors who must attract attention by pulling on a bell at the hours of 10, 11, 12, and 1.0 and 4, 5, or 6 in the afternoon. A bar-restaurant is open throughout the year but is closed on Mondays. From the large terraces there are panoramic views. It is said that 32 towns and villages can be seen on a clear day. Sant Honorat is another monastery with an attached church, 1.5km below the top. The third monastery, the 15th century Gràcia is built under an impressive overhanging rock on the west side.

Although there is a drivable road to the top, the easy walk from Randa village, following the road but taking advantage of a number of obvious short cuts, makes a pleasant half day. The walk described here is a variation which is more of a challenge, using a rough path which follows the base of the crags for a considerable distance. There are a number of shallow caves, but a close inspection is not advised as the rock here is very loose.

Randa village is reached from either Algaida, Montueri or Llucmayor. Park in the reasonably wide street entering the village, after passing a bar.

Type of walk: Easy, except for the section from Gracia to the top at the north end, which is by a rough path not always easy to follow. The start of this path is also quite steep and loose, although it improves and levels out further on.

Starting point:	Randa village
Time:	2hr 45min
Distance:	7km
Highest point reached:	543m
Total height climbed	250m
Grade:	B
Map:	Porreras 1:50,000

Take the signposted road towards Cura. Go through a metal gate at a hairpin bend and follow the path until it re-joins the road near the entrance

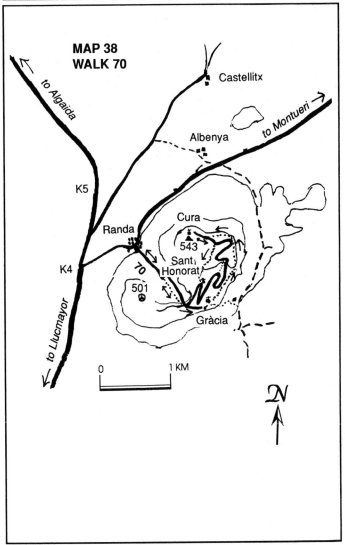

gate of Gràcia. Follow the road in front of Gràcia to the end of the terrace. Go through the gap in the wall and up the steep scree path. This bit is soon over and a comparatively good path is found among some colourful shrubs including lavender, pink-flowered cistus and yellow euphorbias. The path has some ups and downs but is mainly contouring. At times it seems to disappear, but can always be found again with the aid of occasional painted arrows and cairns. Eventually the path turns east, still below the crags, but now rises onto the grassy summit plateau and joins another path which comes up from the Albenya-Randa road.

Follow this path southwards and then turn right along the surfaced road to reach the large group of buildings at the top. To return, follow the road and whatever short cuts appear worthwhile on the way back down to Randa.

Randa - Gràcia	30min
Gràcia - Cura	1hr 15min
Cura - Randa	1hr

ASPHODELUS AESTIVUS

Path below cliffs of Randa (Walk 70)

A HIGH LEVEL WALK FROM VALLDEMOSSA TO POLLENSA

Every year Mallorquin walkers organise a very tough three-day walk from Andratx to Pollensa. This is usually only attempted by the very young and the superfit, and still very few actually complete the rather gruelling course. The following walk from Valldemossa to Pollensa has been devised for those who indulge in walking for pleasure rather than regarding it as a challenge. Even so it is quite a strenuous undertaking requiring skills in route-finding and some easy scrambling.

This walk takes in several mountains over 1,000m. It can be done in three days with overnight stops at Soller and Lluc, but the section from Soller to Lluc is very long. If preferred, it could be done in two stages by providing for an overnight bivvy at the attractive spring, the Font d'es Prat.

The route only touches surfaced roads for very short distances at Soller, Cuber and Lluc. Otherwise it takes the walker through wild country, reaches the tops of Teix, Sa Galera, L'Ofre, Sa Rateta, Massanella and Tomir and enjoys some spectacular scenery. In part it follows an ancient track once used by pilgrims travelling on foot to the monastery of Lluc from Soller.

Day 1

The walk begins in Valldemossa, easily reached by bus from Palma. Leave the village by Son Gual and head up the Cairats valley to the Font des Poll. Opposite this a signpost labelled Serra des Cairats points the way up a wide path which soon doubles back, rising through woodland and eventually up to Teix (1,062m) by the SW ridge. There is a short, easy descent to the little plain known as the Pla de Sa Serp, where there is a freshwater spring. The route now rises slightly over the Puig d'es Vent at 1,004m and follows the crest of the ridge along bare rock with superb views over to the Puig Mayor and the peaks that will be followed on the next stage of the trek. This ridge runs north-east, and before it rises to a final top a right-angled left turn is made to Sa Galera.

The descent to Soller begins by going down to the col between Sa Galera and the Puig des Morro. From here route-finding is fairly complex. Go down the centre of the valley floor to reach a *sitja* (an old charcoal hearth) and a ruined building. An overgrown track leads out to the right and down the right-hand side of the valley. A cairn at the end of an uphill section shows where to leave this track and turn left. After passing a branch back up the valley and another one leading down, the path seems to end at a brushwood fence. This is easily stepped over and the way found down to another little path which leads in zigzags to a small enclosure. After going over a stile of branches the path descends to a marker post where we turn right. The path soon improves, going through a gate with a stile leading below the cliffs and down to some cave houses built under them.

Now a drivable road, the route winds through terraces. Go through a gate by a water tank, turn left, cross a bridge and turn right. Then go under a railway viaduct, turn right at a T-junction and follow the lane to reach Soller by the petrol station. The centre of the town is about ten minutes away. The Hotel Guia next to the station is recommended if it is open.

Day 2a

Next day walk along to the village of Biniaraix. By the washplace at the end of the village there is a signpost showing the way to the beautiful walk up the *barranc,* the gorge which falls from the tiny upland hamlet of the Cases de L'Ofre. The cobbled and stepped path winds enchantingly up through terraces of olive trees into the ever-narrowing valley below the towering cliffs of Cornadors.

When the houses are reached, nestling in their green and sheltered hollow, the left path is taken past another freshwater spring. This track leads up to the Coll de L'Ofre. Before the col take the track right which contours round to the south side of L'Ofre. Shortly after going through a gap in a wall red waymarks show the route up to the top of L'Ofre.

From the top there is a delightful walk along the ridge and over the Puig Franquesa to Sa Rateta. To the left there are views over the Cuber Reservoir to Puig Major and to the right across the Comasema valley to the striking sugarloaf peaks of S'Alcadena and Alaro. From the top of Sa Rateta the way down to the Cuber dam is roughly north-east (steep crags prevent any wandering astray): a cairn shows the entrance to a hidden valley with a cairned path leading downwards. Lower down cairns show the place to strike left, crossing a gully and then going through a fence to reach easier ground.

From the dam walk to the main road and turn right. Continue for about 150m then leave the road to follow a large open *canaleta* for about 2km. At this point a path coming up from Almalutx is met. This crosses over the open channel by a bridge. The path now leads over the Coll des Coloms and onto the Font des Prat. The delicious freshwater here is under a stone roof and protected by an iron railing and door. (Possible bivouac site.)

Day 2b

From the spring a waymarked path leads up an attractive and uninhabited valley, the Comellar des Prat, right up to the Coll des Prat and down over the other side to Comafreda. This way is the way of the pilgrims and quite pleasant and easy to follow.

However, the ascent of Massanella is one of the highlights of this walk and should not be missed. Before the col is reached there is a big red M for Massanella painted on a boulder. This shows the way up to the col between Massanella and the Puig de Ses Bassetes. There isn't exactly a path, but several painted waymarks show the general direction. To reach the col itself it is necessary to scramble up a little rock wall several metres high. There is nothing difficult about it but it does involve trusting one's boots on sloping holds with nothing much for the hands until after a couple of steps up a good jug can be gripped with the right hand. Once this little rock scramble is negotiated there is nothing as difficult on the rest of the route.

Make a rising traverse across scree to the foot of a rocky spur and go up this until a way can be found leading back left to the ridge. There are some cairns but they are hard to see in the rocky wilderness so it is best to rely on your own judgement to pick out the best way. Once on the ridge it is easy walking along to the top of Massanella.

There are two ways of descent which will no doubt be familiar to those who have been to Mallorca previously. For newcomers it is probably easiest to follow the waymarked path down from the top to the sloping plateau below the summit. When the engraved stone is reached follow the path south, rather than go down to the spring, the Font de S'Avenc. Either way, the route is very well-marked down to the Coll de S'Arbona. Turn left on the col and after about 15 minutes of descent look out for paint marks, recently renewed, showing a shortcut down through the woods to Comafreda. The farm track leads down to a gate onto the road near the petrol station.

From the Coll de Batalla go down a minor road to the monastery of Lluc. There are rooms to be had very reasonably, and a restaurant serving evening meals from 08.00 pm. There are also self-catering facilities. If the weather is cold ask for a room *con calefaccion* (with heating).

Day 3

To begin the last stage of the walk go out of the main gate and turn left, then left again, and first right into the football ground. Go through the fence and follow the track until it joins the main road. After turning left for 150m, the main road should be left for the minor road on the right leading to the Binifaldo bottling plant. (It is worth mentioning that an easier option for the last day is to follow the old road from Binifaldo as in Walk 26.)

238

The route up Tomir starts between the gate to the plant and the forest fence. The way is well-marked and easy to follow. On reaching the summit ridge a left turn is made to reach the summit. Go down towards the col between Tomir and the Puig des Ca. This passes the remains of a large snow-pit. Follow the track south along the broad col and, after going through a boundary wall, turn left into a shallow gully. There is an easy way up the little crag at the top by means of a sloping ledge. From the west top double back, then go over the main top and on down the ridge towards the Coll de Miner. It is necessary to come down on the north side of the wall which crosses this col, as there is a high locked gate in it. In this area too, it is as well to keep a low profile as walkers are not too welcome.

Avoid following the new track to Fartaritx del Raco and, where it bends left, cut over the hill to pick up the track that contours along the high cultivated plateau of Fartaritx. When the enclosing wall of Fartaritx Gran is reached, look for the way down to the left shortly after crossing a stream. A delightful mule track winds down through a wild garden of flowering shrubs and arrives in the Vall den March by a house known as Ca'n Huguet.

Now follow the track alongside the stream. Shortly after it turns left and crosses the stream, turn right along a rather overgrown footpath leading to Pollensa. The stream must be crossed again and as the footbridge has collapsed long ago, it may have to be paddled. Most often the stream-bed is dry, but on rare occasions there is a raging torrent and in this case recourse must be had to going round by the main road. In the town, follow the Calle de la Huerta towards the centre, turn left by the Banco Central, then right and left again to arrive in the main square where very welcome refreshment may be had. Rooms are usually available at the Hostal Juma at a corner of the square.

Further details of the route may be found by reference to the following walks: 57, 55, 45, 43, 30(c), 26, 24(a), 23 and 22.

APPENDIX 1: ALPHABETICAL REFERENCE SECTION

Accommodation

For the benefit of those who prefer to travel independently, here are the names and telephone numbers of some selected hotels. (This information has been taken from Tourist Office publications and has not been personally verified.) (H = Hotel, HS = Hostal, R = Residencia which is a hotel without a restaurant.)

Cala San Vicente	Open	Rooms	Tel.no.
Molins H****	1.05 - 1.11	90	53 02 00
Cala San Vicente H***	1.04 -31.10	38	53 02 50
Don Pedro H***	1.01 -31.12	136	53 00 50
Simar H***	1.05 -31.10	120	53 03 00
Niu H*	1.04 -31.10	24	53 01 00
Mayol HS**	1.04 -31.10	40	53 04 40
Oriola HS**	10.02 -31.11	23	53 19 98
Pinos, Los HS**	1.04 -31.10	19	53 12 10
Vistamar HSR*			
(Annexe of Don Pedro)	1.04 -31.10	11	53 00 50

Puerto de Pollensa			
Daina H***	1.4 -31.10	60	53 16 00
Illa D'Or H***	1.4 -31.10	119	53 11 00
Pollensa Park H***	1.4 -31.10	316	53 13 50
Pollentia H***	1.4 -31.10	70	53 12 00
Ses Pins HR***	1.1 -31.10	55	53 10 50
Uyal H***	1.4 -30.09	105	53 15 00

Pollensa			
Juma HSR*	1.1 -31.12	8	53 00 07

Puerto de Soller	Tel no.		Tel.no.
Rocamar H*	63 13 83	Eden Park H***	63 12 00
Los Geraneos	63 14 40	Miramar H*	63 13 50
Costa Brava H*	63 15 50	Monte Azul H*	63 15 13
Marina	63 14 61	Atalaya Club	63 14 03
Eden H***	63 16 00	Hostal Es Port HS***	63 16 50

Soller			
Pension 'La Guia' H*	63 02 27	Monumento	63 01 18
Pension 'Nadal'	63 11 80		

Estate agent: Immobiliaria Alcover, Paseo Es Traves, 07108, Puerto de Soller. Tel 63 18 67. English spoken, and usually have flats to let in the port for long or short periods.

Tour operators: Major tour operators such as Thomson and Intasun normally offer winter holidays in the above resorts. But try *Alternative Mallorca* who offer apartments and hotels in lesser-known places as well as courses in bird-watching,

240

painting and other activities. Enquiries to Michael Walsh at 60 Steinbeck Road, Leeds LS7 2PW. *Classic Collection Holidays* also have a brochure on Mallorca with hotels in small and attractive places such as Deyà, Valldemossa, Banyalbufar and Estellencs. May to October. Enquiries to Classic Collection Holidays, Travel and Leisure Limited, 9 Liverpool Terrace, Worthing, West Sussex BN11 1TA.

Banks: Most of the main resorts have several banks, but there is only one in Cala San Vicente. Opening hours are 09.00 to 14.00, but they also may close for lunch from 11.30 to 12.30. There are fairly frequent holidays when the banks close all day and most hotel notice-boards give this information. Changing money is simple, using Traveller's cheques or Eurocheques. Passports must be shown and they usually want to know where you are staying. The exchange rate is usually more favourable in banks than in hotels and travel agencies.

Boats: There are several regular boat services running in summer which can be very useful to walkers. The following are 1990 timetables, summer only. When summer begins and ends may depend on the weather. Times may vary from year to year so it is advisable to check the notice-boards displayed in the ports.

Formentor - Daily service, except Sundays
Journey time 30 minutes

Dep. Puerto de Pollensa				Dep. Formentor					
10.00	11.00	13.00	15.30	10.30	11.30	13.00	15.00	16.00	17.00

Sa Calobra and Torrente de Pareis - Daily service
Journey time 50 minutes.

Dep.Pto. de Soller			Dep. Sa Calobra		
10.00	12.30	15.00	12.00	14.00	16.45

Deyà - Tuesdays only.
Journey time 30 minutes

Dep. Pto.de Soller		Dep.	Deyà
10.00	15.00	12.30	17.15.

Cala Tuent - Saturdays only
Journey time 50 minutes

Dep. Pto. Soller	Dep. Cala Tuent
10.00	16.45.

Bus travel: Although walkers are strongly advised to hire a car for getting to the start of walks, there are some occasions when public transport can be used. The best place to get hold of timetables is at a bus station, although some tourist offices supply them and many hotels display local ones Sometimes they are posted up on bus stops. Many services are locally organised and bus companies only supply timetables for their own services.

The following timetables were operating in the winter of 1990 and will give an indication of frequency and times. Although there seems to be little change from year to year, there are usually some minor alterations. More buses run in the summer, from the beginning of April to the end of September, but vary according to demand. Walkers are not well served by buses, especially in the mountains.

Although there is a service from Soller along the C710 to Puerto Pollensa, returning in the evening, this only runs at weekends in winter. In summer there is a daily service from Ca'n Picafort to Puerto Soller, which would be a great benefit to walkers in the winter.

There are many buses from Palma radiating in all directions, details of which can easily be obtained if you are staying in Palma. Most walkers will be based in the north of the island so only timetables relevant to this area are included here.

Timetables: (N.B. These are 1990 timetables. Readers are reminded that they may be changed at any time).

Airport-Palma: For those who book flight only it is useful to know that an airport bus runs into the Plaza Espana in Palma, right to the bus station where buses leave for the north, and the railway station where trains depart for Soller. Buses leave the airport every 30 minutes from 07.05 to 24.05 and leave the Plaza Espana for the airport from 06.30 to 23.30.

Palma - Pollensa - Puerto Pollensa: The bus stop in Palma is in the bus station next to the Inca railway station in the Plaza España.

	Monday - Saturday				Sundays/Holidays		
Palma	10.00	13.30	17.30	19.15	10.00	16.30	20.30
Pollensa	11.00	14.30	18.30	20.15	11.00	17.30	21.30
Puerto Pol.	11.15	14.45	18.45	20.30	11.15	17.45	21.45
Puerto Pol.	07.15	09.00	14.00	17.30	08.00	14.45	18.45
Pollensa	07.30	09.15	14.15	17.45	08.15	15.00	19.00
Palma	08.30	10.15	15.15	18.45	09.15	16.00	20.00

Pollensa - Puerto Pollensa: There is a bus station in Pollensa, two minutes walk downhill from the main square. The bus stop in Puerto Pollensa is on the sea-front opposite the bar YUM YUM The journey takes 15 minutes and only the starting times are given.

Pollensa - Puerto Pollensa
Weekdays
06.45 07.30 08.15 09.30 10.15 11.00 12.30 13.30 14.30 15.45 16.30
17.00 17.45 18.30 19.15. 20.15

Sundays/Holidays
07.30 08.30 09.30 10.15 11.00 12.00 13.00 14.15 16.00 16.30 17.00
17.30 18.15 19.15 20.15 21.30

Puerto - Pollensa
Weekdays
07.15 08.30 09.00 10.00 11.00 11.45 12.45 14.00 15.00 16.00 16.45
17.30 18.00 19.00 19.30 20.45

Sundays/Holidays
08.00 08.45 10.00 11.00 11.45 12.45 13.15 14.45 16.15 16.45 17.45
18.45 19.45 20.45 21.45

Pollensa - Cala San Vicente: In Cala San Vicente the bus stop is outside the Bar Miguel in the Calle Temporal, not far from the bank. Sometimes it picks passengers up outside the Don Pedro but in busy times it is best to walk to the bus stop.

Pollensa - Cala San Vicente

Weekdays	08.15	11.15	14.30	18.30
Holidays	09.30	12.15	17.30	

Cala San Vicente - Pollensa

Weekdays	08.45	12.30	14.45	18.45
Holidays	10.00	12.30	17.45	

Cala-San Vicente - Puerto Pollensa - Llenaire: This is a daily service, except Sundays, and in summer only.

Llenaire - Cala San Vicente

9.50   11.50   15.50

Pto.Pollensa to Cala San Vicente

9.15   10.00   12.00   16.00   18.15.

Cala San Vicente - Pto. Pollensa - LLenaire

9.30   10.15   12.15   16.15   18.30

Puerto Pollensa - Alcudia - Ca'n Picafort: This service is especially useful to birdwatchers as it can be used to get to the Albufera. This is a winter timetable, from 1 November to 31 March.

Pto.Pollensa		10.30	12.00		16.45
Alcudia	09.25	10.45	12.15	15.30	17.00
Pto.Alcudia	09.30	10.50	12.20	15.35	17.05
Tucan	09.35	10.55	12.25	15.40	17.10
Ciudad Lagos	09.40	11.00	12.30	15.45	17.15
Ca'n Picafort	09.55	11.15	12.45	16.00	17.30
Ca'n Picafort	09.45	11.15	12.45	16.00	17.30
Ciudad Lagos	10.00	11.30	13.00	16.15	17.45
Tucan	10.05	11.35	13.05	16.20	17.50
Pto Alcudia	10.10	11.40	13.10	16.25	17.55
Alcudia	10.15	11.45	13.15	16.30	18.00
Pto Pollensa	10.30	12.00		16.45	

Palma - Valldemossa - Deyà - Puerto Soller: This service is very useful to walkers based in Soller, especially when the 09.30 bus from Puerto Soller is running. (Not on Sundays in winter, but check locally.) In Palma tickets can be obtained from the Bar Ca'n Meca, at the corner of Avda Juan March, and the Calle Archiduque Luis Salvador. The bus leaves from the opposite side of the road. In Soller this bus stops in the Plaza America and not near the railway station where other buses depart.

Winter service 1 November - 30 April

Palma	07.30*	10.00	12.00*	15.00	19.00
Valldemossa	08.00*	10.30	12.30*	15.30	19.30
Deyà	08.15*	10.45	12.45*	15.45	19.45
Puerto Soller	08.45*	11.15	13.15*	16.15	20.15

Puerto Soller	07.30	09.30*	14.30	16.00*	17.30
Deyà	08.00	10.00*	15.00	16.30*	18.00
Valldemossa	08.20	10.30*	15.30	17.00*	18.30
Palma	08.50	11.00*	16.00	17.30*	19.00

* Not on Sundays and Holidays

Summer service from 1 May to 31 October

Palma	07.45	10.00	12.00	16.15	19.30
Valldemossa	08.15	10.30	12.30	16.45	20.00
Deyà	08.30	10.45	12.45	17.00	20.15
Puerto Soller	09.00	11.15	13.15	17.30	20.45

Puerto Soller	07.30	09.30	14.30	16.00	18.00
Deyà	08.00	10.00	15.00	16.30	18.30
Valldemossa	08.20	10.30	15.30	17.00	19.00
Palma	08.50	11.00	16.00	17.30	19.30

Soller - Puerto Pollensa: This very important service for walkers in the Soller area unfortunately only runs at weekends in winter, from approximately 1 November to 31 March, but is a daily service in summer. The bus stop is outside the railway station in Soller. (In good weather on Sundays the bus can be full when it arrives in Puerto Soller.)

Soller	09.00		18.25
Puerto Soller	09.30		18.10
Ses Barques	09.45		17.50
Army base	10.05		17.35
Escorca	10.20		17.20
Lluc	10.35		17.00
Pollensa	11.20		16.20
Cala San Vicente	11.30		16.10
Puerto Pollensa	11.45		16.00*

* 1 hour later in summer

Ca'n Picafort - Alcudia - Puerto Soller: A daily service in summer, in 1990 from 2 May to 31 October.

Ca'n Picafort		09.15	15.15
C.Lagos		09.30	15.30
Pto.Alcudia		09.40	15.40
Alcudia	07.00	09.50	15.50
Pto.Pollensa	07.10	10.00	16.00
Cala San Vicente		10.10	16.10
Puerto Soller	(approx.) 12.10		18.10
Return from Pto. Soller	09.30	16.30	18.00

Car Hire Some package holidays offer 'free' or reduced car hire as part of the deal, especially during the winter months. (It's not really free as you find you have to pay the insurance.) If this does not apply, then it is cheaper to hire locally than to book a car in advance with one of the international companies. The smallest and cheapest cars are the Seat (i.e.Fiat) Pandas, which are good for driving along narrow mountain roads, but sometimes have starting problems. Note that the spare wheel, jack and wheel brace are under the front bonnet. International driving permits are no longer required, but a current driving licence and your passport must be produced when hiring a car.

Chemists The sign for a chemists shop is a green cross. Many medicines for which a prescription would be required in Great Britain can be bought over the counter. However, these are not handed over just for the asking and a detailed description of symptoms will be required. Staff are usually very helpful and many speak English. After normal hours, one chemist in each town is usually open until late at night. Details are posted in the windows of all chemists.

Complaints All hotels, shops, bars, garages and any place offering services to the public are compelled by law to have a supply of a complaints form or *hoja de reclamaciones* (pronounced 'O ha day rek-lam-ath-ee-oh-neys'). These are only for very serious complaints and should only be resorted to after every attempt has been made to get things put right in a friendly way. If a polite approach to a manager or owner has not worked, then simply asking for the form may bring about a dramatic change of attitude as it is a very serious matter to have a complaint registered. The forms are in triplicate: one copy for the offending organisation, one to be sent to the Oficina de Turismo, Avenida Jaime III, Palma, and one copy to be retained by the complainant.

Currency The monetary unit is the peseta (pta). There are coins of 1, 5, 25, 50, 100, 200 and 500 pesetas and banknotes of 100, 200, 500, 1,000, 2,000 and 5,000 pesetas. A 5-peseta coin is called a duro. During the last six years, the rate of exchange has varied between 170 and 220 pesetas to one pound An easy rule-of-thumb for those who dislike mental arithmetic is to pretend that 200 ptas = £1.00.

Drinks There are no licensing laws as in Britain and there are very many bars where drinks are served all day. All bars also serve coffee and soft drinks and often food as well. All supermarkets and most village shops sell wine, beer and spirits. Some good Mallorquin wines are made at Felanitx and at Binisalem by Franje Roja. Beer, *cerveza*, pronounced 'thair-baytha' is generally good. Draught is *de barril* or *a presion*.

Driving Getting to the start of the walks often means driving along narrow winding roads. The roads themselves are mainly good, but there can be problems when coaches going in the opposite direction are met with. The drivers are always very good and expert at edging past with only an inch or two to spare. The worst place for this is the narrow winding corniche road between Andratx and Soller, but at the time of writing (1990) this is being improved. Another problem when driving about the island is the lack of signposting and lack of advance warning of turns. Go very slowly when you know you going to make a turn and expect it to be a sudden one.

Driving offences The traffic police are very strict and on-the-spot fines of the order of 2,000 ptas are quite common. It is as well to be aware of the following Spanish laws:

1. Always use the seat belts.
2. Always indicate you are pulling out when overtaking anything, including parked cars and cyclists, and allow 1m clearance at least.
3. Always dip headlights when coming up behind another vehicle as well as when approaching.
4. Pay particular attention to all *ceda el paso* (give way) signs and to Stop signs. Some road junctions can be confusing, but 'Stop means Stop' as I was told by the policeman charging me an on-the-spot fine at the Tucan crossroads near Alcudia. (The signs still seem wrong at this point; the Stop sign is at what appears to be a minor road and the give way sign at the major road.)
5. Give way to all vehicles coming from the right.
6. Keep to the speed limit of 110km on C roads and 90km on other roads, or other speeds as shown locally.
7. Never cross unbroken white lines in the centre of the road. 'No overtaking' signs back up these white lines.
8. Do not park facing oncoming traffic or within 3m of a corner.
9. Obey the priority signs on narrow roads and bridges. You have priority at a square sign with a white arrow pointing up and must give way at a round sign with a red arrow pointing up.
10. Each car in Spain should carry a set of spare bulbs, but car hire companies do not provide these. Any fine incurred will be refunded by the car hire company.

If you are stopped by the police for any offence whatsoever it is no use pleading ignorance of the law and highly inadvisable to argue. The best course of action is to apologise; *lo siento*, or *lo mucho siento*. If it is not a very serious offence then you may be let off with a warning, but it is far more likely that you will be charged and required to pay a fine *(una multa)*. If this is the case you will be given a slip of paper, explaining what is to happen. The policeman booking you will then fill in a form describing the offence and ask you to sign it. He will sign it too and give you a copy to keep.

Food (*See also markets and restaurants*) Mallorquin cuisine is similar to that of Catalonia on the mainland. Fish dishes are a specialty and so are *tapas*, which are wonderful titbits served with drinks in many bars. They are usually laid out behind glass on the counter and you can point to the ones you want. Small or large helpings are offered and a large one can make quite a substantial meal. Food in hotels catering for English people sometimes tends to be rather bland, although the tendency now is for most meals to be self-service and there is often an excellent buffet with a good salad selection. You may like to sample the following dishes when you have the opportunity:

Angulas: small eels fried whole in batter
Arroz brut: rice soup with meat
Bacalao: dried codfish with tomatoes in a casserole
Butifarra: Catalan spiced sausage
Calamares: squid, usually served *a la romana* or deep fried, in rings
Caldera de peix: fish soup with rice and slices of bread
Capo a lo Rei en Jaume: capon, cock or turkey stuffed with marzipan and sweet

potatoes and slightly fried
Caracoles: snails cooked in a garlic mayonnaise sauce
Chorizo: a strong spicy sausage
Coca mallorquin: a kind of pizza, often including fish
Empanada: meat and vegetable pie
Ensaimada: a very light flaky bun sprinkled with icing sugar, often eaten for breakfast or taken on picnics
Escaldums: a casserole of chicken and potatoes in an almond sauce
Espinagada: a savoury pie of eels and highly seasoned vegetables
Frito mallorquin: a fry-up of liver, kidneys, green peppers, leeks and garlic
Gambas: prawns
Gazpacho: a cold soup made from tomatoes, onions, peppers, cucumbers, garlic, oil and vinegar
Graixonere: fish with vegetables and eggs
Greixera: mixed pressed cold meats with egg, artichokes, peas, beans and herbs
Guisantes a la catalana: peas fried with ham and onions
Langosta a la catalana: lobster sautéed in wine and rum with herbs and spices
Lechona asada: roast suckling pig (The most famous speciality)
Lenguado: sole, usually grilled with fresh herbs
Mejillones a la marinera: mussels cooked in a spicy sauce
Pa amb oli: bread spread with oil and topped with ham and tomatoes
Paella: a classic Spanish dish. The best are cooked to order and take at least half an hour. It is a combination of rice with poultry, various seafoods, and pork, plus onions, tomatoes, peppers and garlic. Normally served in an iron dish straight from the oven.
Paella catalana: spicy sausage, pork, squid, tomato, chilli pepper and peas
Paella marinera: fish and seafood only
Paella valenciana: the traditional dish with chicken, mussels, shrimps, prawns, peas, tomatoes and garlic
Salmonetes: red mullet. Sobrasada: pork-liver sausage, bright red with pimento
Sopa mallorquina: a very filling soup, almost a stew, made from garlic, onions, vegetables in season and bread
Tortilla española: omelette with potatotes
Trempo: a summer salad with mixed vegetables
Trucha a la navarra: trout stuffed with bacon or smoked ham
Tumbet: a type of ratatouille with aubergines, peppers, tomatoes and potatoes cooked in olive oil
Zarzuela: a mixture of various fish in a hot spicy sauce.

Markets Anyone self-catering will enjoy buying fresh fruit and vegetables at the open markets. There is such a superb selection even in the depths of winter and the prices are very reasonable. They are good places to buy food for packed lunches too, especially the local oranges. A visit to one of these markets is a colourful and entertaining event and highly recommended. Most of them open early in the morning and finish by lunch time.

Alcudia	Tuesday, Sunday	Pollensa	Sunday
Andratx	Wednesday	Puerto Pollensa	Wednesday
Calvià	Monday	Sa Pobla	Sunday
Inca	Thursday	Sineu	Wednesday
Palma	Saturday		

Medical matters When booking a holiday make sure that you have adequate insurance cover. Note that if you intend rock climbing it is often excluded from insurance cover so that special arrangements should be made, for example with the BMC. There are doctors in all towns and a hospital in Palma, which can be reached in under two hours from the most distant parts of the island. First class specialist and emergency treatment is available. *(See also Chemists)*

Photography Bring all the film that you are likely to need as it is a lot more expensive to buy in Mallorca. Colour prints can be developed in 24 hours. Kodak transparencies can be sent to Madrid and should be returned within a week Remember that the light is very bright and it is easy to overexpose, especially near the sea or white buildings.

Police There are three different police forces in Spain and all are armed. The *Policia Municipal* wear blue uniforms and are attached to local town halls and the *Policia Nacional* wear brown uniforms and berets or hats with a red stripe. The national police force is the Guardia Civil, whose uniforms include patent leather hats. The Guardia Civil have the most power. All three services may be called upon if you need help

Post Offices The post offices, *correos*, are open from 09.00-14.00 and from 16.00-19.00, Monday to Saturday. It is best to buy stamps *(sellos)* at a tobacconist *(estanco)* or from any shop selling postcards or from a hotel reception desk. Mail boxes are yellow with a red stripe. A box labelled *extranjero* is for foreign-bound mail. Mail can be sent to a post office to be collected if you do not know what your address will be. The form of address is:
Mr and Mrs A.B.Smith
Lista de Correos
Puerto Pollensa
Mallorca
Baleares
Spain.
Telephones are quite independent of post offices. (q.v.)

Railways *(See trains)*

Restaurants There is a wide choice of places to eat in every resort. Many bars also serve meals and most hotels offer meals to non-residents. Your own hotel will probably offer specialties at extra cost which can be ordered instead of the standard fare. Menus and prices are usually posted outside the entrance so that you can see what is available before deciding where to eat, but it is a good plan to ask someone with local knowledge to recommend somewhere. There is a wide range of prices but paying more does not always mean a better meal, but may mean a more elaborate service. In tourist places the menu is often in several languages including English. In smaller places with more authentic local cooking it pays to know some of the words which may be on the menu. (See Food, p. 246 and Language notes, p.251.) The *menu del dia* is always very good value. This is a two or three course meal including bread and wine, 1990 price about 600 ptas.

Shops and shopping *(See also Markets)* Shopping for food is easy everywhere on the island. Even the smallest villages have a general store and they are nearly all self-service. Hours are 09.00-13.00 and 16.00 or 16.30-20.00. Some shops close on Saturday afternoons. If you go to Palma for a day's shopping and sightseeing, remember the long siesta. Even the cathedral closes in the afternoon

Taxis These are cheaper than in Britain and can be good value for four people sharing. They are usually found in main squares or in front of hotels, or the reception desk at the hotel will call one. The green sign *Libre* means free and any taxi displaying this can be flagged down. There is usually a board near the taxi rank displaying the standard fares to nearby places. If you want to go on a long journey you will probably have to pay the fare both ways even if you are not returning. It is best to agree on the price before setting off. Tips of 5-10% of the fare are customary.

Telephones The telephone system has been modernised and most telephones have automatic dialling systems and can be used for international calls. They take 5-, 25- and 50-peseta coins, which are lined up on top of the dialling box which is a push-button type. Coins not used are refunded when you hang up. Most bars have telephones which can be used for local calls. The dialling tone is a single intermittent note and the engaged sign a very rapid intermittent note. To make a call to England, first dial 07 for the international line, pause until a continuous high-pitched tone is heard, dial 44 for Great Britain, then the area code omitting the first 0 (e.g. 61 for Manchester, not 061). A good supply of 50-peseta coins are needed, but it is cheaper after 8.00 pm and before 8.0 am, after 2.0 pm on Saturday and all day on Sunday. If the coins won't go in the slot it means the box is full and you will have to find another telephone. Hotels will usually make calls for you, but there is often a surcharge. To make a personal call ask the operator for *persona a persona* and to reverse the charges ask for *cobro revertido.*

Theft In Palma and the busy resorts of the south coast it is necessary to be on guard against handbag-snatchers and pickpockets, as in many places today. Never accept a free carnation for your buttonhole; this is a ploy to gain free access to your wallet. Car thieves operate in many areas all over the island and it is never safe to leave valuables or anything at all in a car when you go off walking for the day. Leave the car empty, with the seats tipped foward to show there is nothing hidden underneath. Many friends have had cars broken into and all sorts of items taken, from cameras and good clothes to old trainers and a few groceries.

Toilets There are very few public toilets in Mallorca and most people use those in bars and restaurants. There are usually pictorial signs for men and women, some of them a bit ambiguous. A useful phrase to know is *dónde estan los servicios, per favor* (where are the toilets, please?).

Tourist offices The Spanish National Tourist Office at 57, St.James' St., London SW1A 1LD (telephone 071-499-0901) will supply lists of accommodation and a brochure but do not undertake bookings. The main tourist office in Palma is in Avenida Jaime III, 10, tel. 71-22-16. There is also a kiosk in the Plaza Espana offering some information and maps of Palma There are local tourist offices in some of the resorts, although some of these only open in summer.

Trains There are two railway lines on the island, Palma-Inca and Palma-Soller. The line to Arta was closed some years ago. It is the Soller line which is of special interest to walkers and may be used by the independent traveller going to stay in Soller, or by walkers staying in Palma to get there for the day. The two lines have adjacent stations in the Plaza Espana. From the bus station, go past the Inca line to reach the station for Soller. The Soller line was built in 1912 and although now electrified it still uses very old and attractive carriages with brass fittings. The train ride itself is highly recommended for its own sake. The 10.40 train from Palma is a special tourist train which stops at a viewpoint high above the Soller valley for ten minutes while everyone leaps out with their cameras. This train can be very crowded especially at peak holiday times, and unless you are early at the station you may find that it is standing room only on the platforms between the carriages. There is also an old tram which runs between Soller and the port, which also gives an exciting and scenic ride.

Train times

Palma	08.00	10.40	13.00	15.15	19.45	22.00*
Bunyola	08.26	11.08	13.26	15.40	20.10	22.25*
Soller	09.00	11.45	14.00	16.15	20.45	23.00*

* Sundays and holidays only

Soller	06.45	09.15	11.50	14.10	18.20	21.00*
Bunyola	07.15	09.45	12.15	14.35	18.45	21.25*
Palma	07.45	10.15	12.50	15.10	19.20	22.00*

* Sundays and holidays only

Tramway

Departures from Soller

05.55	07.00	08.00	09.00	10.00	11.00	11.30	12.00	12.30
13.00	14.00	15.00	16.00	16.30	17.00	17.30	17.55	19.00
20.00	20.45							

Departures from Puerto

06.20	07.30	08.25	09.30	10.30	11.30	12.00	13.00	13.25
14.30	15.30	16.30	17.00	17.30	17.55	18.30	19.30	20.20
21.10								

Water Although it is perfectly safe to drink the tap-water, in some of the coastal resorts it is often quite strongly saline and has an exceedingly unpleasant taste. Best to buy the excellent spring water available everywhere in 5-litre bottles.

APPENDIX 2: LANGUAGE NOTES

Introduction

Many people in Mallorca speak some English especially in the major tourist centres and in large hotels. Many others, particularly in the smaller villages and in the country do not know a single word of English or any other languages except Castilian Spanish and Mallorquin. (Some older country people only speak Mallorquin.) These are the people most likely to be met while walking and it is well worthwhile taking the trouble to learn a few words and phrases so as to be able to pass the time of day with them.

The official language of Mallorca is about to change from Castilian Spanish to Mallorquin. Mallorquin is a dialect of Catalan and includes words of French and Arabic origin. The written language can be mastered, for reading purposes, by those with a little knowledge of French and Spanish, but the spoken language is another matter entirely. Between themselves, most of the islanders speak Mallorquin, so that overheard conversations on buses and in bars and shops are frequently totally incomprehensible to visitors. However, if you try and speak a little Spanish in shops and so on, you will find that people are delighted that you are making the effort and will help you all they can.

One of the best ways of learning is to listen to cassettes or radio programmes such as the BBC sometimes produce. Castilian is pronounced exactly as it is spelt, so that if the rules are known a reasonable attempt at pronunciation can be made. Stress is on the last syllable unless indicated otherwise by a stress accent, (e).

Key to pronunciation

The following guide is given for reference and to introduce a few words of vocabulary. It is no substitute for listening to people talking on cassettes, radio or in real life.

a	between a in lass and in father	adiós	goodbye
b	as English	banco	bank
c	before i and e like **th** in thin	cinco	five
	before anything else as in cat	cliente	customer
ch	as in church	chico	boy
d	at beginning of word, like **d** in dog	dos	two
	in other places, like **th** in though	verdad	true
e	as in men, but at end of word as in day	leche	milk
f	as English	fácil	easy
g	before a,o,u, or consonant, as in gas	gasolina	petrol
	before e & i as **ch** in loch	gente	people
gu	before a, like gw	agua	water
h	always silent	hombre	man
i	between i in bit and in machine	litro	litre
j	like **ch** in loch	ajo	garlic
k	as in English	kilo	kilo
l	as in English	libro	book
ll	like **lli** in million	me llamo	I'm called

m	as English	mantequilla	butter
n	as English	naranja	orange
ñ	as ni in onion	los niños	the children
o	between top and for	oficina	office
p	as English	pan	bread
q	like English k	quizás	perhaps
r	slightly rolled	el norte	the north
rr	strongly rolled	carretera	main road
s	voiceless, as in sin	seis	six
t	as English	tienda	shop
u	as in boot	usted	you
v	like a soft English b	vaso	glass
x	at end of word, like tch	Felanitx (placename)	
	between vowels, like gs	taxi	taxi
y	like y in yes	mayor	main
y	the word y, as in machine	y	and
z	as th in thick	manzana	apple

N.B. The three double letters ch, ll and rr are considered as separate letters by the Spanish Academy so they have separate sequences in Spanish dictionaries.

Brief glossary

Some very basic words and phrases are included here because it can be useful to have reference to them without carrying a separate phrase book in your rucksack. Note: Question marks and exclamation marks are always used upside down at the beginning of a question or exclamation.

Everyday words and expressions

hello	hola	thats all right	de nada
good morning	buenos días	thank you very much	muchas gracias
good afternoon	buenas tardes	excuse me, sorry	perdoneme
goodnight	buenas noches	I'm sorry	lo siento
goodbye	adiós	I'm English	soy Inglés (man)
see you tomorrow	hasta mañana		soy Inglesa (woman)
see you later	hasta luego	I don't understand	no comprendo
yes/no	si/no	what did you say?	¿qué dijo?
please	por favor	what is that	¿qué es eso?
thank you	gracias		

would you repeat please?	¿puede repetir, por favor?
more slowly, please	más despacio, por favor
do you speak English?	¿habla Inglés?
I don't speak Spanish	no hablo Espanol
there is, there are	hay
is there a bank near here?	¿hay un banco por aqúi?
where is the post office?	¿dónde esta correos?
where are the toilets?	¿dónde estan los servicios?
men	señores/hombres/caballeros
women	señoras/mujeres
open/closed	abierto/cerrado

today/tomorrow/next week hoy/mañana/la próxima semana

where can I buy...? ¿dónde se puede comprar...?

  a newspaper, stamps un periódico, sellos   I'll have this tomo esto, llevo esto

I'd like that quiero eso   how much is it? ¿cuánto es?

Accommodation

do you have a room? ¿tiene una habitación?

double, single doble, individual

tonight esta noche

for two/three nights para dos/tres noches

how much is the room? ¿cuanto es la habitación?

with bath/without bath con baño/sin baño

Bar and restaurant vocabulary

drinks	bebidas	I'll have/we'll have	tomo/tomamos
breakfast	desayuno	a black coffee	café solo
lunch/dinner	comida/cena	two black coffees	dos cafés solos
I'd like/we'd like	quiero/queremos	white coffee	café con leche
three white coffees	tres cafés con leches	beer	cerveza
tea with milk	té con leche		
tea with lemon for me	té con limón para mi		
a bottle of mineral water	una botella de agua mineral		
fizzy/still	con gas/sin gas		
orange juice	zumo de naranja		
soup	sopa		
hors d'oeuvres	entremeses	the house wine	el vino de la casa
eggs, egg dishes	huevos	a glass of red wine	un vaso de vino tinto
fish, fish dishes	pescados		
sea food, shell fish	maríscos	white wine	vino blanco
vegetables	verduras/legumbres	a dry sherry	un jeréz seco
cheese	queso	meat, meat dishes	carne
fruit	fruta	game	caza
anything else?	¿algo más?	ice-cream	helados
nothing, thank you	nada más, gracias	desserts	postres ·
the bill, please	la cuenta, por favor	sandwich	bocadillo
two packed lunches	dos picnics	packed lunches	picnics
for tommorow	para mañana	en coche,	a pie

Getting about

by car, on foot

how can I/we get to Soller ¿cómo se llega a Soller?

where is. .. ¿donde esta...

the bus station? la estación de autobús?

the bus stop? la parada de autobús?

for Pollensa para Pollensa

how much is the fare? ¿cuánto vale el billete?

return ida y vuelta

single sencillo/solamente ida

where is the road to Inca? ¿donde esta la carretera de Inca?

how do I/we get to Alcudia? ¿para ir a Alcudia?

Especially for walkers

where is the footpath to...?	¿donde esta la senda a...?		
may we go this way?	¿se puede pasar por aqui?		
is it far?	¿esta lejos?	very near?	¿muy cerca?
how far?	¿a que distancia?	left/right	izquierda/derecho
how long?	¿cuanto tiempo?	straight on	todo recto
first left	la primera a la izquierda		
second right	la segunda a la derecha		
in front of the church	en frente de la iglesia	a right of way	derecho de paso
behind the hotel	detrás del hotel	private hunting	coto privado de caza
at the end of the street	al final de la calle		
after the bridge	después del puente	please close	cierren, por favor
where are you going?	¿adonde va/van?	dogs on guard	cuidado con el perro
I'm going/we're going to	voy a/vamos		

Car travel

where can I/we rent a car?	¿donde se puede alquilar un coche?	car repair shop	taller
		garage	garaje
how much is it per day?	¿cuánto es por día?	standard	normal
how much is it for a week?	¿cuánto es por una semana?	premium petrol	super
		fill it up please	lleno, por favor
petrol	gasolina		
petrol station	gasolinera estación de servicio	10, 20, 30 litres	diez, veinte, treinta litros
		may I/we park here?	¿ se puede aparcar aquí?

Road signs

Most are international, but you may see these:

¡Alto!	Halt!	Despacio	Slow
Aparcamiento	Parking	Desviación	Diversion
Calzada deteriorada	Bad road	Desprendimientos	Falling stones
Calzada estrecha	Narrow road	Pare!	Stop!
Ceda el paso	Give way	Peligro	Danger
Cruce peligroso	Dangerous crossroads	Prohibido adelantar	No overtaking
		Prohibido aparcar	No parking
Curva peligrosa	Dangerous bend	Puesto de socorro	First aid post
Cuidado	Caution		

Emergencies

Help! Fire!	¡Socorro! ¡Fuego!	it's urgent	es urgente
Police	Policia, Guardia Civil		
I've had a breakdown	mi coche se ha estropeado		
there's been an accident	ha habido un accidente		
call a doctor quickly	llamen a un medico, rapidamente		

Placenames

Most places in Mallorca have two names, Castilian and Mallorquin, both of which are in common use. At the time of writing Mallorquin is about to become the official language. Whether this means that placenames become standardised remains to be seen. It seems probable that both names will continue to be used, as after all both names have appeared in many books, maps and other printed material which still exists. The names are fairly similar as a rule, such as La Calobra, Sa Calobra, and La Puebla, Sa Pobla.

Some placename prounciations

Cala San Vicente	Kah-lah San Bee-then-tay	Soller	Sol-yair
		Ternelles	Tern-ell-yes
Lluc	L'yook	Valldemossa	Vall-day-moh-sah
Mallorca	My-orka	Pollensa	Pol-yen-sa

Days of the week

	Castilian	Catalan			Castilian	Catalan
Monday	Lunes	Dilluns	Friday		Viernes	Divendres
Tuesday	Martes	Dimarts	Saturday		Sabado	Dissabte
Wednesday	Miercoles	Dimecres	Sunday		Domingo	Sabat
Thursday	Jueves	Dijous				

The Catalan has been given for the days of the week because notices about opening times of shops, museums etc. are often only given in this language.

APPENDIX 3: FURTHER READING

Walking guidebooks

Beese, Gerhard. *Richtig wandern: Mallorca.* 2nd ed.Koln Dumont, 1990.

Crespi-Green, Valerie. *Landscapes of Mallorca: a countryside guide.* 2nd ed. London. Sunflower Books, 1987.

Heinrich, Herbert. *12 classic hikes through Majorca.* Palma, Editorial Moll, 1987.

ICONA. *Son Moragues: guia de paseo.* Palma, 1982.

Llofriu, Pere. *Caminant per Mallorca.* (Manuals d'introduccio a la naturalesa, 8.) 2nd ed. Palma. Editorial Moll, 1989.

Palos, Benigne. *Itineraris de Muntanya: excursions a peu per la Serra de Mallorca.* 2nd ed. (Manuals d'introduccio a la naturalesa, 5). Palma. Editorial Moll, 1984.

Palos, Benigne. *Valldemossa com a centre d'excursions.* Mallorca. Editorial Moll, 1989.

Ponce, Paco. *Mallorca: ein Mallorquiner zeigt seine Heimat.* Gerlen, 6601 Saarbrucken-Ensheim, West Germany, Repa-Druck. 2nd ed. n.d.

Natural history books

General

Parrack, James D. *The naturalist in Majorca.* Newton Abbot. David and Charles, 1973. (o.p.)

Birds

Bannerman, David & Bannerman, W.Mary. *The birds of the Balearics,* illus. by Donald Watson. Croom Helm, 1983.

Busby, John. *Birds in Mallorca.* Christopher Helm, 1988.

Heinzel, Herman & others. *The birds of Britain and Europe with North Africa and the Middle East.* London. Collins, 1972.

Peterson, Roger, & others. *A field guide to the birds of Britain and Europe.* 4th ed. London. Collins, 1983.

Serra, Joan Mayol. *The birds of the Balearic islands.* Tr. from the Catalan by Hannah Bonner. Mallorca. Editorial Moll, 1990.

Stoba, Ken. *Bird watching in Mallorca.* Milnthorpe, Cumbria Cicerone Press, [1990].

Watkinson, Eddie. *A guide to bird-watching in Mallorca.* 2nd ed. Alderney, J.G.Sanders, 1982.

Flowers

Beckett, Elspeth. *Wild flowers of Majorca, Minorca and Ibiza;* with keys to the flora of the Balearic island. Rotterdam Balkema, 1988.

Bonner, Anthony. *Plants of the Balearic island.* (Manuals d'introduccio a la naturelesa, 1). Palma. Editorial Moll, 1982.

Polunin, Oleg and Huxley, Anthony. *Flowers of the Mediterranean.* Chatto and Windus, 1972.

Polunin, Oleg. *Flowers of Europe; a field guide.* Oxford U.P., 1969.

Straka, Herbert, & others. *Führer zur Flora von Mallorca/Guide to the flora of Majorca.* Gustav Fischer Verlag. Stuttgart/New York, 1987. (In German, English, Spanish and French.)

Geology

Adams, A.E. *Mallorcan geology: a geological excursion guide.* Cardiff. Dept. of Extra Mural Studies, University College, 1988.

General Interest

Berlitz travel guide: *Majorca and Minorca.* English ed. dist. by Cassell, 1982.

Facaros, Dana & Pauls, Michael. *Mediterranean island hopping: the Spanish islands; a handbook for the independent traveller.* London. Sphere Books, 1981.

Foss, Arthur. *Majorca.* Faber and Faber. 1972.

Graves, Robert and Hogarth, Paul. *Majorca observed.* London, Cassell, 1965.

Sand, George. *Winter in Majorca.* Trans. and annotated by Robert Graves. Valldemossa, 1956.

Thurston, Hazel. *The travellers' guide to the Balearics: Majorca, Minorca, Ibiza and Formentera.* London. Jonathan Cape, 1979.

Language

BBC. *Get by in Spanish: a quick beginners' course for holidaymakers and business people.* 1977.

Ellis, D.L. & Ellis, R. *Travellers' Spanish.* Pan Books, 1981.

Oliva, Salvador, & Buxton, Angela. *Diccionari Català-Angles* Barcelona, 1985.

Printed by
Carnmor Print & Design, London Road, Preston

MALLORCA
GENERAL LOCATION MAP

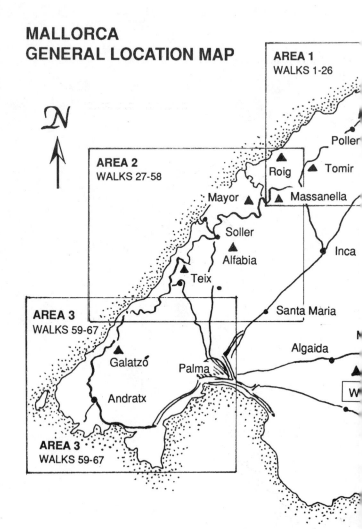

$\mathcal{N}$
↑

AREA 1
WALKS 1-26

AREA 2
WALKS 27-58

AREA 3
WALKS 59-67

AREA 3
WALKS 59-67

Poller

Roig ▲   ▲ Tomir

Mayor ▲   ▲ Massanella

Soller

▲ Alfabia

Inca

▲ Teix

Santa Maria

▲ Galatzó   Palma

Andratx

Algaida

W